Beyond Scarcity

MENA DEVELOPMENT REPORT

Beyond Scarcity

Water Security in the Middle East and North Africa

WORLD BANK GROUP

ISBN (paper): 978-1-4648-1144-9
ISBN (electronic): 978-1-4648-1181-4
DOI: 10.1596/978-1-4648-1144-9

Cover photo: Pier Giorgio Carloni/Shutterstock.com. Used with permission; further permission required
for reuse.

Cover design: Critical Stages, LLC

Library of Congress Cataloging-in-Publication Data has been requested

MENA Development Report Series

This series features major development reports from the Middle East and North Africa region of the World Bank, based on new research and thoroughly peer-reviewed analysis. Each report aims to enrich the debate on the main development challenges and opportunities the region faces as it strives to meet the evolving needs of its people.

Titles in the MENA Development Report Series

Beyond Scarcity: Water Security in the Middle East and North Africa (2018) by World Bank

Jobs or Privileges: Unleashing the Employment Potential of the Middle East and North Africa (2015) by Marc Schiffbauer, Abdoulaye Sy, Sahar Hussain, Hania Sahnoun, and Philip Keefer

The Road Traveled: Dubai's Journey towards Improving Private Education: A World Bank Review (2014) by Simon Thacker and Ernesto Cuadra

Inclusion and Resilience: The Way Forward for Social Safety Nets in the Middle East and North Africa (2013) by Joana Silva, Victoria Levin, and Matteo Morgandi

Opening Doors: Gender Equality and Development in the Middle East and North Africa (2013) by World Bank

From Political to Economic Awakening in the Arab World: The Path of Economic Integration (2013) by Jean-Pierre Chauffour

Adaptation to a Changing Climate in the Arab Countries: A Case for Adaptation Governance and Leadership in Building Climate Resilience (2012) by Dorte Verner

Renewable Energy Desalination: An Emerging Solution to Close the Water Gap in the Middle East and North Africa (2012) by World Bank

Poor Places, Thriving People: How the Middle East and North Africa Can Rise Above Spatial Disparities (2011) by World Bank

Financial Access and Stability: A Road Map for the Middle East and North Africa (2011) by Roberto R. Rocha, Zsofia Arvai, and Subika Farazi

From Privilege to Competition: Unlocking Private-Led Growth in the Middle East and North Africa (2009) by World Bank

The Road Not Traveled: Education Reform in the Middle East and North Africa (2008) by World Bank

Making the Most of Scarcity: Accountability for Better Water Management Results in the Middle East and North Africa (2007) by World Bank

Gender and Development in the Middle East and North Africa: Women in the Public Sphere (2004) by World Bank

Unlocking the Employment Potential in the Middle East and North Africa: Toward a New Social Contract (2004) by World Bank

Better Governance for Development in the Middle East and North Africa: Enhancing Inclusiveness and Accountability (2003) by World Bank

Trade, Investment, and Development in the Middle East and North Africa: Engaging with the World (2003) by World Bank

All books in the MENA Development Report series are available for free at https://openknowledge.worldbank.org/handle /10986/2168

Contents

Figures

Maps

Tables

Foreword

Water security is a central challenge for the development and stability of the Middle East and North Africa region—a challenge of interest far beyond the water sector. That is why we hope that the findings from this report will spark discussion, not just among a technical audience, but also among a range of regional actors and policy makers, including representatives from governments, the private sector, civil society, and utilities.

Given its relative scarcity, water has always been a source of opportunities and risks in the Middle East and North Africa region. For millennia, investments and innovations in water management have contributed to social and economic development and to extraordinary accomplishments, facilitated by secure water supplies and irrigated agriculture. One might wonder: What makes today's water challenges different from a decade or even a century ago? And how can water security contribute to the region's economic, social, and environmental well-being, and its path to peace and stability?

The answer to these questions lies in the rapid evolution of the Middle East and North Africa's socioeconomic, environmental, and political context. This context is characterized by high rates of population growth, about 2 percent annually, and particularly the expansion of cities, with the region's urban population expected to double by 2050, to nearly 400 million.

Increasing consumption, paired with undervalued water, inadequate governance arrangements, and weak enforcement is leading to the depletion of water resources—especially groundwater—at an unprecedented rate. Unmanaged trade-offs in the water-energy-food nexus are also contributing to an overexploitation of water resources.

Climate change poses another set of pressures on this rapidly evolving context. The negative impacts of climate change on water availability call for urgent action to allocate and use water more wisely. Climate change is also bringing about more frequent and severe climatic events.

This will in turn increase drought and flood risks, which will harm the poor disproportionately.

It is an unfortunate fact that many of the most fragile countries are also those with the greatest water stress. Tragically, the Middle East and North Africa region has been in turmoil for several years now. Conflict and increased water stress are revealing the vulnerabilities of existing water management systems, which once delivered services to its citizens and are now failing when they are needed the most.

While the resource challenges will remain daunting, the Middle East and North Africa has an opportunity to expand the use of innovations in institutions and technology. As highlighted in this report, improved water resource assessment and allocation mechanisms have demonstrated more productive use of water in many parts of the world, yet they remain relatively underused in the region. The Middle East and North Africa could overcome scarcity as a constraint on growth and well-being, and increase its ability to withstand shocks and protracted crises, such as climate variability and drought or a refugee influx, while also addressing immediate humanitarian needs such as water and food security.

Given the complex and rapidly evolving social context, this report also shows that water security is about much more than just coping with water scarcity. It entails ensuring the delivery of affordable and high-quality water to citizens in order to reinforce relationships between service providers and customers and to contribute to a renewed social contract calling for greater transparency and accountability.

Water security also requires managing the impacts of migration on water supplies to ensure, against a backdrop of historic levels of displacement, that both host and refugee communities enjoy equitable and reliable access without degrading water resources.

Moving forward on this critical agenda requires action at three levels: Existing regional networks of public officials, such as the programs and councils supported by the League of Arab States and the Food and Agricultural Organization of the United Nations, are key to developing the political commitment for needed policy reforms and public and private investments. At the technical level, governments need to work with the private sector and participate in regional exchanges among water professionals, such as the Arab Countries Water Utility Association, which provide opportunities to learn and share good practices on water solutions. Civil society, especially the region's youth, have a key role in raising awareness of the value of water and the need for actions in support of a sustainable future.

The stakes are high. The region will need to redouble its efforts to manage its age-old water challenges in this era of acute scarcity.

The World Bank stands ready to work in partnership with governments, civil society, the private sector, as well as regional and international organizations to enhance the region's water security.

Hafez Ghanem   Guangzhe Chen
Vice President   Senior Director
Middle East and North Africa Region   Water Global Practice
The World Bank   The World Bank

Acknowledgments

This report is the outcome of multiple studies and consultations carried out and commissioned by the World Bank. The work was led by Claudia Sadoff and Edoardo Borgomeo, with Anders Jägerskog, Dambudzo Muzenda, Sandy Ruckstuhl, and colleagues across the Middle East and North Africa (MENA) Water Practice, and Regional and Country Management Units. Support and guidance was provided by Steven Schonberger (MENA Water Practice Manager), Franck Bousquet (MENA Regional Programs and Partnerships Director), Guangzhe Chen (Senior Director, Global Water Practice), and Shanta Devarajan (Senior Director, Development Economics).

World Bank colleagues who contributed to the report include Richard Abdulnour, Naif Abu-Lohom, Abdulhamid Azad, Daniel Camos Daurella, Stephane Dahane, Mouhamed Fadel Ndaw, Adnan Ghosheh, Osama Hamad, Gabriella Izzi, Philippe Marin, Alex McPhail, Yogita Mumssen, Francois Onimus, Iyad Rammal, Amal Talbi, Maheen Zehra, and Sally Zgheib. The team also wishes to express its sincere appreciation for inputs provided by the Program Leaders for Sustainable Development in the region: Suhail Jme'An, Ashish Khanna, Andrea Liverani, Bjorn Philipp, and Maria Vagliasindi.

A World Resources Institute team comprising Betsy Otto, Charlie Iceland, Tianyi Luo, and Rutger Hofste contributed a background paper on water stress and water demand in the region. Rens van Beek of Utrecht University authored a background paper on sustainable water use in the region. This report also draws on a commissioned geospatial analysis performed by Deltares (Sheila Ball, Marta Faneca Sanchez, and Marijn Kuijper) to estimate groundwater stress and exposure in the MENA region. Dr. Jarrah AlZubi and Ali Karnib are thanked for providing insightful recommendations on the MDG+ datasets.

Specific contributions were received from Matar Hamed Al Neyadi (Undersecretary of the United Arab Emirates Ministry of Energy), Rachael McDonnell (International Centre for Biosaline Agriculture), and Dale Whittington (University of North Carolina at Chapel Hill).

The team gratefully acknowledges the contribution of Claudia Ringler and Tingju Zhu (International Food Policy Research Institute) for providing the data on the welfare change resulting from improved irrigation water service delivery from the IMPACT model. Data on the economic costs of inadequate water supply and sanitation were provided by Guy Hutton (UNICEF) and Franziska Gaupp, Jim Hall, and Kevin Wheeler (University of Oxford).

The team wishes to thank the report's peer reviewers and other colleagues not previously mentioned who provided valuable, insightful comments during the review process: Ghazi Abu Rumman, Omer Karasapan, Claire Kfouri, Julian Lampietti, Pilar Maisterra, Sajjad Shah, Caroline van den Berg, Dorte Verner, Marcus Wijnen, and William Young.

The team is especially grateful to Shawki Barghouti for his guidance, detailed comments, and continued support during the development of the report.

The report has also benefited from the comments, ideas, and data shared by academics and practitioners. The task team would like to thank Marta Antonelli (Swiss Federal Institute of Aquatic Sciences), Malin Falkenmark (Stockholm International Water Institute), Michael Gilmont (University of Oxford), Matti Kummu (Aalto University), and Michael Talhami (International Committee of the Red Cross).

The early findings of this report were presented at the 2017 Arab Water Week, held in Amman, Jordan, on March 19–23. The task team wishes to thank the participants at that presentation for comments received both during and after the consultation seminar. Consultations were also held in March, 2017 in Jordan and in the West Bank and Gaza, and in July, 2017 in Cairo, at the Technical Committee meeting of the Arab Ministerial Water Council of the League of Arab States. The many useful comments and suggestions received during those consultations have strengthened this report.

Finally, the team wishes to acknowledge the hard work of the production team. Pascal Saura, as well as Deborah Appel-Barker, Erin Barrett, Susan Graham, Patricia Katayama, and Jewel McFadden, guided the editing and production process; Bruno Bonansea produced the maps, Sharon Faulkner and Lalima Maskey supported the teams throughout, and Francis Gagnon of Voilá Information Design provided skillful information design advice.

About the Water Global Practice

Launched in 2014, the Word Bank Group's Water Global Practice brings together financing, knowledge, and implementation in one platform. By combining the Bank's global knowledge with country investments, this model generates more firepower for transformational solutions to help countries grow sustainably. Please visit us at www.worldbank.org/water or follow us on Twitter at @WorldBankWater.

Abbreviations

ACWUA	Arab Countries Water Utilities Association
BlWSI	Blue Water Sustainability Index
FAO	Food and Agricultural Organization of the United Nations
IFPRI	International Food Policy Research Institute
IOM	International Organization of Migration
JMP	Joint Monitoring Programme (WHO/UNICEF)
MDGs	Millennium Development Goals
MENA	Middle East and North Africa
SDGs	Sustainable Development Goals
SDG 6	the water SDG (Sustainable Development Goal)
UNICEF	United Nations Children's Fund
UN-Water	United Nations Water
WHO	World Health Organization
WRI	World Resources Institute

Note: All currency amounts are in U.S. dollars, unless otherwise noted.

The Middle East and North Africa Region

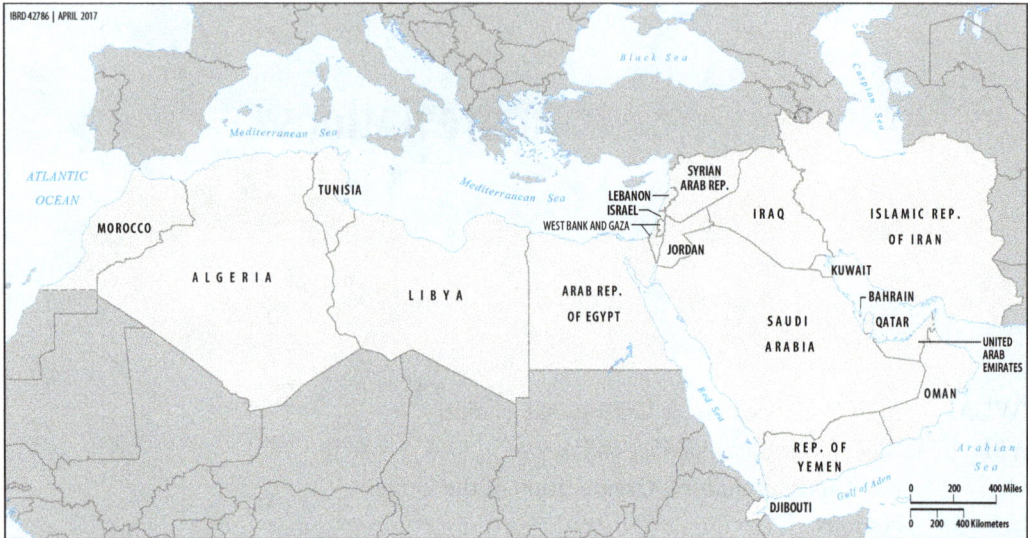

Source: World Bank.

The Middle East and North Africa (MENA) region includes the following countries and economies:

Algeria, Bahrain, Dijbouti, the Arab Republic of Egypt, the Islamic Republic of Iran, Iraq, Israel, Jordan, Kuwait, Lebanon, Libya, Morocco, Oman, Qatar, Saudi Arabia, the Syrian Arab Republic, Tunisia, the United Arab Emirates, West Bank and Gaza, and the Republic of Yemen.

The Gulf states and the six members of the Gulf Cooperation Council (the GCC countries) are Bahrain, Kuwait, Oman, Qatar, Saudi Arabia, and the United Arab Emirates.

The Maghreb consists of Algeria, Libya, Morocco, and Tunisia.

The Mashreq consists of Jordan, Iraq, Lebanon, the Syrian Arab Republic, and West Bank and Gaza.

Executive Summary

The Region's Water Challenges—and the Region's Water Solutions—Extend Far beyond Water Scarcity

Of all the challenges the Middle East and North Africa region faces, it is least prepared for water crises. The World Economic Forum asked experts and leaders in the region: "For which global risks is your region least prepared?" The majority of respondents identified water crises as the greatest threat to the region—greater even than political instability or unemployment (World Economic Forum 2015).

The Middle East and North Africa is the most water scarce region in the world.[1] Over 60 percent of the region's population lives in areas with high or very high surface water stress, compared with a global average of about 35 percent (figure ES.1). Over 70 percent of the region's gross domestic product (GDP) is generated in areas with high to very high surface water stress, compared with a global average of some 22 percent.

The region's current water challenges go far beyond age-old constraints of water scarcity. While the region's water scarcity challenges have been apparent for hundreds of years, newer challenges are adding both hazards and complexity. The complexities of the water-food-energy nexus, climate change, droughts and floods, water quality, transboundary water management, and the management of water in the context of fragility, conflict, and violence compound the challenge of water scarcity. Meeting these challenges will depend as much on better governance of water resources as on more and better resource endowments, infrastructure investments, and technologies.

Many countries in the region are already eroding their water resource base. For millennia, investments and innovations in water management have been made across the region. However, accelerating economic and population growth coupled with poor governance have now overwhelmed these efforts in many countries. Unsustainable volumes of water are

FIGURE ES.1

Share of GDP Produced and Population Living in Areas of High or Very High Water Stress in the Middle East and North Africa Compared with World Averages

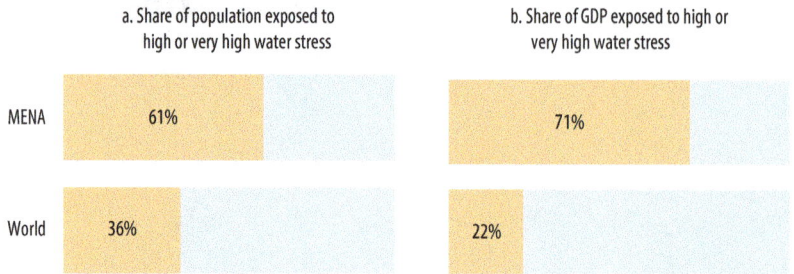

Source: Estimates for the Middle East and North Africa from the World Bank. World averages were taken from Veolia Water and IFPRI 2011.

being withdrawn, degrading ecosystems and aquifers (figure ES.2). Overdrawing water from rivers and aquifers is equivalent to living beyond one's means—drawing down or depreciating a country's natural capital and undermining its longer-term wealth and resilience.

A fundamental development challenge for the region is to take the actions necessary to navigate sustainable pathways toward water security. Sustainable pathways would anticipate and manage the inevitable increases in water scarcity and water-related risks—against a backdrop of climate change, urbanization, growing fiscal constraints, and widespread fragility and conflict. Planning and action are needed to strengthen the resilience of economies and societies to protect them from water-related disasters. Planning and management are also needed to deliver water services that are affordable for both users and government budgets, and to mitigate the costs and social disruptions that can be expected to result from extreme scarcity, sudden supply interruptions, contamination, floods, or droughts.

Water challenges can compound existing and emerging instabilities and can contribute to unrest and conflict. Failure to address water challenges in the Middle East and North Africa can have significant negative spillover effects both within and outside the region.

Water security exists when water is effectively, sustainably, and equitably managed both to leverage its productive potential and to mitigate its destructive potential. Water security has been defined as "the availability of an acceptable quantity and quality of water for health, livelihoods, ecosystems and production, coupled with an acceptable level of water-related risks to people, environments and economies" (Grey and Sadoff 2007 p. 545). Water security goes beyond water scarcity to take account not

FIGURE ES.2

Sustainability of Water Withdrawals, by Source, as a Percentage of Total Withdrawals, Selected Countries and Economies

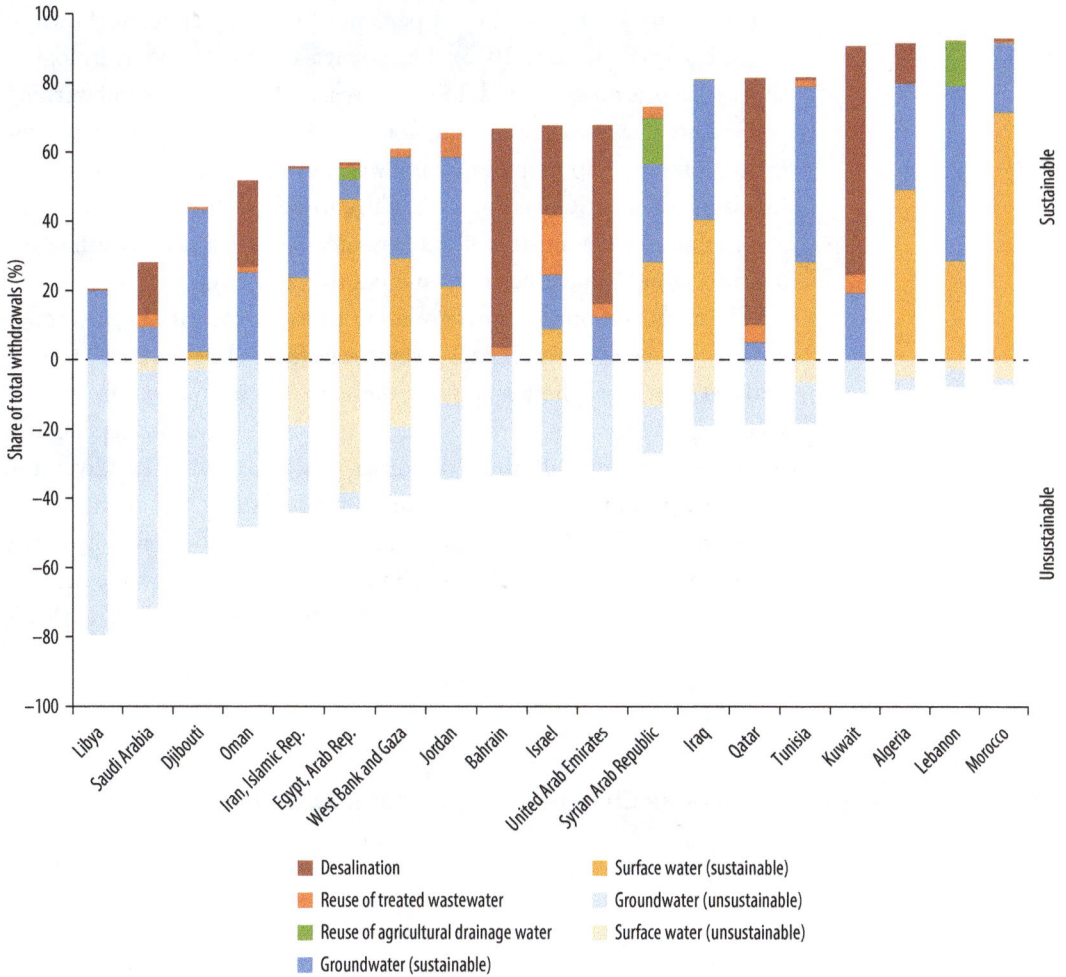

Sources: World Bank calculations, based on desalination capacity from Global Water Intelligence 2016a; data on all other categories are from FAO AQUASTAT (database).

Note: The percentage of unsustainable groundwater and surface water withdrawals was estimated for this study using the Blue Water Sustainability Index. No data are available for the Republic of Yemen on sustainability of water use. Caution should be used in comparing data on annual freshwater withdrawals, which are subject to variations in collection and estimation methods. For Iraq, the Syrian Arab Republic, and West Bank and Gaza, the breakdown between surface and groundwater withdrawals was not available, and withdrawals were split equally between the two categories. In absolute terms, the Arab Republic of Egypt has the largest volume of reuse of agricultural drainage water and Saudi Arabia the largest desalination capacity in the region.

only of a country's water resource endowment, but also of the productive and protective actions the country has taken to secure water. Some of the most water-scarce countries in the world are also arguably some of the most water secure—while some of the most water-rich countries in the world struggle to protect their populations from water-related disasters and to provide improved drinking water access.

Countries that fail to achieve water security forgo potential growth, increase vulnerabilities to hydrological shocks, and may potentially compound social and political fragility. The Middle East and North Africa region has the greatest expected economic losses from climate-related water scarcity, estimated at 6–14 percent of GDP by 2050, as shown in figure ES.3 (World Bank 2016). The impacts of scarcity and hydrological shocks, such as droughts and floods, increase where forecast and warning systems are weak, stormwater and flood management are inadequate, irrigation infrastructure is minimal, and water stored in reservoirs and aquifers is insufficient. Governments' failure to deliver basic water services, and to mitigate the impacts of water-related hazards and risks, can erode legitimacy and compound social and political fragility.

The risks and opportunities relating to water security in the region have never been greater. Because water scarcity has been a central feature of the region throughout its history, there is potential for complacency in accepting the limitations that water scarcity implies, or for dependence on incremental or traditional responses to water challenges. Given the rapid growth of the region's economy and population, incremental solutions are increasingly inadequate and unaffordable. Fortunately, at the same time, many countries have demonstrated success in implementing innovative programs to diminish wasteful nonrevenue water (water that is

FIGURE ES.3

The Economic Impacts of Climate Change–Induced Water Scarcity, by 2050

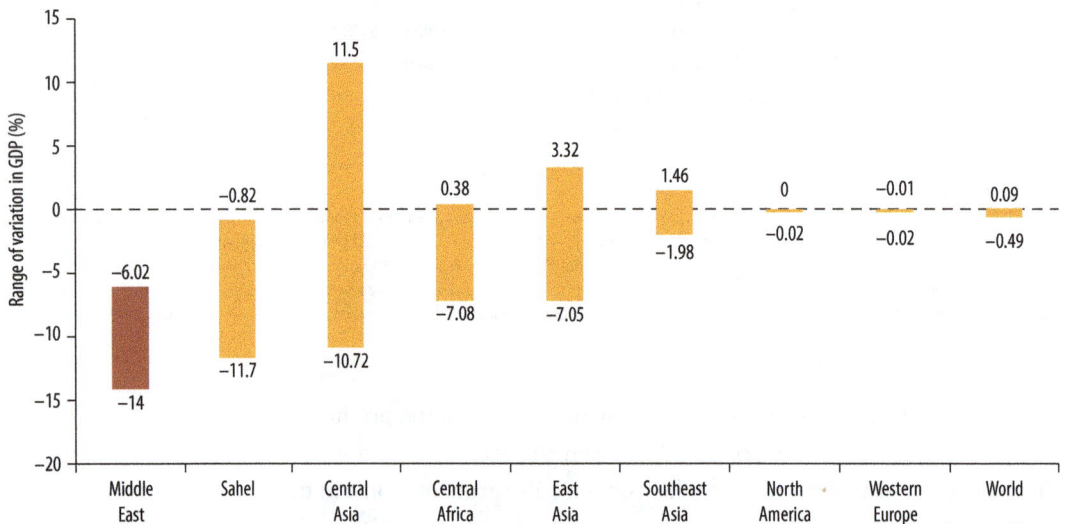

Source: World Bank 2016.

Note: The range of impacts is determined by the type of policies implemented to cope with water scarcity, from a business-as-usual policy (−14 percent) to a policy seeking to reallocate water to the most productive uses (−6 percent).

produced and lost before it reaches the customer), to increase water productivity, and to produce nonconventional water through wastewater recycling or desalination. The cost-effectiveness of these technologies is also rapidly improving, changing the landscape of options for the next generation of water management.

Achieving water security in the Middle East and North Africa requires a new way of looking at water management. The policies, incentives, and institutional weaknesses in many countries have led to inefficient and low-value water use as well as unreliable water services and unregulated water usage and wastewater discharge. Despite water scarcity, the region's water service fees are very low, and its effective water subsidies are the highest in the world (Kochhar et al. 2015). These policies promote resource degradation, aggravate fiscal deficits, and compound vulnerabilities. The way in which water is delivered, allocated, priced, and managed can have profound implications for the region's economic growth. It will influence the structure of its economies and its environmental sustainability, along with social inclusion and regional stability.

Now and in the future, a broader range of tools, technologies, and policies will need to be considered, debated, and implemented. Investments in water infrastructure, information systems, institutions, and technologies will be needed. Societies will need to move beyond the traditional approach to managing scarcity by augmenting supplies, and consider controversial solutions. These may include policies that create incentives for water conservation and water use efficiency, including fees, fines, permitting, and pricing,[2] as well as wastewater recycling and reuse; and the reallocation of water from rural to urban users and from agriculture to industry. Furthermore, social inclusion must be central to the delivery of water services and protection of poor and marginalized populations from water-related risks.

This report provides a regional assessment of the status of water security in the Middle East and North Africa. It describes existing water-related challenges, and it outlines emerging opportunities. It explores three questions that are fundamental to water security:

1. Are the region's water resources being managed sustainably and efficiently?
2. Are water services being delivered reliably and affordably?
3. Are water-related risks being appropriately recognized and mitigated?

This regional assessment provides a foundation to identify the most significant water-related issues and potential entry points for action in the

Middle East and North Africa region. It aims to motivate comprehensive assessments of water security at the national level and to stimulate dialogue on water security.

Question 1. Are the Region's Water Resources Being Managed Sustainably and Efficiently?

The Middle East and North Africa is a global hotspot of unsustainable water use. The region is using far more water than is available on a renewable basis (see map ES.1). In some countries, more than half of current water withdrawals exceed sustainable limits. Failure to address excessive water use can lead to the depletion and degradation of both surface and groundwater resources, which compromises livelihoods and development opportunities for future generations.

The region as a whole faces extreme scarcity, but each country has a different water resource endowment that will shape its broader water challenges. Some countries rely most heavily on groundwater, as shown in figure ES.4. Others rely more heavily on large transboundary rivers. Scarcity is so great in the Gulf states, for example, that there is a strong focus on nonconventional water resources, such as desalination (see figure ES.5) and wastewater recycling for nonpotable uses as alternatives to the continued withdrawal of nonrenewable fossil groundwater. Understanding and diversifying the range of potential water resources in the region is essential.

Groundwater is often used in the absence of alternative sources, or as a buffer against drought, and it may not be apparent beforehand when this crucial resource might fail. Ongoing groundwater overabstraction may reach a critical point where fossil aquifers are depleted and where renewable aquifers are drawn down to the point that abstraction is no longer economically feasible. When aquifers are close to depletion, water quality deteriorates to the point of rendering the water unsuitable for human consumption. It is difficult to predict when aquifers may become compromised, given the large uncertainties in total groundwater storage (Richey et al. 2015).

Water quality in the region is degraded by unsustainable water consumption, brine discharge from desalination, pollution, and untreated wastewater. The cost of poor water quality in the region is estimated to range from 0.5 to 2.5 percent of GDP every year (World Bank 2007). The impacts of this mismanagement range from health damage from the spread of waterborne diseases to the loss of ecosystem services and fisheries that result from the pollution of fresh and marine water bodies. The International Union for Conservation of Nature estimates that in the Arabian Peninsula alone, 17 percent of freshwater species are threatened

(continued on next page)

MAP ES.1

Global Blue Water Sustainability Index for Surface Water, Groundwater, and Combined Surface and Ground Water, 1960–2010 Average

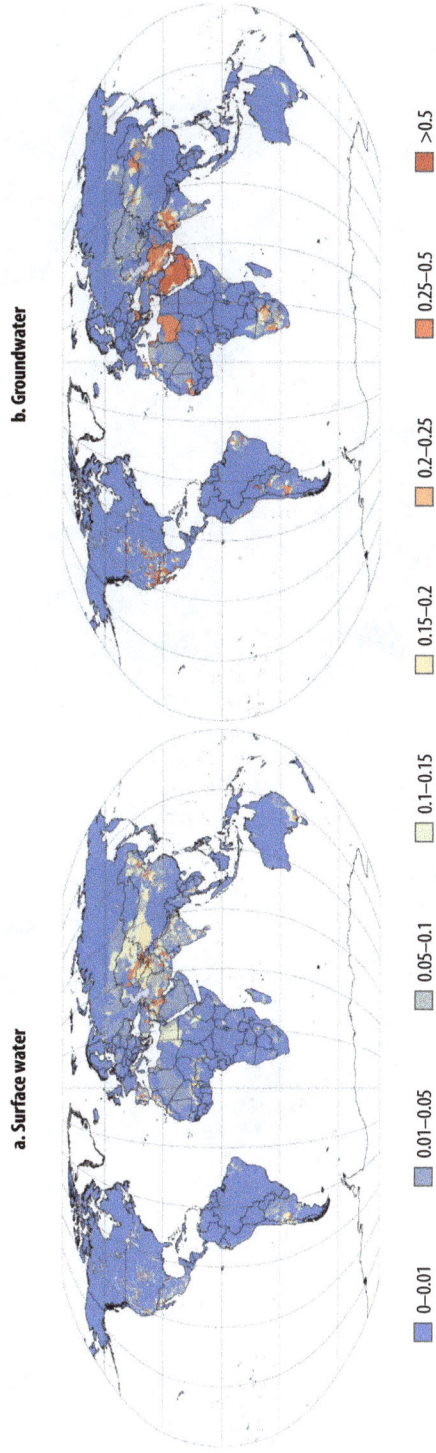

a. Surface water

b. Groundwater

0–0.01 | 0.01–0.05 | 0.05–0.1 | 0.1–0.15 | 0.15–0.2 | 0.2–0.25 | 0.25–0.5 | >0.5

MAP ES.1   *Continued*

c. Index total

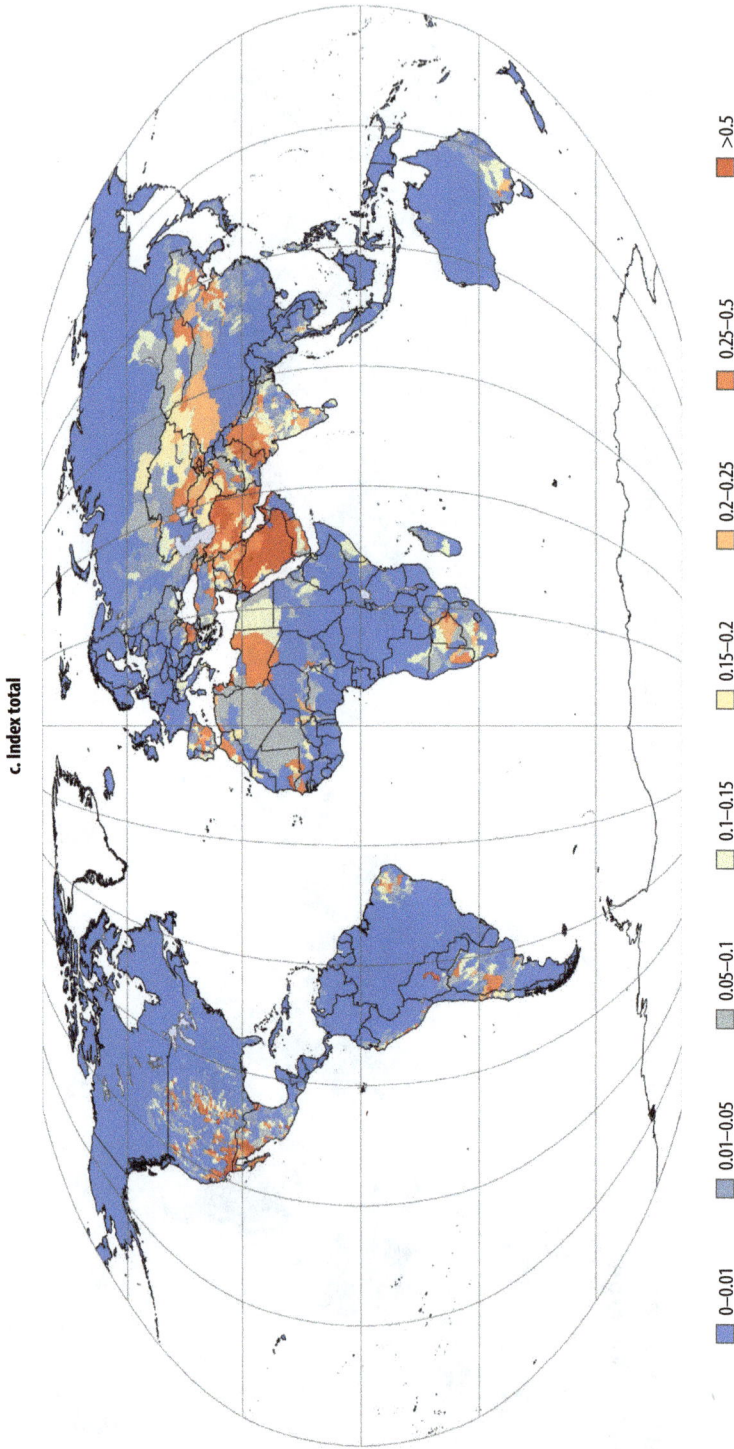

Legend:

- 0–0.01
- 0.01–0.05
- 0.05–0.1
- 0.1–0.15
- 0.15–0.2
- 0.2–0.25
- 0.25–0.5
- >0.5

Source: Wada and Bierkens 2014.

Note: The Blue Water Sustainability Index (BIWSI) measures the portion of water use that is unsustainable. The index is a dimensionless quantity ranging from 0 to 1 that expresses the portion of consumptive water use that is met from nonsustainable water sources. Blue = sustainable; red = unsustainable. Nonsustainable *surface water* use is estimated as the amount of environmental flow requirements not satisfied due to surface water overabstraction. Nonsustainable *groundwater* use is estimated as the difference between groundwater abstraction and natural groundwater recharge plus recharge from irrigation return flows.

FIGURE ES.4

Water Withdrawals, by Source, as a Percentage of Total Withdrawals, by Country and Economy, 2010

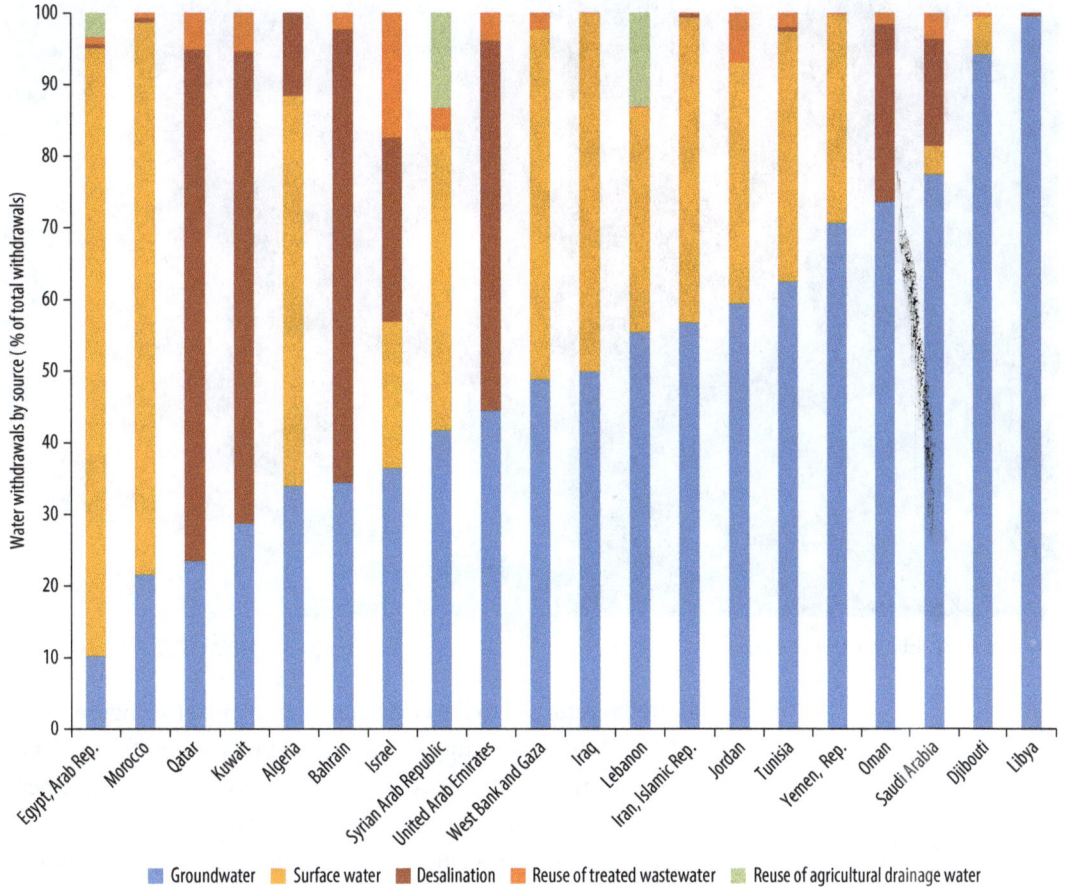

Sources: World Bank calculations. Data on desalination capacity come from Global Water Intelligence 2016a. Data on all other categories are from FAO AQUASTAT.

Note: For Iraq, the Syrian Arab Republic, and West Bank and Gaza, the breakdown between surface and groundwater withdrawals was not available and withdrawals were split equally between the two categories. In absolute terms, the Arab Republic of Egypt has the largest volume of reused of agricultural drainage water, and Saudi Arabia the largest desalination capacity in the region. Caution should be used in comparing data on annual freshwater withdrawals, which are subject to variations in collection and estimation methods.

with extinction (García et al. 2015). The semi-enclosed nature of the Gulf also means that discharged untreated wastewater accumulates in a "pollutant trap" that threatens marine ecosystems and human activities and livelihoods that rely on marine resources (Van Lavieren et al. 2011).

More than half of the wastewater collected in the Middle East and North Africa is returned to the environment untreated, resulting in both health hazards and wasted water resources. There are significant opportunities for recycled water to meet increasing water demands in the region. While over half of the wastewater is not even collected, 57 percent of the wastewater

FIGURE ES.5

Desalination Capacity, by World Region, 2016

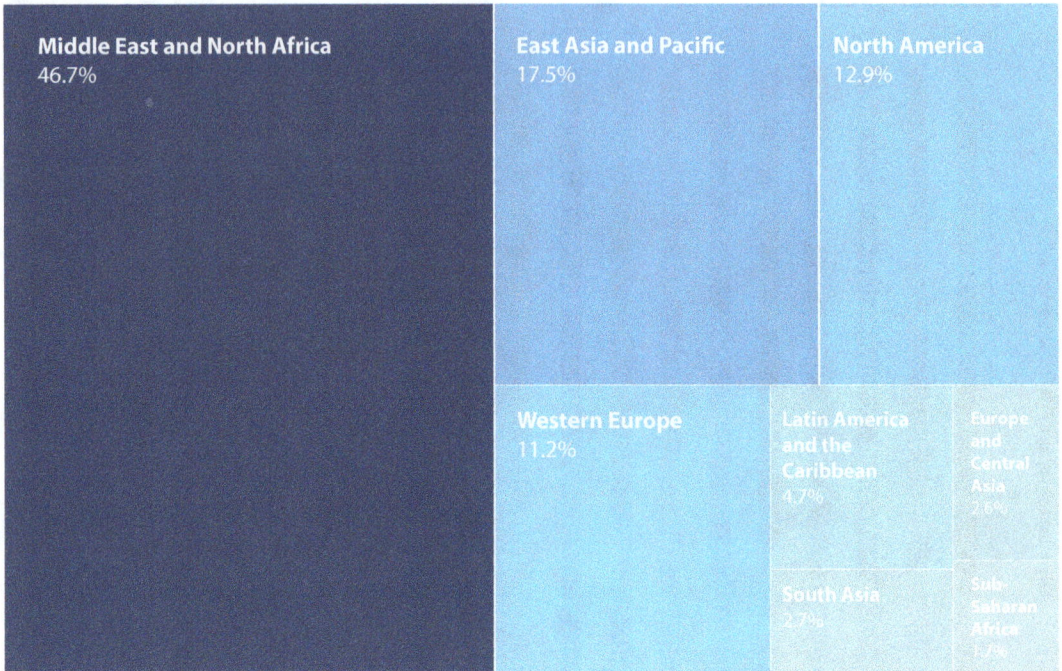

Source: Data from Global Water Intelligence 2016a.

that is collected is returned to the environment untreated (see figure ES.6). The Arab Republic of Egypt, Jordan, and Tunisia treat a significant part of their collected wastewater, but they still have not been able to implement reuse of this water at scale (see figure ES.7). This may be a missed opportunity to respond to landscape, industrial, or agricultural water demands at a relatively low cost. Recent studies from the region also underscore the economic feasibility of managed aquifer recharge using treated wastewater as part of a wider strategy to diversify supply (Zekri et al. 2014).

Total water productivity in the Middle East and North Africa is only about half the world's average. There are striking differences in total water productivity across the region—which features some of the most water productive as well as some of the least water productive countries in the world. Agriculture accounts for nearly 80 percent of the region's water use, somewhat higher than the world average of about 70 percent. Agriculture tends to produce the lowest economic returns from water. Globally, on average, the economic returns to agricultural water are about half that of municipal water, and one-third that of industrial water (Aylward et al. 2010).

The region has some of the world's highest losses of freshwater resources in its food supply chain on a per capita basis. Some Middle Eastern and North African countries lose between 80 to 177 cubic meters per capita

FIGURE ES.6

Share of Collected Wastewater That Is Untreated, Treated, and Reused in Irrigation

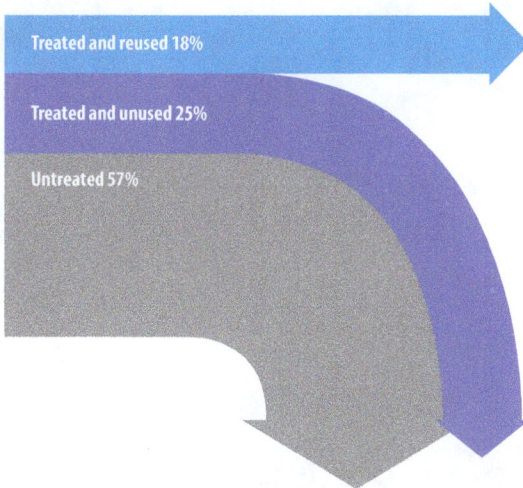

Treated and reused 18%

Treated and unused 25%

Untreated 57%

Source: World Bank, using data from FAO AQUASTAT (database).
Note: The figure was generated by summing country-level data on wastewater treated and reused from FAO AQUASTAT. Country-level data are based on estimates provided by the governments and are subject to variations in estimation methods and year of collection.

per year of freshwater resources from "field to fork" (Kummu et al. 2012). Agricultural losses, processing losses, and losses at the distribution and consumption stages are all responsible for this waste. At the consumption stage alone, the UN Food and Agricultural Organization estimates that food waste in the Middle East and North Africa is 32 percent (FAO 2011). In the area of water-intensive fruits and vegetables, this proportion increases to around 60 percent.

High water subsidies and weak monitoring and enforcement mechanisms undermine incentives for efficient water use. They encourage overexploitation and in many countries perpetuate a pattern of low-value uses and low water productivity. Part of the water challenge in the Middle East and North Africa lies in managing demands and putting the right incentives in place to save water. These are politically sensitive issues, yet this management is essential to improving water services delivery and water resources productivity. Water service fees can signal resource scarcity and encourage conservation. They can also provide financing for water resources protection, infrastructure maintenance, and service delivery.

Water governance issues—in particular, the failure to create incentives that signal extreme water scarcity and promote water conservation—are the common denominator of water management in the Middle East and North Africa. Excessive consumption and resource depletion are the predictable consequences of undervalued water, weak governance arrangements, and

FIGURE ES.7

Share of Wastewater That Is Reused versus Share That Is Treated

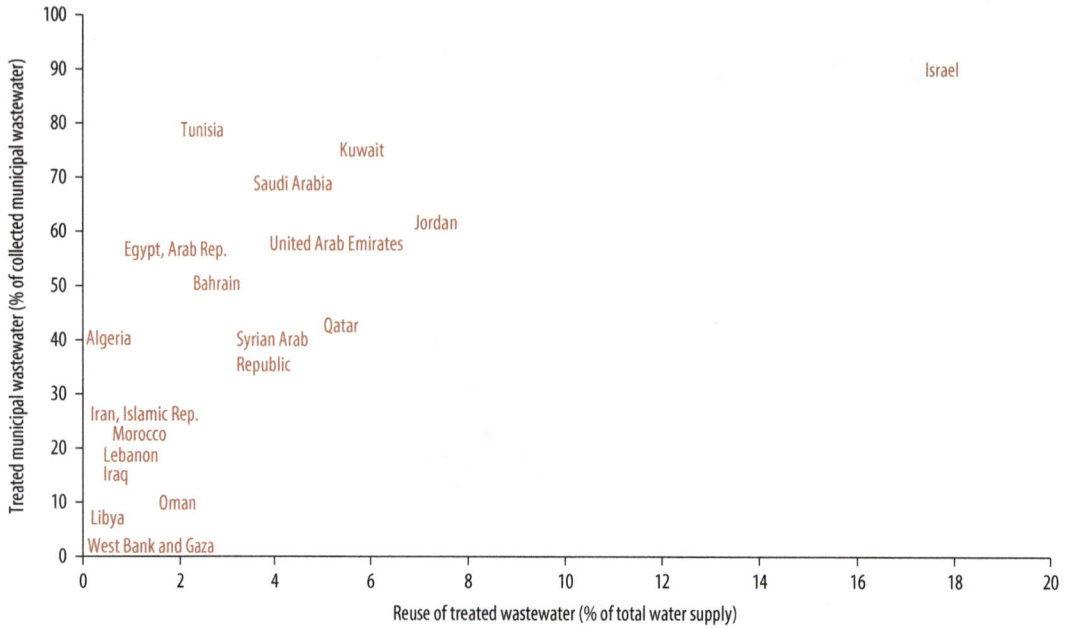

Source: World Bank, using data from FAO AQUASTAT (database).
Note: Data on wastewater produced, treated, and reused in the Middle East and North Africa sourced from FAO AQUASTAT. Country-level data are based on estimates provided by governments and are subject to variations in estimation methods and year of collection. There are no data for Djibouti.

inadequate enforcement. Lack of legal frameworks, inadequate enforcement, and poor institutional coordination prevent the region from exploiting recent advances in wastewater treatment and reuse technologies.

There is important scope for strengthening the sustainability and efficiency of water management in the region. To better manage the region's water resources and sustainably balance water supply and demand, there are essentially three nonexclusive strategies that can be pursued to strengthen water security:

1. Use (or lose) less water, to reduce demand

   Demand management strategies include water service fees and pricing that reflect the resource's scarcity and promote conservation; incentives and technologies to enhance productivity and efficiency; control of losses and leakage.

2. Reallocate water, to realign demand

   Regulations and market-based tools include planning and prioritization of high value water uses balanced with safeguards for social equity and stability; water rights, subsidies, and pricing policies; regulations and enforcement to control unplanned overexploitation.

3. Provide (or create) more water, to meet demand
   Supply side responses include development of a diversified portfolio of conventional and nonconventional water resources; coordinated use of surface and groundwater; stormwater capture, wastewater recycling and reuse.

Question 2. Are Water Services Being Delivered Reliably and Affordably?

Water supply and sanitation services account for a very large share of water use in some Middle Eastern and North African countries, although they globally represent a relatively small share of water use (around 10 percent). In the Gulf States and in West Bank and Gaza, municipal water demands account for almost half of all abstractions. Projected population growth and migration to urban centers are increasing municipal water demands across the region (Tropp and Jägerskog 2006).

The Middle East and North Africa region has had one of the best performances globally in terms of increasing access to improved water supply and sanitation since 1990; however, conflict has reversed progress in many countries. United Nations Children's Fund (UNICEF) and World Health Organization (WHO) data suggest that progress on water and sanitation has barely kept up with population growth, especially in urban areas (UNICEF and WHO 2015, 17). Access still needs to be extended to hard-to-reach rural locales and conflict-affected areas. Access gains have been reversed by ongoing armed conflict and migration in the region, causing untold human suffering as well damaging infrastructure and diminishing institutional capacity.

Access is essential but is only one aspect of water services. The international benchmarks of the Sustainable Development Goals (SDGs) raise the performance bar for the region by addressing the reliability and quality of water services. The reliability, affordability, and quality of water supply and sanitation services are quite mixed in the region. Statistics mask the reality of intermittent supply. High subsidy rates obscure the affordability of services, both in relation to households' ability to pay and to the government's ability to afford continued subsidization. Improvements in the quality of water services are important to ensure customers' satisfaction and their willingness to pay for water services, and hence the financial sustainability of providing water services.

Inadequate water supply and sanitation cost the region some $21 billion per year in economic losses. Mortality due to unsafe water supply and sanitation in a few countries in the Middle East and North Africa, especially those affected by conflict, is greater than global averages. Inadequate water supply and sanitation cost about 1 percent of regional GDP annually, with conflict-affected countries losing as much as 2–4 percent annually (see figure ES.8).

Improving the way in which water is stored and delivered to users of irrigation water could lead to an estimated $10 billion welfare gain annually. If all the available surface water allocated to agriculture in the Middle East and North Africa could be stored and delivered efficiently to irrigated agriculture, agricultural production would increase 1–8 percent, and the variability in production of some commodities would decrease. Countries that could reap the greatest relative benefits are Egypt, the Islamic Republic of Iran and the Syrian Arab Republic—which is not surprising, given that these countries also have the largest proportion of irrigated areas in the region. In absolute terms, the biggest benefits would occur in Egypt and the Islamic Republic of Iran, where irrigated agriculture is a fundamental component of the economy.

FIGURE ES.8

Economic Losses from Inadequate Water Supply and Sanitation, by Country and Economy, 2010

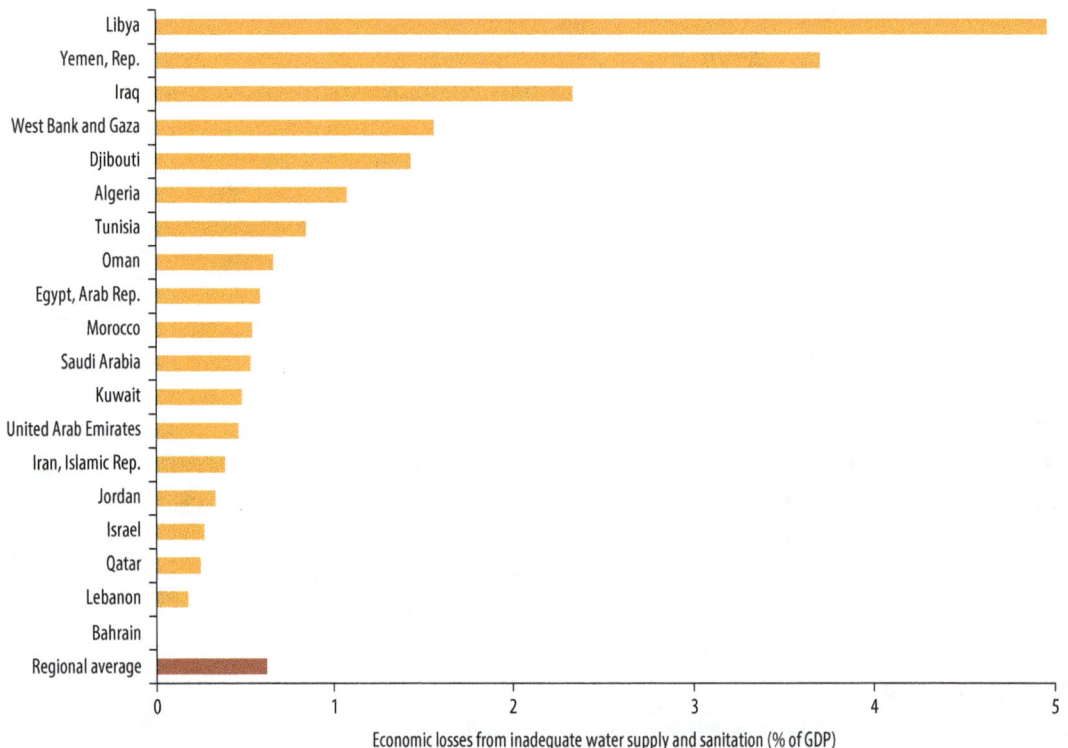

Economic losses from inadequate water supply and sanitation (% of GDP)

Sources: Sadoff et al. 2015; and Hutton 2013.
Note: No data are available for the Syrian Arab Republic.

Despite its scarcity, the region has the world's lowest water tariffs and the highest proportion of GDP (2 percent) spent on public water subsidies. This leads to excessive use of extremely scarce water resources (see figure ES.9). Especially in the agricultural sector, water service fees in the Middle East and North Africa do not reflect the scarcity value of water or the cost of delivery (AWC 2014). The region has some of the lowest water service fees for irrigation water in the world, which enables farmers to grow water-intensive crops and it discourages the adoption of water-saving irrigation technologies (Berglöf and Devarajan 2015). Service fees on drinking water are also very low, with some cities charging seven to eight times lower than elsewhere in the region and the world (see figure ES.10).

Failure to price water services properly undermines the financial sustainability of those services. Average service costs exceed average service charges in most Middle Eastern and North African countries (ACWUA 2014, table 14), indicating a lack of cost recovery. On average, the price charged for water in the Arab region is about 35 percent of the cost of production for conventional sources (surface and groundwater). In the case of desalinated water, only 10 percent of costs are covered by charges (Gelil 2014). Cost recovery is essential to ensure long-term sustainability of water services. Failure to recover costs can also severely undermine a utility's capacity to treat wastewater, leading to deteriorating water quality and degradation of freshwater ecosystems.

FIGURE ES.9

Water Subsidies to Urban Water Utilities as a Share of Regional GDP, by World Region

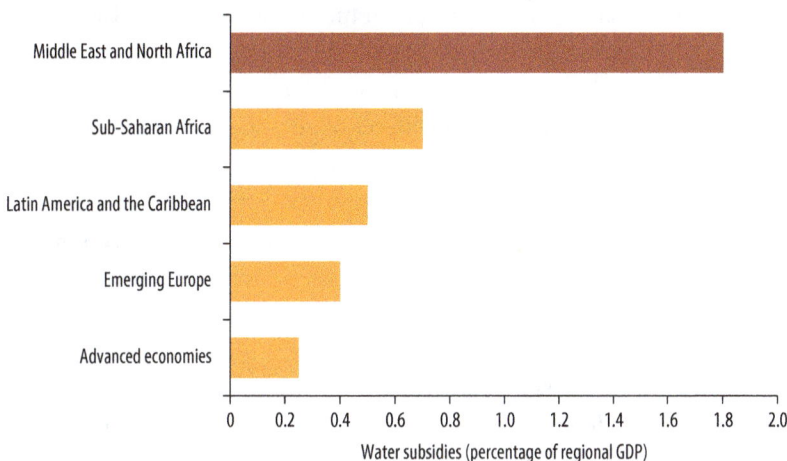

Source: Kochhar et al. 2015.
Note: Subsidies are defined as the difference between actual water charges to water users and a reference price that would cover all costs associated with supplying that water.

FIGURE ES.10

Combined Water and Wastewater Bill per Cubic Meter, Selected Cities in the Middle East and North Africa and Other Regions, 2016

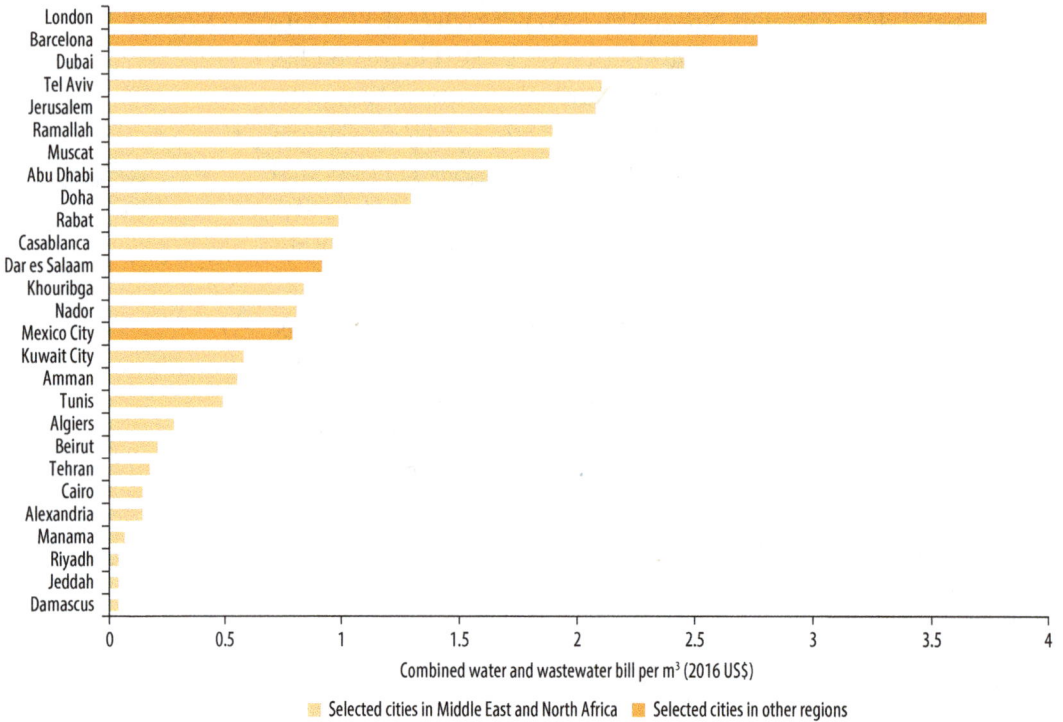

Combined water and wastewater bill per m³ (2016 US$)

■ Selected cities in Middle East and North Africa   ■ Selected cities in other regions

Source: Global Water Intelligence 2016b.
Note: Exchange rates as of July 1, 2016. Average household water use varies by household and by water utility; here it is assumed to be 15 cubic meters (m³) per month.

Subsidies typically benefit wealthier households more than poor households. Wealthier areas can benefit more from subsidized water than poorer neighborhoods, in some cases (Berglöf and Devarajan 2015). In the worst case, poor households may be located in areas unserved by utilities, requiring residents to buy water of dubious quality from vendors in the informal sector at prices much higher than those paid by the rich. Even when the poor have access to piped water, they capture a smaller share of the benefits from the subsidies, because they use less water (Whittington et al. 2015). Available data for selected countries globally suggest that the poorest 20 percent of the population receive less than 10 percent of subsidies incurred by public water utilities, while the richest 20 percent capture over 30 percent of the subsidies (Fuente et al. 2016).

Service providers' dependence on government subsidies diminishes their customer orientation. As a result, utilities are more inclined to prioritize service improvements on the basis of political preference—with differing impacts regarding both service quality and inclusion.

Valuing and pricing water is a politically sensitive issue, but it is essential. All countries should try to design affordable, equitable, and sustainable water service fees and subsidy policies. Fiscal pressures could soon force many countries to do so. A recent survey carried out by the Arab Forum for Environment and Development found that 77 percent of respondents were willing to pay more for water consumption in return for improved social benefits (Saab 2015). The valuation of water services should be framed for what it is: a means of recovering the cost of water service provision and a tool to help preserve water resources for future generations by providing an incentive for current generations to consume water sustainably.

Improving water services could also help strengthen the social compact between governments and citizens. When governments fail to provide water services, citizens' confidence in institutions is weakened. Reversing this trend requires working toward better service quality, greater accountability of water utilities, and clearer understanding of citizens' expectations with respect to water services.

Three main innovations can help improve the quality and reliability of urban and agricultural water services: integrated urban water management, the development of nonconventional water resources, and the use of treated wastewater for agricultural use or managed aquifer recharge. The private sector has been at the forefront in developing many innovations for augmenting water supplies and enhancing efficiency, but great scope exists to extend private sector participation to improve the quality of water services.

Improving the quality of water services also requires improving data collection and monitoring. It is difficult to obtain a comprehensive picture of the quality and reliability of water services in the region, especially for agricultural and industrial users. Monitoring the targets of the new SDGs (in particular SDG 6 on water) provides a tremendous opportunity to build a more evidence-based and comprehensive picture of the status of water services in the Middle East and North Africa.

Question 3. Are Water-Related Risks Being Appropriately Recognized and Mitigated?

While population and economic growth will increase water demands, climate change will be the primary driver for the most pronounced changes in surface water stress across the region. Climate change increases water stress through multiple mechanisms, including reductions in rainfall and increasing temperatures (IPCC 2014), higher evapotranspiration rates and crop water requirements (Verner 2012), and heat extremes

(Lelieveld et al. 2016). Climate change will increase surface water stress in many areas and lead to greater rainfall variability.

Increased surface water stress due to climate change will occur in countries facing politically and environmentally fragile situations. Projections suggest that Iraq, Lebanon, Jordan, Morocco, and Syria will all experience significantly increased water stress driven by climate change (see figure ES.11). On the other hand, socioeconomic change will drive smaller increases in surface water stress in countries such as Algeria, Tunisia, the Republic of Yemen, and the Islamic Republic of Iran.

Climate change contributes to the rise of sea levels, increasing the risk of flooding and salinization of deltas and aquifers in coastal areas of the region. Low-lying deltas such as the Nile and the Shatt-al Arab have been identified as at risk from the impacts of climate change (Tessler et al. 2015), as have low-lying coastal areas such as Morocco's Mediterranean coastal zone (Snoussi, Ouchani, and Niazi 2008). In Alexandria in the Nile Delta, average annual flood losses in 2050 might double, compared

FIGURE ES.11

Future Drivers of Surface Water Stress in the Middle East and North Africa

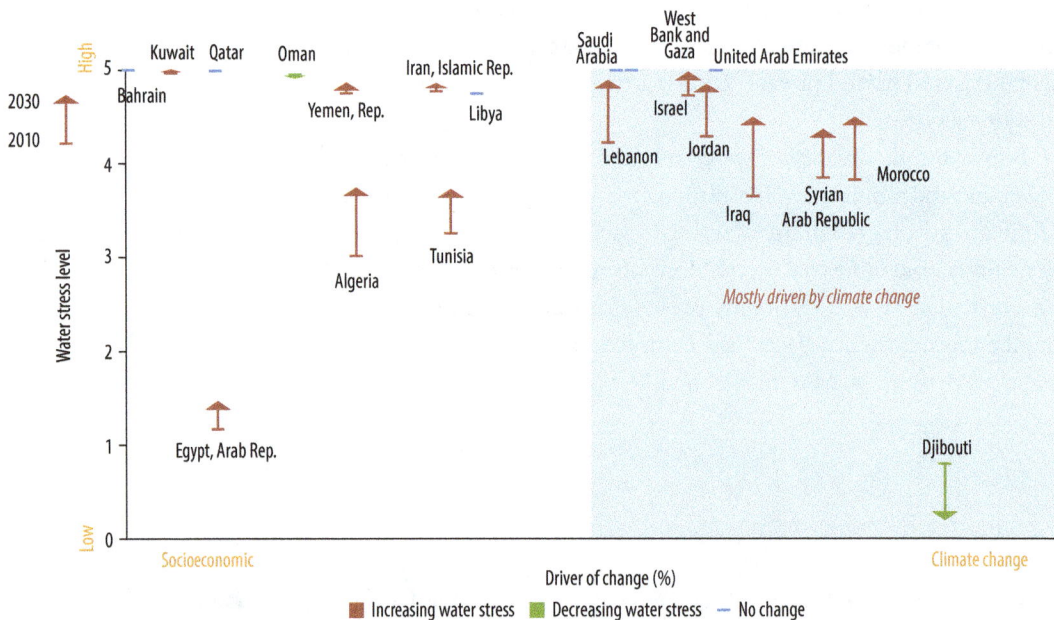

Source: Analysis and calculations based on World Resources Institute Aqueduct™ data.

Note: Water stress is quantified as the ratio of annual water withdrawals to average annual surface water availability under an RCP 8.5 (high emission scenario) and SSP2 (business as usual for socioeconomic change). The position of each country along the horizontal dimension reflects the percent change in water stress, which is driven by climate change (right) or socioeconomic change (left). Future climate change is modeled using an ensemble of climate models for a high emission scenario (RCP 8.5). Socioeconomic change is modeled using a middle-of-the-road scenario where future socio-economic trajectories do not shift markedly from historical patterns (that is, a business-as-usual scenario for population growth and the economy) (O'Neill et al. 2015). Estimates of surface water stress do not account for withdrawals from groundwater and nonconventional water supplies.

with 2005 levels, if the current standard of flood defense is maintained (Hallegatte et al. 2013). Sea-level rise also causes saltwater to intrude into freshwater aquifers and river systems. Coastal areas where groundwater is overexploited are particularly vulnerable to saltwater intrusion into aquifers, because excessive groundwater abstraction makes space for saltwater to flow into freshwater aquifers (Mabrouk et al. 2013). In deltas and river systems like the Shatt-al-Arab in Iraq, the combination of sea level rise and diminished volumes of river outflows allows the tides to push brackish water far upstream in these systems. This can turn river waters and connected groundwater resources brackish, which would have devastating effects on the riverine ecology.

Flood and drought risks are increasing and are likely to harm the poor disproportionately. In the Middle East and North Africa, poorer populations are the most vulnerable to weather-related shocks (Hallegatte et al. 2016; Wodon et al. 2014). Floods are the most frequent natural disaster in the region. The percentage of the region's GDP produced in areas exposed to floods tripled from 1979 to 2009. More severe and intense droughts are expected as a consequence of climate change. Recent droughts have been exceptional relative to the natural variability observed in the last millennium (Cook et al. 2016), increasing concerns that drought conditions will be further exacerbated by climate change.

The interrelationships among the water, food, and energy sectors pose difficult trade-offs and result in unintended consequences. The need for water to produce food, and the need for energy to produce water (for desalination and groundwater pumping), demonstrate the importance of linkages across these sectors for addressing water security. Integrated approaches across the water-food-energy nexus are required to mitigate water-related risks and achieve the SDG targets. The importance of multisectoral, nexus approaches to solving complex resource management problems has been recognized by the League of Arab States in its Strategic Framework for Sustainable Development (Gelil 2014).

Trading water embedded in commodities (virtual water trade) provides a way to transfer water resources from other regions to the water-stressed Middle East and North Africa. The region imports virtual water from around the world (Allan 2001). The United States is the single largest exporter of virtual water to the Middle East and North Africa, followed by Argentina, Australia, and Brazil (see map ES.2) (Antonelli and Tamea 2015). The Middle East and North Africa region is the world's largest importer of wheat, and seven Middle East and North Africa countries are in the top thirty food-importing countries in the world. In the Middle East and North Africa, trade in virtual water can enable a reallocation of water from irrigated

MAP ES.2

Net Virtual Water Trade with the Middle East and North Africa, by World Region, 2015

IBRD 43080 | AUGUST 2017

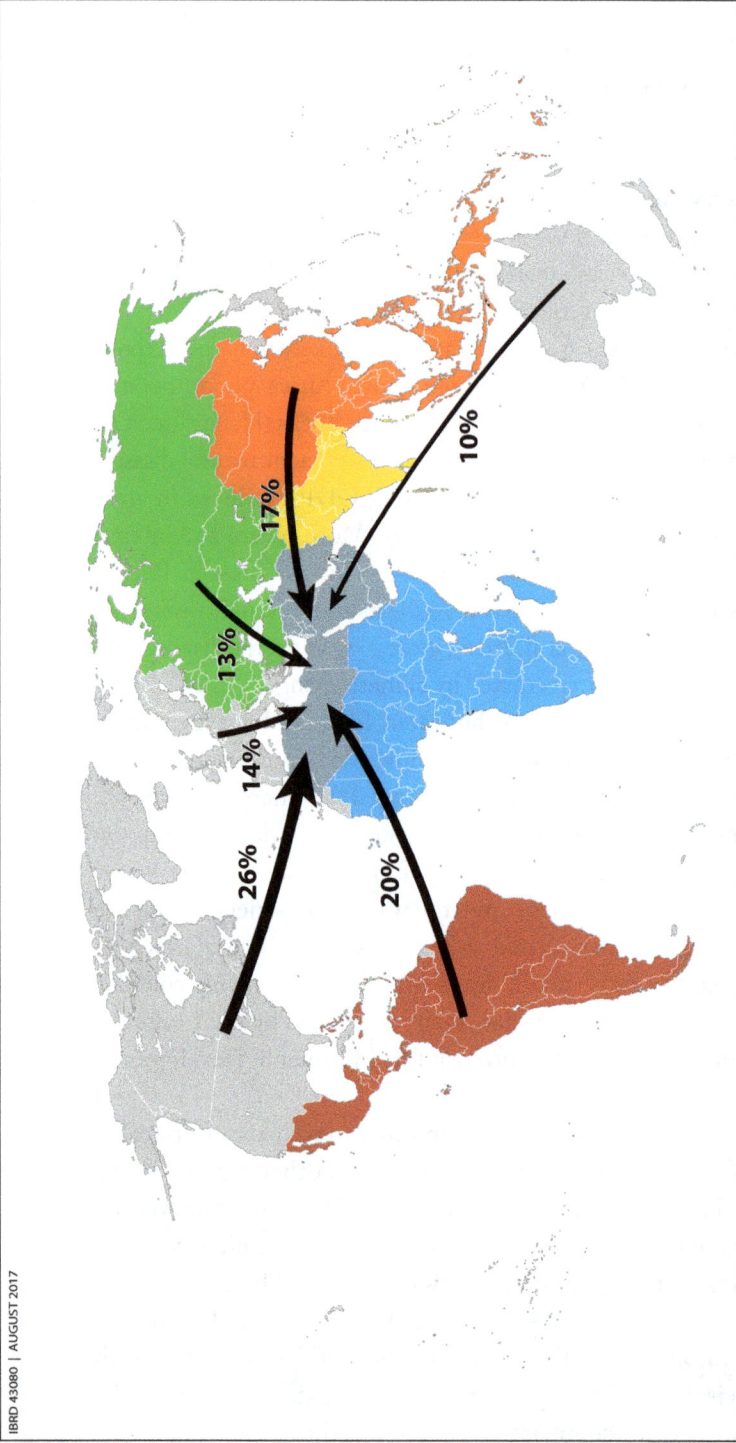

Source: World Bank with data from Antonelli and Tamea 2015.
Note: Thickness of the arrow denotes relative amount of water imported to the Middle East and North Africa from that region.

agriculture to other higher-value sectors, thereby enhancing the region's overall economic productivity of water.

Virtual water can help strengthen water and food security simultaneously, if associated risks are managed. First, the direction of the net water trade needs to be managed. Virtual water imports to the region increased by more than 150 percent between 1986 and 2010 (Antonelli, Laio, and Tamea 2017). Virtual water exports from the region increased by more than 300 percent over the same period, but they have been declining since 2010, following new polices and export restrictions (Antonelli and Tamea 2015). This points to the importance of aligning a country's agricultural and trade policies with its water security goals. Some states are reluctant to become too dependent on imports, because both food and water are seen as issues of national security (Swain and Jägerskog 2016). Food price shocks, transport disruptions, and other systemic risks can affect the trade in virtual water. There are also associated social risks to be managed, because large populations depend on agriculture for their livelihoods.

Reliance on shared transboundary waters adds a layer of uncertainty and potential risks to water resources management and planning in the region. A large part of both surface and groundwater resources in the Middle East and North Africa are transboundary, and some countries rely heavily on these shared resources (see map ES.3). Some 60 percent of surface water resources in the region are transboundary, and all countries share at least one aquifer. The greatest risks arise where countries have both a high percentage of water originating outside their borders and a high reliance on those shared waters. Climate change presents additional challenges because transboundary agreements are often based on multi-year averages, as opposed to percentages of flows. Thus agreements can come under considerable strain when water availability deviates from historical norms. Constructive, transparent, and equitable relationships over transboundary water resources are essential.

Fragility and political instability can slow or reverse gains in water security, and water insecurity in turn can compound fragility. Forced population displacement significantly increases the difficulty of achieving water security. The influx of refugees can exacerbate demographic pressures on limited water resources, leading to social tensions and increased fragility within refugee communities and between refugees and host communities. In particular, there are risks of sexual and gender-based violence toward women and girls who need to access sanitation, cooking facilities, and water points in refugee camps. Investments in water security can potentially help break this vicious cycle of water insecurity and instability, and contribute to stability and resilience (Sadoff, Borgomeo, and de Waal 2017).

MAP ES.3

Major Transboundary Aquifers in the Middle East and North Africa

IBRD 42540 | APRIL 2017

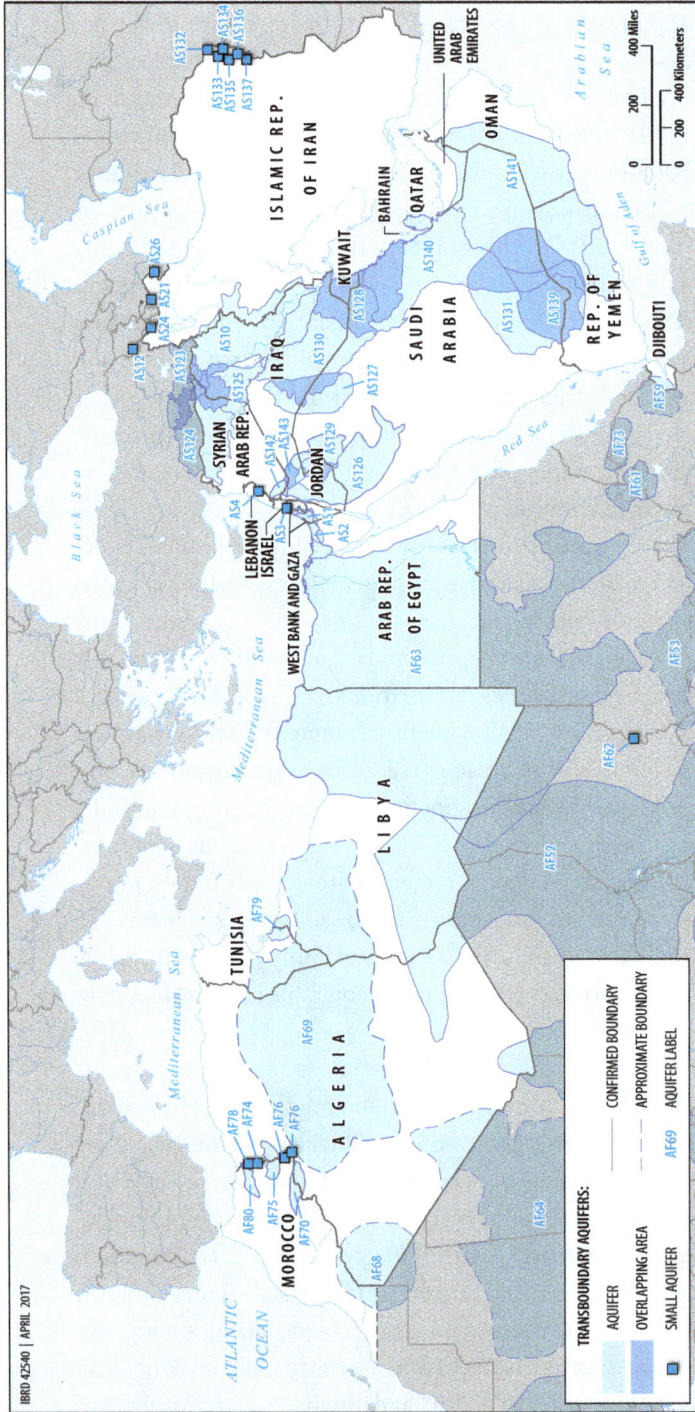

Source: International Groundwater Resource Assessment Centre.

Transforming Water: Opportunities and Solutions for Water Security

Technological and governance innovations—in the region and globally—are accelerating to meet an urgent need for action. Some of the most notable water management innovations in the world are being implemented in the Middle East and North Africa. These innovations include highly successful efforts to increase water use efficiency along with state-of-the-art water recycling and policies that have successfully reallocated water from low- to high-value uses.

A range of new technologies for water resources management and water service delivery are available to promote efficiency. Smart metering, in particular, can be used to improve accuracy in billing, evaluate consumption, and increase users' awareness of their own consumption. As experiences from the region and globally show, smart metering also helps water service providers identify leaks, reduce operating costs, and communicate the value of water to users.

Technology also helps to improve water service delivery, especially for the underserved and the poor. Mobile based systems ensure improved customer service by allowing for real time monitoring of water infrastructure. This is particularly important for identifying and fixing operational issues in rural areas where the status of water infrastructure may be difficult to monitor. Furthermore, mobile technologies promote rapid access to information and data sharing, creating a system of accountability. In turn, this strengthens public participation and promotes a more equitable and transparent allocation of the resource. Finally, evidence from different parts of the world shows that the introduction of mobile water payment options improves collection efficiency and increases utilities' revenues, providing financial strength to extend services to the underserved.

Technologies and practices to recycle water and curb waste are increasingly being used in the region. Several countries have recognized the benefits of recycling water; some aim to recycle all of their wastewater by 2030. Positive experiences in Jordan (As-Samra) and Tunisia (Souhil Wadi) show that wastewater can be safely recycled for use in irrigation and managed aquifer recharge. Recent decreases in the cost of desalination and advances in membrane technology also mean that desalination is increasingly becoming a viable alternative to traditional freshwater resources.

Innovations in integrated urban water management can contribute to improving the quality, reliability, and sustainability of urban and agricultural water services. Integrated urban water management considers the city's urban water services in close relation with its urban development dynamics on the one hand, and with the broader basin context on the other (World Bank 2012). These approaches have been tried, tested, and scaled in many water-scarce regions in the world. Such approaches will encourage cities to create strong synergies within or outside the water basin—for example through the development of wastewater recycling for agriculture or shared desalination with industries.

Water security also requires moving toward a diversified water management portfolio. Diversified solutions lead to greater resilience to systemic shocks—be they climatic or economic. This starts with "closing the water resources loop" rather than thinking of water usage as "once through the system." Examples of diversification include optimizing local surface as well as groundwater storage; developing nonconventional water resources such as desalination, recycling and recharge; reducing leakage; and promoting conservation.

Increased institutional coordination among the water, energy and agricultural sectors is strengthening water management efforts. Successfully reducing water use and reallocating water to higher value uses requires coordination between different ministries, increased regulatory clarity and data sharing. Around the world, successful water management is happening in concert with policies that consider energy and agriculture.

Experiences from the region show that it is possible to implement the right incentives to encourage water savings and reallocation. These incentives can be developed in a way that avoids disproportionate impacts on the poor as well as social unrest. Well-designed incentives include accurate targeting of price changes—for instance by targeting higher consumption users—and public campaigns explaining the reason for pricing changes and the availability of compensatory mechanisms.

Public-private partnerships have also been implemented in the region to tackle the operational constraints of water utilities. The Middle East and North Africa has been the most active place in the world (along with China) regarding public-private partnerships in water management. This has led to improved utility performance over the last six years. Across the region almost 28 million people now have improved water services via public-private utility partnerships.

There is an increasing role for private sector financing of water infrastructure. Most of the public-private partnerships in the region have focused on service efficiency. Now there is growing interest in mobilizing private capital to meet the tremendous financing needs for water infrastructure. Wastewater treatment plants in Bahrain, Egypt, Jordan, and the Islamic Republic of Iran, along with irrigation projects in Morocco, show that the private sector is motivated to bring financing to public-private partnerships and to work toward a creditworthy water utilities that could attract more private sector financing when issues of tariffs, partial subsidies, and assurance of payments are addressed.

Achieving water security means acting together, from the household level to the regional level. From a household water perspective, this means engaging women, who often have the main responsibility for using and conserving water. Women's rights, representation, and resources need to be acknowledged and addressed, both for social inclusion and for sustainable development. Youth should also be engaged in developing the next generation's water expectations and practices.

At the regional level, cooperation on water can foster greater trust and collaboration. The World Bank is supporting regional cooperation across Middle East and North Africa. As part of its regional strategy, the World Bank is promoting regional cooperation around water and other regional public goods and sectors, such as energy and education. The purpose of this action area is not to promote cooperation for its own benefits, but as a means to greater peace and stability in the region (Devarajan 2015). The efforts of the League of Arab States to strengthen water management in the region need to continue. The work by the Arab Countries Water Utilities Association (ACWUA) on benchmarking water utilities and tracking performance of water services across the region will become more valuable as part of the SDGs. Similarly, collaboration between researchers and universities through established and emerging networks, such as the Middle East and North Africa Network of Water Centers of Excellence (MENA NWC) is essential. Finally, nongovernmental organizations (NGOs), such as the regional Israeli, Palestinian, and Jordanian NGO EcoPeace Middle East, and international organizations can contribute with knowledge and financial resources to help Middle Eastern and North African countries and economies address some of their water challenges.

Engaging and educating civil society on water issues and water conservation is also crucial to guarantee success. Changing water management practices to ensure better service delivery and sustainability of water use requires changing the attitudes of individuals and government officials, as much as putting in place institutional incentives and arrangements. Promotion of water conservation in schools is just one potential mechanism to change people's awareness and attitudes about water, alongside media campaigns to raise awareness about water challenges.

While the opportunities and experiences presented here can serve as points of entry for action, solutions will be context-dependent. There is a rich menu of technological, financial, and institutional options, but the right actions will be different for any particular country, river basin, or city. This is because of the diversity of environmental, economic, and sociopolitical characteristics in the Middle East and North Africa.

Some interventions will need to be prioritized during times of protracted crisis, as opposed to interventions and investments that can be carried out during times of post-conflict development. Given the scale of the disruption caused by conflicts, and the protracted nature of some of the region's crises, the traditional approach of waiting for conflicts to end before carrying out reconstruction plans will not work (Devarajan 2015). As discussed in the World Bank's regional strategy, the Middle East and North Africa region requires a dynamic approach that brings in external partners, leverages large scale financing, and moves beyond humanitarian response to longer-term development, wherever and whenever conflict subsides.

The region demonstrates a host of potential solutions to its water management challenges, but clear, strong incentives are needed to spur action. Incentives for water conservation and innovation are needed to change the way water is managed. These can come through policies, pricing, allocation, or regulation. If water becomes unavailable, or too expensive, water users will respond. They will innovate. They will find better ways of doing more with less. They will adopt proven solutions and adapt or create new solutions.

The most important lesson from global and regional experience is that technology, policy, and institutional management must evolve together to achieve water security. Strategies that seek to "desalinate their way out of water insecurity" have made limited progress toward water security. Global experience shows that countries and cities that have arguably overcome the limits of water scarcity have done so through integrated management of both water resources (conventional and nonconventional) and water services and mitigation of water-related risks (figure ES.12). This has allowed them to effectively surpass the constraints of their scant natural water endowments. These cutting-edge water managers are effectively aligning water resource planning, management, institutions, information systems, infrastructure, risk management, and incentives to access and store more water, allocate it more efficiently, and deliver it more effectively to customers. And they have done so while guarding the quality and sustainability of their water resources.

Failure to seize these opportunities will have significant implications for the political, economic, and environmental stability in the region and beyond. As the current conflict and migration crisis unfolding in the Middle East and North Africa shows, failure to address water challenges can have severe impacts on people's well-being and political stability.

The strategic question for the region is whether countries will act with foresight and resolve to strengthen water security, or whether they will wait to react to the inevitable disruptions of water crises.

Governance and Incentives to Seize Emerging Opportunities in Water Resources Management and Water Services Delivery and to Mitigate Water-Related Risks

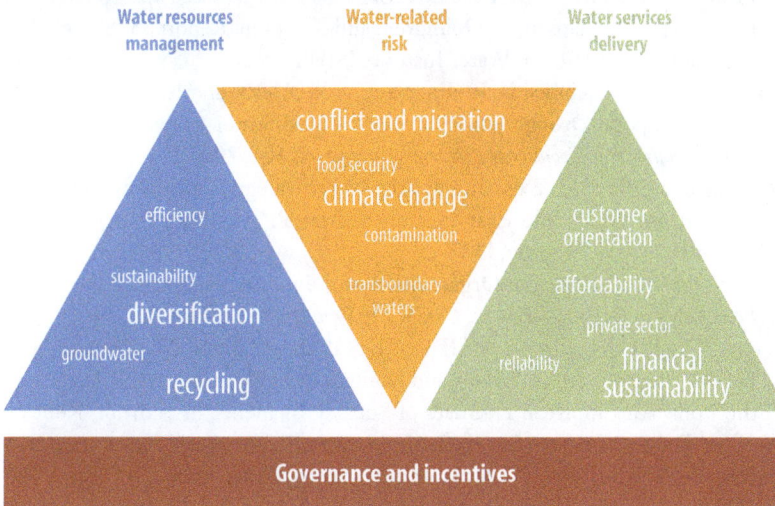

Notes

1. Water stress arises when water withdrawals for human, agricultural, and industrial uses are relatively high compared with the level of renewable water resources—that is, the ratio of water withdrawal to water availability is high.
2. Pricing refers to a fee to cover the costs of service provision.

References

ACWUA (Arab Countries Water Utilities Association). 2014. "Water Utilities Reform in the Arab Region. Lessons Learned and Guiding Principles." ACWUA, Amman, Jordan.

Allan, J. A. 2001. *The Middle East Water Questions. Hydropolitics and the Global Economy*. London: IB Tauris.

Antonelli, M., F. Laio, and S. Tamea. 2017. "Water Resources, Food Security and the Role of Virtual Water Trade in the MENA Region." In *Governance of Environmental Change within a Human Security Perspective*, edited by M. Behnassi. Springer.

Antonelli, M., and S. Tamea. 2015. "Food-Water Security and Virtual Water Trade in the Middle East and North Africa." *International Journal of Water Resources Development* 31 (3): 326–42.

AWC (Arab Water Council). 2014. *3rd Arab Water Forum, Together towards a Secure Arab Water*. Final Report. Cairo: AWC.

Aylward, B., H. Seely, R. Hartwell, and J. Dengel. 2010. "The Economic Value of Water for Agricultural, Domestic and Industrial Uses: A Global Compilation of Economic Studies and Market Prices." Prepared for the United Nations Food and Agricultural Organization (UN FAO) by Ecosystem Economics.

Berglöf, E., and S. Devarajan. 2015. "Water for Development: Fulfilling the Promise." In *Water for Development—Charting a Water Wise Path*, edited by A. Jägerskog, T. J. Clausen, T. Holmgren, and K. Lexén. Report 35. Stockholm: Stockholm International Water Institute (SIWI).

Cook, B. I., K. J. Anchukaitis, R. Touchan, D. M. Meko, and E. R. Cook. 2016. "Spatiotemporal Drought Variability in the Mediterranean over the Last 900 Years." *Journal of Geophysics Research Atmospheres* 121: 2060–74.

Devarajan, S. 2015. "An Exposition of the New Strategy, 'Promoting Peace and Stability in the Middle East and North Africa'." Working Paper 102936, World Bank, Washington, DC.

FAO (Food and Agricultural Organization of the United Nations). 2011. *Global Food Losses and Waste—Extent, Causes and Prevention*. Rome: FAO.

Fuente, D., J. Gakii Gatua, M. Ikiara, J. Kabubo-Mariara, M. Mwaura, and D. Whittington. 2016. "Water and Sanitation Service Delivery, Pricing, and the Poor: An Empirical Estimate of Subsidy Incidence in Nairobi, Kenya." *Water Resources Research* 52: 4845–62.

García, N., I. Harrison, N. Cox, and M. F. Tognelli. 2015. *The Status and Distribution of Freshwater Biodiversity in the Arabian Peninsula*. Gland, Switzerland: IUCN (International Union for Conservation of Nature).

Gelil, I. A. 2014. "Proposal for an Arab Strategic Framework for Sustainable Development, 2015–2025." Arab High Level Forum on Sustainable Development, Economic and Social Commission for Western Asia (ESCWA), United Nations, Amman, April 2–4.

Global Water Intelligence. 2016a. "Global Water Market 2017: Meeting the World's Water and Wastewater Needs until 2020." Global Water Intelligence.

———. 2016b. "Global Water Tariff Survey 2016." Global Water Intelligence.

Grey, D., and C. Sadoff. 2007. "Sink or Swim? Water Security for Growth and Development." *Water Policy* 9 (6): 545–71.

Hallegatte, S., M. Bangalore, L. Bonzanigo, M. Fay, T. Kane, U. Narloch, J. Rozenberg, D. Treguer, and A. Vogt-Schilb. 2016. *Shock Waves: Managing the Impacts of Climate Change on Poverty, Climate Change and Development*. Washington, DC: World Bank.

Hallegatte, S., C. Green, R. J. Nicholls, and J. Corfee-Moriot. 2013. "Future Flood Losses in Major Coastal Cities." *Nature Climate Change* 3: 802–06.

Hutton, G. 2013. "Global Costs and Benefits of Reaching Universal Coverage of Sanitation and Drinking-Water Supply." *Journal of Water and Health* 11 (1): 1–12.

IGRAC (International Groundwater Resources Assessment Centre) and UNESCO-IHP (UNESCO International Hydrological Programme). 2015. "Transboundary Aquifers of the World" (map). Edition 2015. Scale 1 : 50,000,000. Delft, Netherlands: IGRAC.

IPCC (Intergovernmental Panel on Climate Change). 2014. "Climate Change 2014: Impacts, Adaptation, and Vulnerability." Part B: Regional Aspects, Contribution of Working Group II to the *Fifth Assessment Report of the Intergovernmental Panel on Climate Change*, 1327–70. Cambridge, U.K.: Cambridge University Press.

Kochhar, K., C. Pattillo, Y. Sun, N. Suphaphiphat, A. Swiston, R. Tchaidze, B. Clements, S. Fabrizio, V. Flamini, L. Redifer, H. Finger, and an IMF Staff Team. 2015. "Is the Glass Half Empty or Half Full? Issues in Managing Water Challenges and Policy Instruments." Staff Discussion Note SDN/15/11, International Monetary Fund, Washington, DC.

Kummu, M., H. de Moel, M. Porkka, S. Siebert, O. Varis, and P. J. Ward. 2012. "Lost Food, Wasted Resources: Global Food Supply Chain Losses and Their Impacts on Freshwater, Cropland and Fertilizer Use." *Science of the Total Environment* 438: 477–89.

Lelieveld, J., Y. Proestos, P. Hadjinicolaou, M. Tanarhte, E. Tyrlis, and G. Zittis. 2016. "Strongly Increasing Heat Extremes in the Middle East and North Africa (MENA) in the 21st Century." *Climatic Change* 137 (1): 245–60.

Mabrouk, M. B., A. Jonoski, D. Solomatine, and S. Uhlenbrook. 2013. "A Review of Seawater Intrusion in the Nile Delta Groundwater System—The Basis for Assessing Impacts Due to Climate Changes and Water Resources Development." *Hydrology and Earth Systems Sciences* 10: 10873–911.

O'Neill, B. C., E. Kriegler, K. K. Ebi, E. Kemp-Benedict, K. Riahi, D. S. Rothman, B. J. van Ruijven, D. P. van Vuuren, and J. Berkmann. 2015. "The Roads Ahead: Narratives for Shared Socioeconomic Pathways Describing World Futures in the 21st Century." *Global Environmental Change* 42: 169–80.

Richey, A. S., B. F. Thomas, M.-H. Lo, J. S. Famiglietti, S. Swenson, and M. Rodell. 2015. "Uncertainty in Global Groundwater Storage Estimates in a Total Groundwater Stress Framework." *Water Resources Research* 51: 5198–216. doi:10.1002/2015WR017351.

Saab, N. 2015. "Consumption Patterns in Arab Countries." AFED Public Opinion Survey. Arab Forum for Environment and Development.

Sadoff, C. W., E. Borgomeo, and D. de Waal. 2017. *Turbulent Waters: Pursuing Water Security in Fragile Contexts*. Washington, DC: World Bank.

Sadoff, C. W., J. W. Hall, D. Grey, J. C. J. H. Aerts, M. Ait-Kadi, C. Brown, A. Cox, S. Dadson, D. Garrick, J. Kelman, P. McCornick, C. Ringler, M. Rosegrant, D. Whittington, and D. Wiberg. 2015. *Securing Water, Sustaining Growth: Report of the GWP/OECD Task Force on Water Security and Sustainable Growth*. Oxford, U.K.: University of Oxford.

Snoussi, M., T. Ouchani, and S. Niazi. 2008. "Vulnerability Assessment of the Impact of Sea-Level Rise and Flooding on the Moroccan Coast: The Case of the Mediterranean Eastern Zone." *Estuarine, Coastal and Shelf Science* 77 (2): 206–13.

Swain, A., and A. Jägerskog. 2016. *Emerging Security Threats in the Middle East: The Impact of Climate Change and Globalization*. Lanham, MD: Rowman and Littlefield.

Tessler, Z. D., C. Vorosmarty, M. Grossberg, I. Gladkova, H. Aizenman, J. P. M. Syvitski, and E. Foufoula-Georgiou. 2015. "Profiling Risk and Sustainability in Coastal Deltas of the World." *Science* 349 (6248): 638–43.

Tropp, H., and A. Jägerskog. 2006. "Water Scarcity Challenges in the Middle East and North Africa." Occasional Paper 2006/31 for the *Human Development Report 2006*. United Nations Development Programme, New York City.

UNICEF and WHO (United Nations Children's Fund and World Health Organization). 2015. "Keeping Up with Population Growth." In *Progress on Sanitation and Drinking Water 2015. Update and MDG Assessment*. Geneva: WHO Press.

Van Lavieren, H., J. Burt, D. A. Feary, G. Cavalcante, E. Marquis, L. Benedetti, C. Trick, B. Kjerfve, and P. F. Sale. 2011. *Managing the Growing Impacts of Development on Fragile Coastal and Marine Ecosystems: Lessons from the Gulf.* A policy report. Hamilton, Ontario, Canada: UNU-INWEH (United Nations University-Institute of Water, Environment, and Health).

Verner, D. 2012. *Adaptation to a Changing Climate in the Arab Countries: A Case for Adaptation, Governance, and Leadership in Building Climate Resilience.* MENA Development Report. Washington, DC: World Bank.

Veolia Water and IFPRI (International Food Policy Research Institute). 2011. Sustaining Growth via Water Productivity: 2030/2050 Scenarios. http://growingblue.com/wp-content/uploads/2011/05/IFPRI_VEOLIA_STUDY_2011.pdf.

Wada, Y., and F. Bierkens. 2014. "Sustainability of Global Water Use: Past Reconstruction and Future Projections." *Environmental Research Letters.* http://dx.doi.org/10.1088/1748-9326/9/10/104003.

Whittington, D., C. Nauges, D. Fuente, and X. Wu. 2015. "A Diagnostic Tool for Estimating the Incidence of Subsidies Delivered by Water Utilities in Low- and Medium-Income Countries, with Illustrative Simulations." *Utilities Policy* 34: 70–81.

Wodon, Q., A. Liverani, G. Joseph, and N. Bougnoux, eds. 2014. *Climate Change and Migration: Evidence from the Middle East and North Africa.* World Bank Studies. Washington, DC: World Bank.

World Bank. 2007. *Making the Most of Scarcity: Accountability for Better Water Management Results in the Middle East and North Africa.* MENA Development Report. Washington, DC: World Bank.

———. 2012. *Integrated Urban Water Management: A Summary Note.* Washington, DC: World Bank.

———. 2016. *High and Dry: Climate Change, Water, and the Economy.* Washington, DC: World Bank.

World Economic Forum. 2015. *Global Risks 2015.* 10th ed. Geneva: World Economic Forum.

Zekri, S., M. Ahmed, R. Chaieb, and N. Ghaffour. 2014. "Managed Aquifer Recharge Using Quaternary-Treated Wastewater: An Economic Perspective." *International Journal of Water Resources Development* 30 (2): 246–61.

Introduction

Water crises are seen as the greatest risk for which the Middle East and North Africa is least prepared. The World Economic Forum asked experts and leaders from the region: "For which global risks is your region least prepared?" The greatest number of respondents identified water crises—even ahead of issues such as political instability and unemployment—as the most prominent risk for which the region is least prepared to face (figure I.1).

It is well known that the Middle East and North Africa constitutes the most water scarce region in the world—today, the majority of the region's population and gross domestic product (GDP) are exposed to "high" or "very high" water stress.[1] Over 60 percent of the region's population lives in areas with high or very high surface water stress—far exceeding the global average of about 35 percent. Over 70 percent of the region's GDP is generated in areas with high to very high surface water stress, more than triple the global average of some 22 percent.

The region's water challenges go far beyond its age-old constraints of water scarcity, however, and include a growing range and intensity of water-related risks, water governance issues, and broader but related challenges of climate change and conflict. The complexities of the water-energy-food nexus, climate change, droughts and floods, water quality, transboundary water management, and the management of water in the context of fragility, conflict, and violence compound the challenge of water scarcity. While the region's water scarcity challenges have been apparent for millennia, newer challenges are adding both hazards and complexity. The answers to these challenges will be as much about governance as they are about resource endowments, infrastructure investments, or technologies.

Many countries have already passed the damaging tipping point beyond water scarcity and are now eroding their water resource base.

FIGURE I.1

Main Global Risks for Which the Middle East and North Africa Region Is Least Prepared

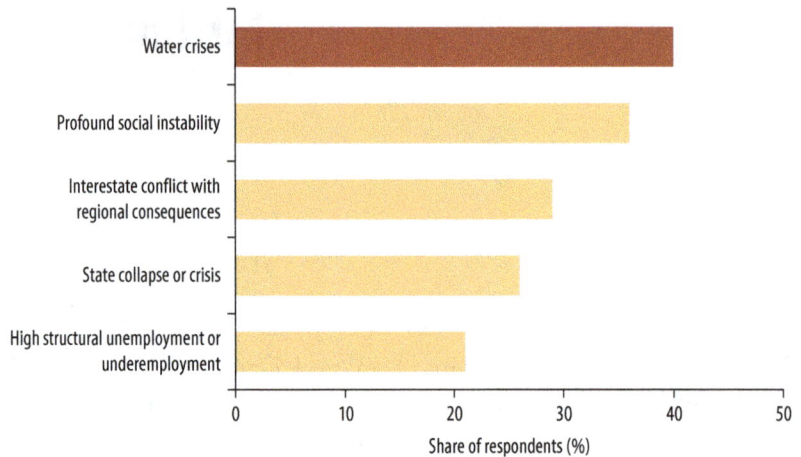

Source: WEF 2015.
Note: Based on survey asking, "For which global risks is your region least prepared?"

For millennia, investments and innovations have been made across the region in water management. But economic and population growth have now overwhelmed these efforts in many countries, and unsustainable volumes of water are being withdrawn, degrading ecosystems and aquifers. Overdrawing water from rivers and aquifers is like living beyond one's means—drawing down or depreciating a country's natural capital, and undermining its longer-term wealth and resilience.

Other countries have arguably overcome the limits of water scarcity by intensively managing both conventional and nonconventional water resources in a way that effectively allows them to surpass the constraints of their scant natural water endowments. Water resource planning, management, institutions, information systems, infrastructure, and incentives can all be aligned in order to access and store more water, allocate it more effectively, use it more efficiently, and even to "produce" nonconventional water through wastewater recycling or desalination. Just as the region's water challenges have evolved, so have the solutions for managing water scarcity, providing water services, and mitigating water-related risks.

A fundamental development challenge for the region is to take the actions necessary to navigate sustainable pathways toward water security that anticipate and manage the inevitable increases in water scarcity and water-related risks—against a backdrop of climate change, growing fiscal constraints, and widespread fragility and conflict. Planning and action are needed to strengthen the resilience of economies and societies to water-related hazards, to deliver water services that are affordable both from the perspective of users and government budgets, and to mitigate the costs and social disruptions that can be expected to result from extreme scarcity, sudden supply interruptions, contamination, floods, or droughts.

Countries in the region that fail to achieve water security are not only forgoing potential growth; they are also heightening their vulnerability to hydrological shocks and potentially compounding social and political fragility. The region is expected to experience the greatest economic losses in the world from climate-related water scarcity, reaching 6–14 percent of GDP losses by 2050. Growth is being undermined by water scarcity, unreliable water supplies, and the water-related illnesses that result from inadequate clean water and sanitation. The impacts of scarcity and hydrological shocks such as droughts and floods are heightened where forecast and warning systems are weak, stormwater and flood management are inadequate, irrigation infrastructure is limited, and stored water in reservoirs and groundwater aquifers is insufficient. The failure to deliver basic water services, and to mitigate the impacts of water-related hazards and risks, can erode government legitimacy and compound social and political fragility.

Both the risks and opportunities for water management in the region have never been greater. Because water scarcity has been a central feature of the region throughout its history, there is potential for complacency in accepting the limitations that water scarcity implies, or for dependence on incremental or traditional responses to water challenges. Given the rapid growth of the region's economy and population, incremental solutions and continued subsidies are becoming increasingly inadequate and unaffordable. Fortunately, at the same time, many countries have demonstrated success in implementing aggressive programs to diminish nonrevenue water, increase water productivity, and produce nonconventional water through wastewater recycling or desalination. The cost-effectiveness of these technologies is also rapidly improving, changing the landscape of options for the next generation of water management.

To achieve water security, a new consciousness is needed about the way in which water is managed in the region. In many countries, policies, incentives, and institutional weaknesses have enabled inefficient and low-value water use. But there is simply not enough water to continue in this way. Those policies today are leading to resource degradation and rising fiscal deficits.

Moving forward, a broader range of tools and technologies will need to be considered, debated, and implemented. Investments in water infrastructure, information systems, institutions, and technologies will be needed. Societies will also need to consider and discuss controversial solutions such as water service fees; wastewater recycling and reuse;

the reallocation of water from rural to urban users and from agriculture to industry; and the imperative for social inclusion in the delivery of water services and protections against water–related risks.

This report provides a regional assessment of the status of water security in the Middle East and North Africa region, describes existing water-related challenges, and outlines emerging opportunities to achieve water security. It explores three questions that are fundamental to water security:

1. Are the region's water resources being managed sustainably and efficiently?
2. Are water services being delivered reliably and affordably?
3. Are water-related risks being appropriately recognized and mitigated?

The assessment provides a foundation to identify the most significant water-related issues and potential "entry points" for action in the Middle East and North Africa region, to motivate more comprehensive assessments of water security at the national level, and to enhance the dialogue on water security (box I.1).

BOX I.1

Ten Years on from *Making the Most of Scarcity*: How Is This Report Different from Previous World Bank Studies on Water in the Middle East and North Africa?

In 2007, the World Bank published a flagship report highlighting the key water challenges facing the Middle East and North Africa Region. The report, entitled *Making the Most of Scarcity: Accountability for Better Water Management in the Middle East and North Africa*, provided an assessment of the factors determining water service delivery outcomes and the successes and failures of water reform in the region. The 2007 report emphasized three areas that ought to be considered to ensure that water management becomes financially, socially, and environmentally sustainable over the long term: recognizing the political nature of water reforms; understanding the centrality of nonwater policies in influencing water outcomes, and improving the accountability of government agencies and service providers to the public.

The current report differs in that it focuses on assessing the status of water resources and water risks in the Middle East and North Africa, in addition to water services. It provides an up-to-date analysis of the status, trends, and impacts of water risks and opportunities for each country in the region. Furthermore, the report considers and quantifies issues related to exposure to water stress, sustainable water use, nonconventional water resources, the water-energy-food nexus, and current conflicts.

Note

1. Water stress arises when water withdrawals for human, agricultural, and industrial uses are relatively high compared to the level of renewable water resources—that is, when there is a high water-withdrawal-to-availability ratio.

CHAPTER 1

Water Security

Why Water Security Matters

Water insecurity threatens global prosperity. It acts as a drag on growth that can cost the global economy some $500 billion per year. The drag is strongest in countries already experiencing water stress, and those with low incomes and high dependence on agriculture (Sadoff et al. 2015). Roughly one-quarter of global GDP is produced in areas with high or very high water scarcity.[1] About 35 percent of the world's population lives in water-scarce areas,[2] and water-related diseases affect more than 1.5 billion people annually (UNICEF and WHO 2015). Increasing awareness of the impacts of water insecurity on human well-being and economic prosperity is reflected in the Word Economic Forum's *Global Risks* report, where water-related risks have been consistently ranked among the top 10 global risks (WEF 2015).

Water security is a state in which water is effectively and sustainably managed, both to leverage its productive potential and to mitigate its destructive potential. Water security has been defined as "the availability of an acceptable quantity and quality of water for health, livelihoods, ecosystems and production, coupled with an acceptable level of water-related risks to people, environments and economies" (Grey and Sadoff 2007). This definition and others (see, for instance, Grey et al. 2013; Hall and Borgomeo 2013) highlight the importance of risk management in the construct of water security. More recently, UN-Water developed a definition of water security that explicitly captures interactions with wider social, economic, political, and environmental systems, as "the capacity of a population to safeguard sustainable access to adequate quantities of acceptable quality water for sustaining livelihoods, human well-being, and socio-economic development, for ensuring protection against waterborne pollution and water-related disasters, and for preserving ecosystems in a climate of peace and political stability."[3]

Water security goes beyond water scarcity to take into account not only a country's water resource endowment but also the productive and protective actions it has taken to secure water. Some of the most water-scarce countries in the world are also arguably some of the most water secure, while some of the most water-rich countries in the world struggle to protect their populations from water-related disasters and/or provide improved drinking water access.

Water security can be thought of as the outcome or the goal of water resources management—a dynamic goal that will evolve as hydrological, economic, political, and social circumstances change. Chronic scarcity, growing demand, and increasing hydrological extremes are driving the need for strengthened water resources management, conservation, and efficiency; and for diversified portfolios of water sources—including nonconventional water sources, such as reuse and desalination. Progress toward water security requires continuous monitoring, investment, and coordinated policy linking sustainable water management and service provision, in order to strengthen the resilience of communities, countries, and economies to environmental stresses and reduce the risk of contributing to political fragility.

When a water-related challenge arises, it can trigger or worsen wider economic and political crises. Water challenges can compound existing and emerging instabilities and can contribute to unrest and conflict. When institutions fail to address water insecurity—for instance, when they fail to protect populations from the consequences of a flood or provide basic water services—government credibility may be undermined and the social contract weakened. When water insecurity adversely affects populations, it fuels perceptions that governments are not doing enough, exacerbating grievances, and destabilizing already-fragile situations (see, for instance, Harris, Keen, and Mitchell 2013; Sadoff, Borgomeo, and de Waal 2017).

Without enhanced water security, it will be difficult to achieve the Sustainable Development Goals (SDGs). SDG 6, the so-called water SDG, seeks to "ensure availability and sustainable management of water and sanitation for all." This SDG moves significantly beyond the water-related objective that was articulated under the Millennium Development Goals (MDGs), which was to halve, by 2015, the proportion of the population without sustainable access to safe drinking water and basic sanitation. The MDG for drinking water was met, ahead of the target deadline, in 2010. The MDG for sanitation was not achieved. Looking forward, SDG 6 calls for full global access to both drinking water and sanitation. It also includes new objectives with targets relating to water quality, reuse, scarcity, transboundary cooperation, and integrated water resource management. In addition to SDG 6, water resource challenges are inherent in several other SDGs, including the goals for food security (SDG 2), energy (SDG 7), resilient infrastructure (SDG 9), aquatic eco-systems (SDG 14), and terrestrial ecosystems (SDG 15).

The importance of water security is recognized in the Arab Ministerial Water Council's Water Security Strategy. This strategy, adopted in 2011, lays out a joint framework for action to tackle the water crisis facing the Middle East and North Africa region. Its priorities include raising water productivity; adopting integrated water policies; developing nonconventional water resources, with a focus on renewable energy desalination and water treatment; signing agreements on shared water resources in the Arab region; and incorporating climate change adaptation into national water policies (AMWC 2012).

The Region's Water Challenge in a Global Context

Nowhere is the challenge of water security greater than in the Middle East and North Africa region, which is the world's most water-stressed region. Water stress arises when water withdrawals for human, agricultural, and industrial uses are relatively high compared to the level of renewable water resources—that is, the water-withdrawal-to-availability ratio is high. Water stress in the Middle East and North Africa, measured with water withdrawals as a percentage of total renewable surface freshwater availability, is greater than any other region in the world, as shown in figure 1.1. Water stress is measured in terms of water usage relative to the natural endowment of surface freshwater resources, so it does not capture the contribution of nonconventional water supplies or groundwater resources that may have been developed to relieve water stress.

The surface water resources of the Middle East and North Africa are not only the scarcest; they are also the most variable and unpredictable in the world. Compared to other regions, surface freshwater availability in the Middle East and North Africa varies greatly from year to year (figure 1.1). On average, across the region, annual surface water availability can deviate by as much as 75 percent from the annual means. Strong year-to-year variability means that the region is prone to multiyear droughts and intense rainfall events, which lead to catastrophic flooding. As a consequence, the availability of soil moisture—so-called *green water*[4]—is also prone to large variability in the region. Several agricultural systems in the region are rainfed. Therefore, any changes (or variations) in rainfall will severely affect agricultural output (Allan 2001; Antonelli and Tamea 2015).

FIGURE 1.1

Water Stress and Year-to-Year Variability in Surface Water, by World Region

a. Year-to-year variability   b. Surface water stress

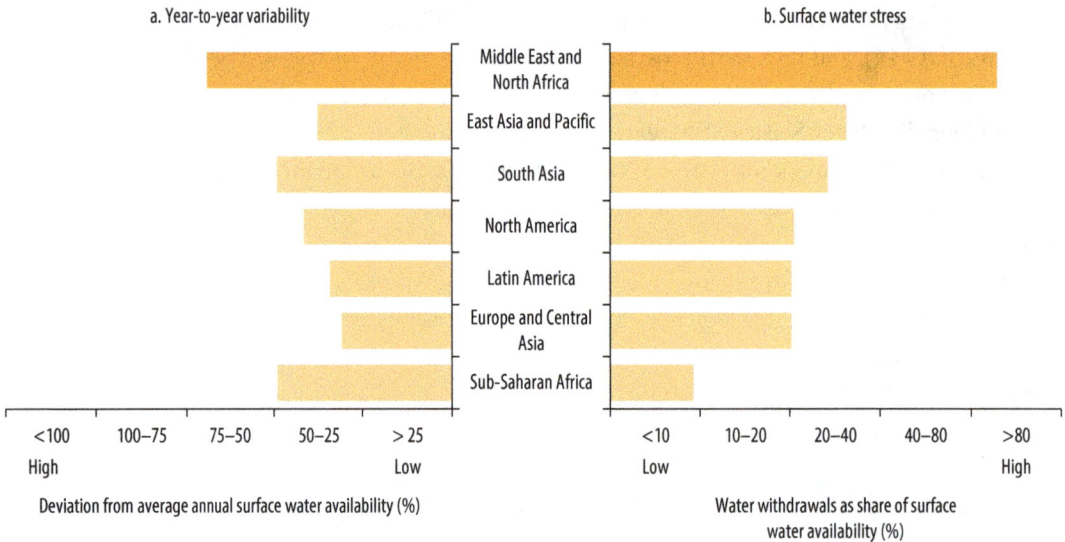

| | Middle East and North Africa | |

<100   100–75   75–50   50–25   > 25   <10   10–20   20–40   40–80   >80
High   Low   Low   High

Deviation from average annual surface water availability (%)   Water withdrawals as share of surface
water availability (%)

Source: World Resources Institute Aqueduct™ database.
Note: Water stress measures total water withdrawals as a percentage of total surface water availability. It does not account for dependence on transboundary water sources or nonconventional water sources. Year-to-year variability measures the percent deviation from mean annual surface water availability.

Over 60 percent of the population of the Middle East and North Africa lives in areas of high or very high water stress, compared to some 35 percent for the rest of the world. Ensuring the provision of water services for communities in situations of high water stress requires particular diligence and planning because there are likely to be fewer feasible alternatives for self-provision. Figure 1.2 shows the percentage of the population in the Middle East and North Africa region that lives in areas of high or very high water stress relative the percentage of the world's population living in areas of high or very high water stress (Veolia Water and IFPRI 2011).

Roughly 70 percent of the region's economic activities are produced in areas of high or very high water stress, more than three times the global average of 22 percent. Figure 1.2 shows the percentage of GDP in the region that is produced in areas of high or very high water stress relative the percentage of the GDP worldwide that is produced in areas of high or very high water stress (Veolia Water and IFPRI 2011). This largely reflects the high economic output of the highly water-stressed Gulf states.

Despite a long history of water management and recent advances in nonconventional water supplies, chronic extreme scarcity and inadequate governance are driving unsustainable water use in the region. Chronic scarcity, variable hydrology, poor governance, and soaring demand are causing overexploitation of the region's scarce water resources. Map 1.1

FIGURE 1.2

Share of GDP Produced and Population Living in Areas of High or Very High Water Stress in the Middle East and North Africa Compared with World Averages

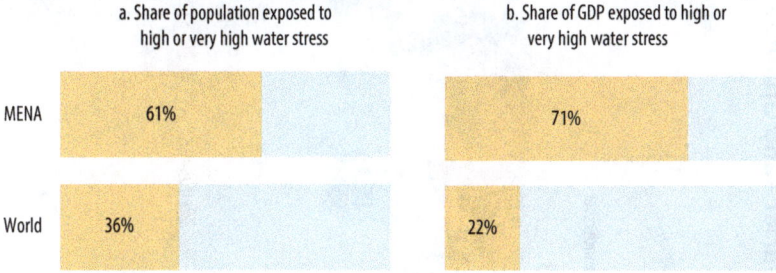

a. Share of population exposed to high or very high water stress

MENA	61%
World	36%

b. Share of GDP exposed to high or very high water stress

MENA	71%
World	22%

Source: Estimates for the Middle East and North Africa are from World Resources Institute Aqueduct data. World averages are from Veolia Water and IFPRI 2011.
Note: High or very high water stress imply that water withdrawals are 40 percent or more of surface water resources availability.

shows the sustainability of water use, measured with the Blue Water Sustainability Index.[5] This indicator measures the portion of human water consumption that is unsustainable; that is, the portion of surface water consumption that exceeds environmental flow requirements[6] plus the portion of groundwater consumption that is nonrenewable because it exceeds natural recharge.[7]

The Middle East and North Africa region, along with Central Asia and parts of South and East Asia, stands out as areas in which water resources are being unsustainably exploited. Across the Middle East and North Africa region, the indicator ranges from 0.1 to more than 0.5, suggesting that in some parts of the Middle East and North Africa more than half of the water consumption is unsustainable (map 1.1, panel c). This is significantly higher than values for many other parts of the world. Surface water overabstraction is a concern in the Mashreq and particularly in the Nile region, where about one-tenth of surface water consumption is unsustainable or is sustained at the expense of environmental flows (panel a). Groundwater overabstraction (panel b) is concentrated in the Arabian Peninsula, the Maghreb, and the Islamic Republic of Iran.

The region is especially a global hotspot for groundwater overexploitation. Groundwater resources are being abstracted at a rate faster than they are being replenished, which is leading to overexploitation and persistent groundwater depletion. Groundwater abstraction accounts for a large portion of all water withdrawals in Middle Eastern and North African countries and economies. At the same time, estimates of the total groundwater reserves in the region that can be economically and sustainably exploited are highly uncertain. Countries in the Middle East and

MAP 1.1

Global Blue Water Sustainability Index for Surface Water, Groundwater, and Combined Surface and Groundwater, 1960–2010 Average

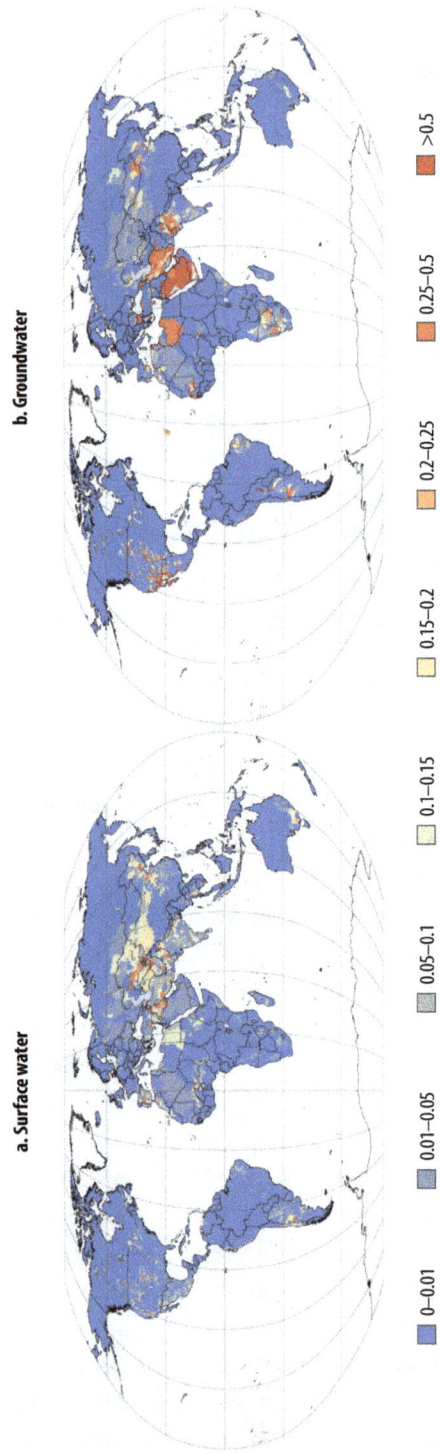

a. Surface water

b. Groundwater

0–0.01	0.01–0.05	0.05–0.1	0.1–0.15	0.15–0.2	0.2–0.25	0.25–0.5	>0.5	

c. Index total

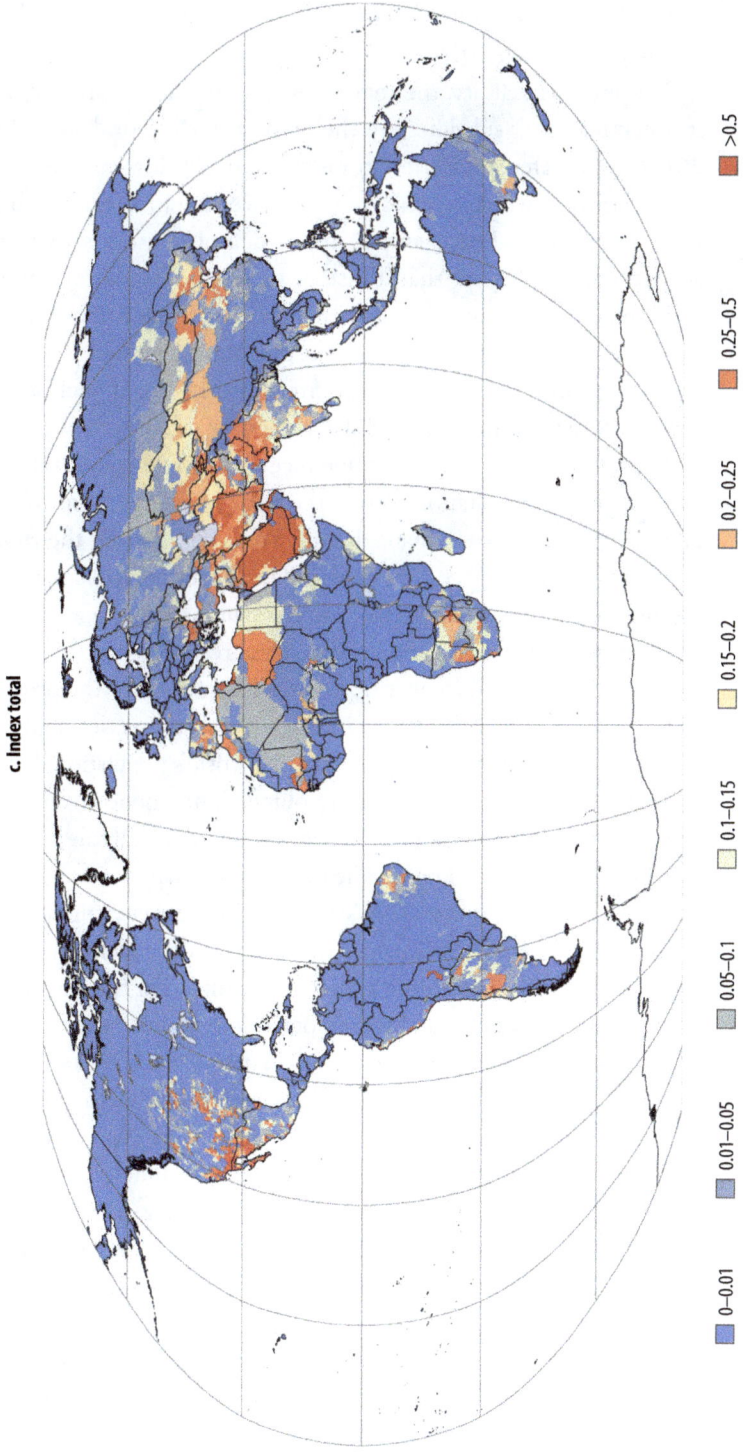

■ 0–0.01 ■ 0.01–0.05 ■ 0.05–0.1 □ 0.1–0.15 □ 0.15–0.2 ■ 0.2–0.25 ■ 0.25–0.5 ■ >0.5

Source: Wada and Bierkens 2014.

Note: The Blue Water Sustainability Index (BWSI) is a dimensionless quantity ranging from 0 to 1 that expresses the portion of consumptive water use that is met from nonsustainable water sources. Blue = sustainable; red = unsustainable. BWSI measures the portion of water use that is unsustainable. Nonsustainable surface water use is estimated as the amount of environmental flow requirements not satisfied due to surface water overabstraction. Nonsustainable groundwater use is estimated as the difference between groundwater abstraction and natural groundwater recharge plus recharge from irrigation return flows. The Middle East and North Africa stand out as a global hotspot for unsustainable surface water and groundwater use.

North Africa, such as Jordan and Oman, have started to develop databases to monitor groundwater abstraction, yet data on the portion of groundwater that can be economically exploited are still lacking in the region (Wijnen and Hiller 2016).

Despite this scarcity, the region's water service fees are very low, and its effective water subsidies are the highest in the world (Kochhar et al. 2015). Low water service fees translate into very low cost recoveries for water utilities, which instead rely on government subsidies to finance their operations. For example, high-income Kuwaitis (whose water service fees are higher than those in most Middle Eastern and North African countries) pay less for their household water than low-income, water-rich Liberians and only about one-third as much, on average, as consumers in other water-scarce areas of the world such as Mexico, Singapore, and Namibia (Berglöf and Devarajan 2015).

High water subsidies undermine incentives for efficient water use and encourage overexploitation. Part of the water challenge in the Middle East and North Africa lies in managing demands and putting the right water saving incentives in place. These are politically sensitive issues, yet they are essential to improve water services delivery and water resources productivity. Water service fees are essential to signal resource scarcity and encourage conservation, and to provide financial resources for the protection of water resources, maintenance of infrastructure, and service delivery.

The region is home to 6 percent of the world's population, but has just 1 percent of the world's freshwater resources. Thus, nonconventional water resources—and desalination, in particular—play a critical role in the region's water supply portfolio. The Middle East and North Africa now accounts for almost 50 percent of the world's desalination capacity (figure 1.3). The oil-rich Gulf countries, in particular, are heavily dependent on desalination for water security. The steady growth of desalination has been enabled in part by low energy prices and technological improvements, which have lowered plant operations costs. Innovations in nano-membranes and renewable energy desalination (World Bank 2012a) may contribute to wider adoption of nonconventional supply sources across the region (AWC 2014).

Middle Eastern and North African countries and economies are well aware that desalination is not a panacea to solve water scarcity (World Bank 2012b). Furthermore, the subsidization of desalinated water supplies, both from fiscal resources and through energy pricing, may become less affordable against a backdrop of uncertain global energy prices and resulting fiscal pressures. Phasing out energy subsidies in some countries may increase the cost of water production in general and of desalination in particular.

The region treats a relatively high percentage of its collected wastewater (about 40 percent), but there is little recycling of this potential resource.[8] Wastewater treatment levels in the region are higher than in Asia,

FIGURE 1.3

Desalination Capacity, by World Region, 2016

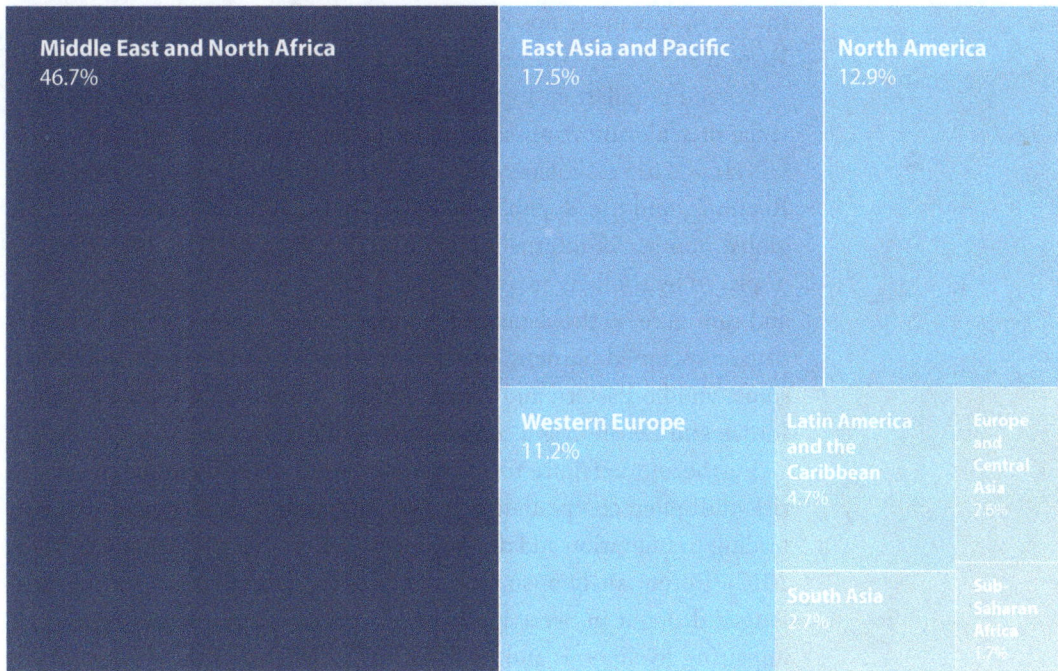

Middle East and North Africa 46.7%	East Asia and Pacific 17.5%	North America 12.9%
	Western Europe 11.2%	Latin America and the Caribbean 4.7%	Europe and Central Asia 2.6%
		South Asia 2.7%	Sub-Saharan Africa 1.7%

Source: Data from Global Water Intelligence 2016.

Latin America, and Sub-Saharan Africa (Qadir 2010). The region's wastewater treatment level is comparable to the average for upper-middle-income countries (38 percent).[9] High-income countries treat 70 percent of their generated wastewater on average, lower-middle-income countries treat 28 percent, and low-income countries on average treat 8 percent of the wastewater they generate (Toshio et al. 2013). These averages do not reflect the large disparities across the region in the level of treatment, as the resources available for wastewater treatment vary and so does the efficiency of treatment. Recycling of treated wastewater that is generated from domestic and industrial activities has a potential role to play in meeting water demands in the Middle East and North Africa—for example, in groundwater recharge (also known as managed aquifer recharge) or irrigated crop systems. Despite its perceived advantages, the uptake of water recycling in the region has not been extensive because of a range of challenges, including institutional barriers, social acceptability, financing, and cost recovery.

The region includes crucial transboundary freshwater resources. Freshwater resources that are drawn from shared rivers and aquifers add a layer of complexity and potential tensions to water challenges in the Middle East and North Africa. The most important rivers in the region—the Nile, the Jordan, and the Tigris-Euphrates—are all transboundary. In addition, there are many important regional aquifer systems. This transboundary dimension of water management also implies that decisions made upstream outside of the region can affect Middle Eastern and North African countries and economies.

Forced population displacement significantly compounds the challenge of achieving water security in the region (IDMC and NRC 2016; UNHCR 2015). Violence and conflict in Iraq, Libya, the Syrian Arab Republic, and the Republic of Yemen have led to recent spikes in the global number of internally displaced people (UNHCR 2015). People displaced by conflicts are often deprived of access to water and sanitation and can increase the demand for water in host communities. Refugees place unplanned burdens on water services and the water resources of some Middle Eastern and North African countries, as recently seen in Jordan and Lebanon as a consequence of the Syrian crisis.

Furthermore, failure to address water-related challenges can act as a risk multiplier, compounding risks from fragility, conflict, and violence, leading to migration and displacement (Sadoff, Borgomeo, and de Waal 2017). Recent analyses suggest that government failure to address prolonged drought in Syria contributed to political unrest and conflict by impairing livelihoods and exacerbating food insecurity, which contributed to migration from rural to urban areas (De Châtel 2014). Longstanding underinvestment in drought preparedness and policy failures to properly address the crisis fostered dissatisfaction toward the government, especially among those who were most severely affected and who felt they were forced to resettle as a consequence of these conditions (De Châtel 2014; Jägerskog and Swain 2016). In the Republic of Yemen, a drought in 2008 caused the displacement of thousands of people (IRIN 2008). In the southern governorates of Iraq, more people were forced to migrate because of water scarcity issues than violence and conflict (IOM 2012). In both countries, these environmental shocks and their social and economic consequences escalated fragility in already tenuous circumstances.

Climate risks in the Middle East and North Africa are also extreme. The region is expected to have the greatest economic losses from climate-related water scarcity as a share of GDP by 2050 (World Bank 2016). The many impacts of climate change on water scarcity have the potential to impair economic activities in the region, causing reductions in GDP of between 6 percent and 14 percent of GDP by 2050 (World Bank 2016). The range of impacts depends on the underlying economic and climate trajectories used in the analysis, as well as two different policy scenarios. The business-as-usual scenario leads to a GDP decline of 14 percent,

FIGURE 1.4

The Economic Impacts of Climate Change–Induced Water Scarcity, by 2050

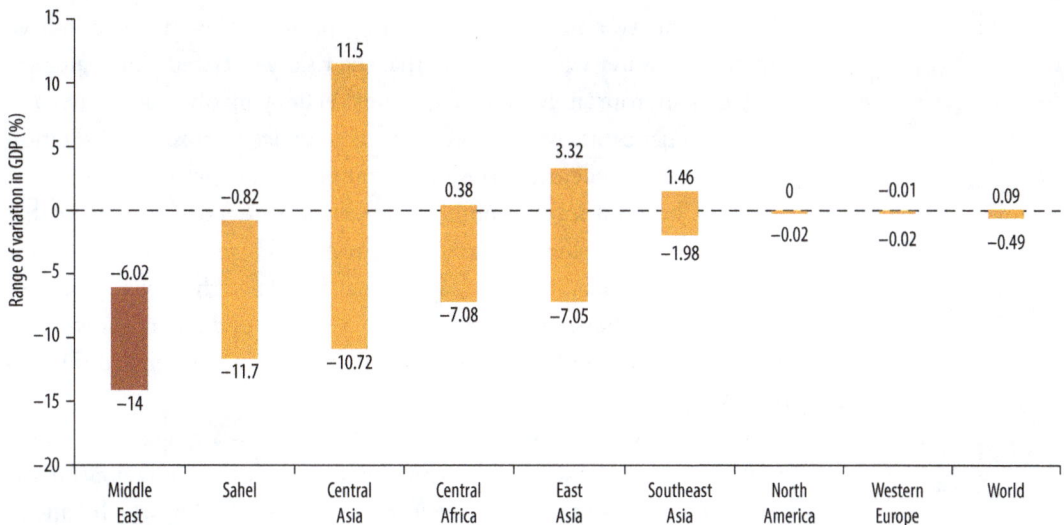

Source: World Bank 2016.

Note: The range of impacts is determined by the type of policies implemented to cope with water scarcity, from a business-as-usual policy (−14 percent) to a policy seeking to reallocate water to the most productive uses (−6 percent).

while a scenario encouraging water allocation to higher-value uses leads to a GDP decline of 6 percent (figure 1.4).

The projected losses in the Middle East and North Africa imply that even under baseline growth projections, policies and reform would be required to cope with water scarcity induced by climate change. Projected increases in water demand from population growth, especially in urban areas, could lead to further unregulated exploitation of groundwater resources. Increasing temperatures from climate change will lead to increased water requirements from agriculture. There will also be other climate effects, including, importantly, sea-level rise and more extreme rainfall events (Verner 2012). Another important aspect of climate change in the region is that water availability will become more uncertain. Likely impacts are that larger volumes of water will arrive during shorter time periods, leading to changing patterns of groundwater recharge and flash floods, as well as less green water, because arid soils are typically less able to absorb heavier rains. This will impair prospects for rainfed agriculture in the region. As uncertainty prevails, vulnerable and marginalized groups will face the greatest risks, and may be more likely to face the resulting economic and health challenges.

Elements of Water Security in the Middle East and North Africa

Water security aims to leverage the opportunities and productive potential of water while ensuring that the risks associated with water are managed appropriately. Assessing water security involves going beyond metrics of per capita water availability or statistics on access to sanitation facilities. Water security considers a range of water-related outcomes, such as a harmful level of pollutants in river waters or an unaffordable water tariff. It considers the role of policies and investments—and their economic and social consequences—that influence these water-related outcomes. Furthermore, water security seeks to understand how water management influences broader social, economic, and environmental outcomes.

Achieving water security involves actions across a range of elements related to water resources management and service delivery. This is reflected in the Sustainable Development Goals. SDG 6, which aims to "ensure availability and sustainable management of water and sanitation for all," moving beyond basic access targets and calling for the protection of water resources from overexploitation and pollution. It includes targets relating to water quality, reuse, scarcity, transboundary cooperation, and integrated water resource management—all of which are elements that strengthen water security (box 1.1).

To assess water security in the Middle East and North Africa region, this report focuses on three major elements of water security: management of water resources, delivery of water services, and mitigation of water-related risks. The rationale for this grouping comes from the recognition that as water resource constraints become binding, it is not possible to separate the management and allocation of water resources from the reliable delivery of water services, and that, as natural and socioeconomic conditions change, the relationships of water with biophysical and socioeconomic systems change, generating new risks and intensifying old ones. Grouping the elements of water security in these three categories provides an operational framing to assess the status of water security in the Middle East and North Africa region.

The assessment explores three questions that are fundamental to water security:

1. Are the region's water resources being managed sustainably and efficiently?
2. Are water services being delivered reliably and affordably?
3. Are water-related risks being appropriately recognized and mitigated?

BOX 1.1

SDG Goal 6: Ensure Availability and Sustainable Management of Water and Sanitation for All

The Sustainable Development Goals (SDGs) build on the success of the Millennium Development Goals (MDGs) to address a wider range of challenges related to water. SDG 6 has the following targets:

6.1   By 2030, achieve universal and equitable access to safe and affordable drinking water for all.

6.2   By 2030, achieve access to adequate and equitable sanitation and hygiene for all and end open defecation, paying special attention to the needs of women and girls and those in vulnerable situations.

6.3   By 2030, improve water quality by reducing pollution, eliminating dumping and minimizing release of hazardous chemicals and materials, halving the proportion of untreated wastewater, and substantially increasing recycling and safe reuse globally.

6.4   By 2030, substantially increase water-use efficiency across all sectors and ensure sustainable withdrawals and supply of freshwater to address water scarcity and substantially reduce the number of people suffering from water scarcity.

6.5   By 2030, implement integrated water resources management at all levels, including through transboundary cooperation as appropriate.

6.6   By 2020, protect and restore water-related ecosystems, including mountains, forests, wetlands, rivers, aquifers, and lakes.

6.A   By 2030, expand international cooperation and capacity-building support to developing countries in water- and sanitation-related activities and programs, including water harvesting, desalination, water efficiency, wastewater treatment, recycling and reuse technologies.

6.B   Support and strengthen the participation of local communities in improving water and sanitation management.

Source: UN 2015, Sustainable Development Knowledge Platform, available online at https://sustainabledevelopment.un.org/sdgs.

Water resources include the physical availability of surface water and groundwater resources and the demand for water from different sectors, including agriculture, industry, and domestic uses. This question seeks to quantify the water endowment of each country and the current sustainability of water use. To answer the water resources question, this report seeks to capture the characteristics of water security related to water availability and consumption and to measure the extent to which countries have responded to the scarcity of freshwater by diversifying water supply sources—for instance, by investing in efficiency, desalination, or water recycling.

Water services reflect the aspects of water security related to the delivery of water to multiple users. These aspects range from the reliability, quality, and affordability of water provided by urban utilities to the benefits of irrigation water delivery to agriculture. They relate to the financial and operational performance of water utilities, the coverage of water supply and sanitation services, and the capacity of institutions to provide water to users. Water delivery to agriculture and hydropower producers also are components of water security, as is the availability of water for recreational, aesthetic, and spiritual uses. Water service indicators highlight the link between good water service delivery and the social contract between service providers and water users. Some indicators in the water services category are not readily quantified. This report assessed them using the best available data from regional studies (ACWUA 2015).

Risk indicators relate to threats that might arise and the potential factors that can create or compound challenges in the management of water resources and delivery of water services. These include climate-related risks, such as floods, droughts, and sea-level rise; as well as risks associated with dependence on transboundary water resources; contamination of drinking water supplies; unintended impacts from policies in the water sector and in other sectors, such as agriculture or energy; global economic shocks; and fragility, conflict, and violence. Including these wide-ranging risk considerations improves understanding and assessments of the implications of exogenous factors—such as food trade and migration—beyond those related strictly to water, that can become potentially harmful shocks. This area of analysis can also contribute to an understanding of the role water management can play in facilitating social stability and adaptation to climate change.

These elements frame a structured, regional-level assessment across a range of aspects of water security. For the assessment to be meaningful, multiple elements of the water challenge—from the often-cited biophysical water resources indicators (such as water stress) to water services characteristics—are considered. These elements are estimated at the country level based on annual data. While basin-level analysis may be more meaningful from a hydrological sciences perspective, the country-level assessment is better suited to inform broad, national-level dialogues on water security. The selection of diagnostic elements reflects the dimensions of water security that are relevant to the Middle East and North Africa and for which reliable data could be collected. Most of these diagnostic elements are challenging to assess, given data limitations, the complexity of most water issues, and the changing nature of hydrocli-matic conditions (Gleick 2015).

Because this is a regional-level analysis, it is necessarily limited by the availability of regionally comparable, publicly available data. Furthermore, while it provides a first step in collecting information on water security and for constructing an assessment that goes beyond simple water scarcity metrics, this assessment still captures only a portion of the numerous aspects of water security that countries face. It is hoped that more detailed national-level analyses might be carried out along these lines in the future.

Notes

1. Growing Blue, Water in 2050. http://growingblue.com/water-in-2050/.
2. UN-Water, Key Water Indicators Portal.
3. UN-Water, Water Security (http://www.unwater.org/topics/water-security /en/.
4. More precisely, green water is the water in the top soil layer or root-zone. For more on the concept of green water, see Falkenmark and Rockström (2006).
5. Blue water is liquid water in rivers and aquifers. The Blue Water Sustainability Index (BlWSI) is a dimensionless quantity ranging from 0 to 1 that expresses the portion of consumptive water use that is met from nonsustainable water sources. BlWSI measures the portion of water use that is unsustainable. Nonsustainable surface water use is estimated as the amount of environmental flow requirements not satisfied due to surface water overabstraction. Nonsustainable groundwater use is estimated as the difference between groundwater abstraction and natural groundwater recharge plus recharge from irrigation return flows.
6. The environmental flow requirement is here interpreted as the quantity of surface water flow that is needed to sustain healthy aquatic ecosystems. This quantity is rarely measured, so in this report it set to the monthly surface water flow that is exceeded 90 percent of the time, following Wada and Bierkens (2014) and Smakhtin, Revenga, and Döll (2004).
7. Natural groundwater recharge is water drainage through soils that replenishes aquifers.
8. National statistics on treated wastewater are based on self-reported volumes of produced municipal wastewater presented in the AQUASTAT database and are subject to a range of limitations and assumptions, described by Mateo-Sagasta and Salian (2012).
9. The Middle East and North Africa region is characterized by a mix of income levels. Lower-middle-income countries and economies, defined as those with gross national incomes (GNI) per capita of $1,026 to $4,035, include Djibouti, the Arab Republic of Egypt, Morocco, Syria, Tunisia, West Bank and Gaza, and Yemen. Upper-middle-income countries (with GNI of $4,036 to $12,475) include Algeria, Iran, Iraq, Jordan, Lebanon, and Libya. Upper-income countries (with GNI above $12,476) include Bahrain, Israel, Kuwait, Malta, Oman, Qatar, Saudi Arabia, and the United Arab Emirates.

References

ACWUA (Arab Countries Water Utilities Association). 2015. *Water Supply and Sanitation Services in the Arab Region (MDG+ Initiative) First Report.* Amman: ACWUA.

Allan, J. A. 2001. *The Middle East Water Question: Hydropolitics and the Global Economy.* London: I. B. Tauris.

AMWC (Arab Ministerial Water Council). 2012. *Arab Strategy for Water Security in the Arab Region to the Challenges and Future Needs for Sustainable Development 2010–2030.* Cairo: AMWC.

Antonelli, M., and S. Tamea. 2015. "Food-Water-Security and Virtual Water Trade in the Middle East and North Africa." *International Journal of Water Resources Development* 31 (3): 326–42.

AWC (Arab Water Council). 2014. *3rd Arab Water Forum, Together towards a Secure Arab Water.* Final Report. Cairo: AWC.

Berglöf, E., and S. Devarajan. 2015. "Water for Development: Fulfilling the Promise." In *Water for Development—Charting a Water Wise Path*, edited by A. Jägerskog, T. J. Clausen, T. Holmgren, and K. Lexén. Report 35. Stockholm: Stockholm International Water Institute (SIWI).

De Châtel, F. 2014. "The Role of Drought and Climate Change in the Syrian Uprising: Untangling the Triggers of the Revolution." *Middle Eastern Studies* 50 (4): 521–35. doi: 10.1080/00263206.2013.850076.

Falkenmark, M., and J. Rockström. 2006. "The New Blue and Green Water Paradigm: Breaking New Ground for Water Resources Planning and Management." *Journal of Water Resources Planning and Management*, May–June, 129.

Gassert, F., P. Reig, T. Luo, and A. Maddocks. 2013. "Aqueduct Country and River Basin Rankings: A Weighted Aggregation of Spatially Distinct Hydrological Indicators." Working Paper, World Resources Institute, Washington, DC.

Gleick, P. H. 2015. "On Methods for Assessing Water-Resource Risks and Vulnerabilities." *Environmental Research Letters* 10 (11): 104014.

Global Water Intelligence. 2016. "Global Water Market 2017: Meeting the World's Water and Wastewater Needs until 2020." Global Water Intelligence.

Grey, D., D. Garrick, D. Blackmore, J. Kelman, M. Muller, and C. Sadoff. 2013. "Water Security in One Blue Planet: Twenty-First Century Policy Challenges for Science." *Philosophical Transactions of the Royal Society A* 371: 20120406.

Grey, D., and C. Sadoff. 2007. "Sink or Swim? Water Security for Growth and Development." *Water Policy* 9 (6): 545–71.

Hall, J., and E. Borgomeo. 2013. "Risk-Based Principles for Defining and Managing Water Security." *Philosphical Transactions of the Royal Society A* 371: 20120407.

Harris, K., D. Keen, and T. Mitchell. 2013. *When Disasters and Conflicts Collide. Improving the Links between Disaster Resilience and Conflict Prevention.* London: Overseas Development Institute.

IDMC and NRC (Internal Displacement Monitoring Centre and Norwegian Refugee Council). 2016. "Grid 2016. Global Report on Internal Displacement." http://www.internal-displacement.org/assets/publications/2016/2016-global -report-internal-displacement-IDMC.pdf.

IOM (International Organization for Migration). 2012. *IOM Iraq Special Report: Water Scarcity.* https://environmentalmigration.iom.int/iom-iraq-special-report-water-scarcity.

IRIN. 2008. "Drought Displaces Thousands in Mountainous Northwest." May 5. http://www.irinnews.org/news/2008/05/05/drought-displaces-thousands-mountainous-northwest (accessed May 3, 2016).

Jägerskog, A., and A. Swain. 2016. "Water, Migration and How They Are Interlinked." Working Paper 27, SIWI (Stockholm International Water Institute), Stockholm.

Kochhar, K., C. Pattillo, Y. Sun, N. Suphaphiphat, A. Swiston, R. Tchaidze, B. Clements, S. Fabrizio, V. Flamini, L. Redifer, H. Finger, and an IMF Staff Team. 2015. "Is the Glass Half Empty or Half Full? Issues in Managing Water Challenges and Policy Instruments." Staff Discussion Note SDN/15/11, International Monetary Fund, Washington, DC.

Mateo-Sagasta, J., and P. Salian. 2012. "Global Database on Municipal Wastewater Production, Collection, Treatment, Discharge and Direct Use in Agriculture." Food and Agricultural Organization of the United Nations, Rome.

Qadir, M. 2010. "Wastewater Production, Treatment, and Irrigation in Middle East and North Africa." *Irrigation and Drainage Systems* 24 (1): 37–51.

Sadoff, C. W., E. Borgomeo, and D. de Waal. 2017. *Turbulent Waters: Water Security in Fragile Systems.* Washington, DC: World Bank.

Sadoff, C. W., J. W. Hall, D. Grey, J. C. J. H. Aerts, M. Ait-Kadi, C. Brown, A. Cox, S. Dadson, D. Garrick, J. Kelman, P. McCornick, C. Ringler, M. Rosegrant, D. Whittington, and D. Wiberg. 2015. 2015. *Securing Water, Sustaining Growth: Report of the GWP/OECD Task Force on Water Security and Sustainable Growth.* Oxford, UK: University of Oxford.

Smakhtin, V. U., C. Revenga, and P. Döll. 2004. "A Pilot Global Assessment of Environmental Water Requirements and Scarcity." *Water International* 29 (3): 307–17.

Toshio, S., M. Qadir, S. Yamamotoe, T. Endoe, and A. Zahoora. 2013. "Global, Regional, and Country Level Need for Data on Wastewater Generation, Treatment, and Use." *Agricultural Water Management* 130: 1–13.

UNHCR (Office of the United Nations High Commissioner for Refugees). 2015. "Global Trends: Forced Displacement in 2015." http://www.unhcr.org/576408cd7.pdf.

UNICEF and WHO (United Nations Children's Fund and World Health Organization). 2015. *Progress on Drinking Water and Sanitation, 2015 Update and MDG Assessment.* New York: UNICEF.

Veolia Water and IFPRI (International Food Policy Research Institute). 2011. *Sustaining Growth via Water Productivity: 2030/2050 Scenarios.* http://growingblue.com/wp-content/uploads/2011/05/IFPRI_VEOLIA_STUDY_2011.pdf.

Verner, D. 2012. *Adaptation to a Changing Climate in the Arab Countries: A Case for Adaptation Governance and Leadership in Building Climate Resilience.* MENA Development Report. Washington, DC: World Bank.

Wada, Y., and F. Bierkens. 2014 "Sustainability of Global Water Use: Past Reconstruction and Future Projections." *Environmental Research Letters* 9 (10): 1–17.

WEF (World Economic Forum). 2015. *Global Risks 2015.* 10th ed. Geneva: WEF.

Wijnen, M., and Hiller, B. 2016. "Africa Groundwater Strategy—Concept Note." Washington, DC: World Bank.

World Bank. 2012a. *Renewable Energy Desalination: An Emerging Solution to Close the Water Gap in the Middle East and North Africa*. MENA Development Report. Washington, DC: World Bank.

———. 2012b. "Desalination Opportunities and Challenges in the Middle East and North Africa Region." In *Water in the Arab World: Management Perspectives and Innovations*, edited by K. Al-Jamal and M. Schiffer, chapter 26. Washington, DC: World Bank.

———. 2016. *High and Dry: Climate Change, Water, and the Economy*. Washington, DC: World Bank.

CHAPTER 2

Profiling Water Security in the Middle East and North Africa

Managing Water Resources

This section examines the status of water resources in the Middle East and North Africa. It includes a description of the physical freshwater resources base and of water use by sector. The diagnostic elements chosen to reflect these characteristics are based on existing data sets from the Food and Agriculture Organization of the United Nations (FAO), the World Resources Institute (WRI), and the World Bank, as well as novel data sets produced as part of this study by the WRI and Utrecht University.

Six major elements related to water resources are considered: water scarcity, freshwater variability, sustainability of water use, water quality, water productivity, and nonconventional water resources. These six elements were chosen to represent often-cited statistics on water scarcity and variability in the region, as well as other important issues that are often ignored in water stress calculations concerning the sustainability of water use, water productivity, and the ability of countries to deal with low freshwater availability by utilizing nonconventional water supplies.

These elements were selected to look beyond water resource endowments and incorporate responses that countries and economies can make to secure or enhance their natural freshwater resource base. Water resources assessments based solely on measures of natural water resource endowments, such as freshwater availability per capita, may be misleading in that they identify water-stressed regions without accounting for a country's capacity to respond to physical water scarcity. In most countries in the Middle East and North Africa, water endowments are very low, but overall water security may or may not be low, depending, among other factors, on water management practices, such as those promoting water productivity or enhancements to supply. Innovations, reforms, and investments in water security can begin to effectively decouple water security from water endowments. Thus, the diagnostics of water security must be multidimensional and cannot be reduced to a single indicator or measure.

Scarcity and Sustainability

Surface Water Stress

Physical water scarcity is the first, and overriding, theme of the surface water story in the Middle East and North Africa. Physical water scarcity arises from the low availability of water resources compared to demand for water, and can be measured as water stress. When there is a high ratio of water withdrawals to renewable surface water supply, a particular country or location is said to be *water stressed*. Most countries and economies in the Middle East and North Africa region are characterized by high to very high water stress, as shown in the surface water stress map (map 2.1).

The majority of the population in the Middle East and North Africa (over 60 percent) lives in areas of high or very high water stress—far higher than the global average of about 35 percent (figure 2.1).[1] The spatial distribution of the population exposed to surface water stress is shown in map 2.2, and demonstrates that water stress affects populations across the region. Water stress in the Nile region appears low because this calculation does not take into account seasonal variability or upstream developments that may cause water shortages.

The majority of economic output in the Middle East and North Africa is also produced in areas of high or very high surface water stress. On average, 71 percent of the region's gross domestic product (GDP) is generated in areas with high to very high surface water stress (figure 2.2), compared to a global average of some 22 percent (Veolia Water and IFPRI 2011). In absolute terms, this means that about $2.5 trillion of the region's GDP is currently generated in areas of high to extremely high water stress. The Islamic Republic of Iran, Saudi Arabia, and the United Arab Emirates stand out as the countries with the highest absolute economic exposure to water stress (figure 2.3). The geographic distribution of GDP exposure to water stress is shown in map 2.3.

In most Middle Eastern and North African countries and economies, the challenge of managing high levels of water stress is compounded by high levels of year-to-year hydrological variability—and hence uncertainty. This combination of chronic, extreme scarcity coupled with higher than average interannual variability makes water management and allocation particularly challenging (Hall et al. 2014). Figure 2.4 shows surface water variability, calculated as the percent deviation from mean annual surface water availability from 1950 to 2010 (Gassert et al. 2014). The high

MAP 2.1

Baseline Surface Water Stress, Middle East and North Africa, 2010

IBRD 42769 | APRIL 2017

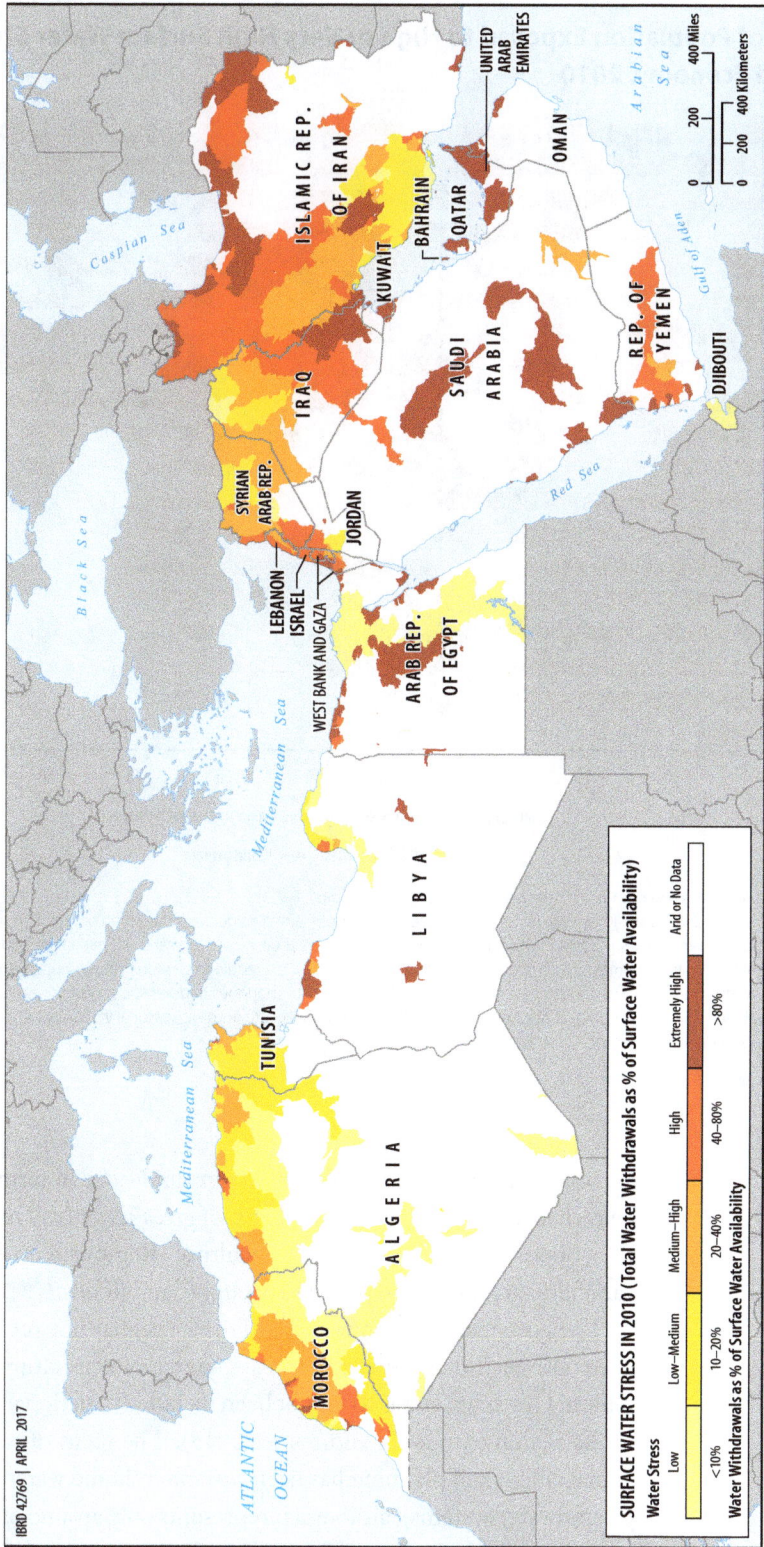

SURFACE WATER STRESS IN 2010 (Total Water Withdrawals as % of Surface Water Availability)

Water Stress

Low	Low–Medium	Medium–High	High	Extremely High	Arid or No Data
<10%	10–20%	20–40%	40–80%	>80%	

Water Withdrawals as % of Surface Water Availability

Source: Analysis and calculations based on World Resources Institute Aqueduct™ data.

Note: Water stress measures water withdrawals as a percent of surface water availability. Values of 40 percent or more indicate areas with high or very high water stress. Water stress does not account for dependence on transboundary water sources or nonconventional water sources. Water stress is estimated using administrative units for each country from the Global Database of Administrative Areas (http://www.gadm.org/).

FIGURE 2.1

Percentage of Population Exposed to High or Very High Surface Water Stress, by Country and Economy, 2010

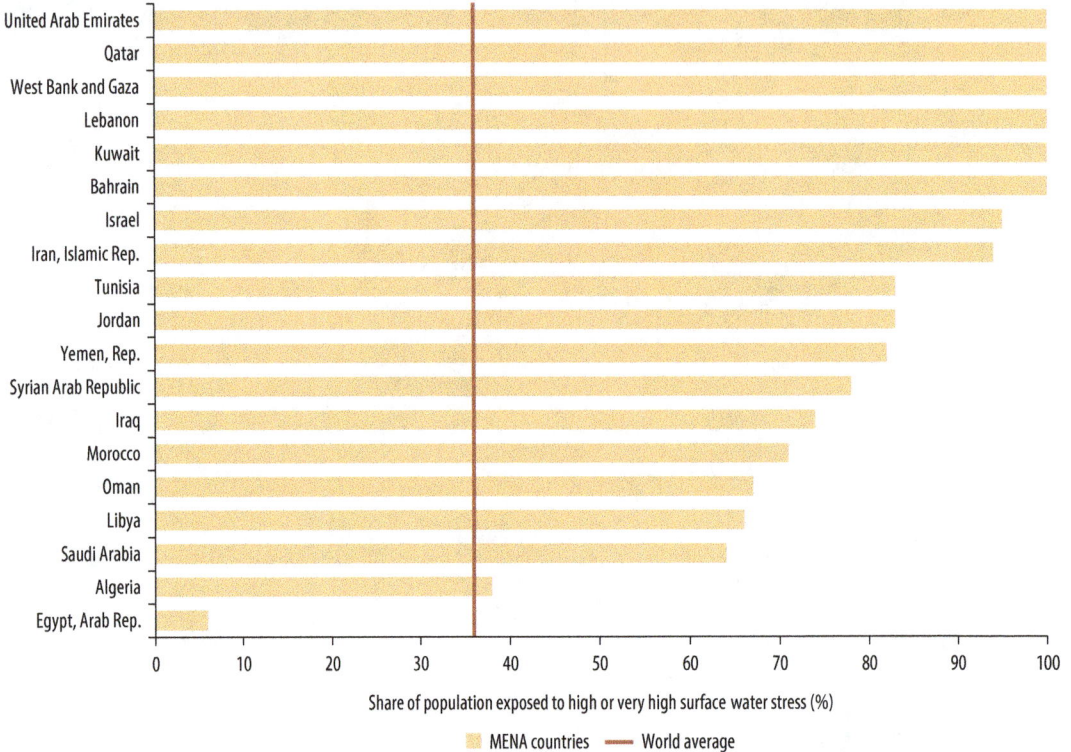

Share of population exposed to high or very high surface water stress (%)

MENA countries — World average

Source: Analysis and calculations based on World Resources Institute Aqueduct™ data.
Note: Areas where water withdrawals are 40 percent or more of surface water supplies are considered to have high or very high stress. Caution should be used in comparing data on annual freshwater withdrawals, which are subject to variations in collection and estimation methods. In addition, inflows and outflows are estimated at different times and at different levels of quality and precision, requiring caution in interpreting the data. This calculation does not account for water stress arising for upstream developments that may cause shortages in downstream countries and economies. Values appear low for the Arab Republic of Egypt, in part because the calculation does not take into account seasonal variability or upstream usage on the Nile River. No data were available for Djibouti.

variability in surface water also affects groundwater in terms of ability to be recharged as well as the prevalence of *green water* (soil moisture)—and thus opportunities for rainfed agriculture. Regions with high levels of variability are also more prone to droughts and floods.

The potential of green water (soil moisture) has not yet been fully utilized, although it represents the main source of agricultural water in the region. Green water has so far not been included in national water budgets in the region (Antonelli and Tamea 2015). The focus of water resources management and planning has been *blue water* (liquid water in surface and groundwater systems), although it represents only around one-third of the world's available freshwater resources. Because green water originates

MAP 2.2

Population Exposure to Surface Water Stress, Middle East and North Africa, 2010

IBRD 42771 | APRIL 2017

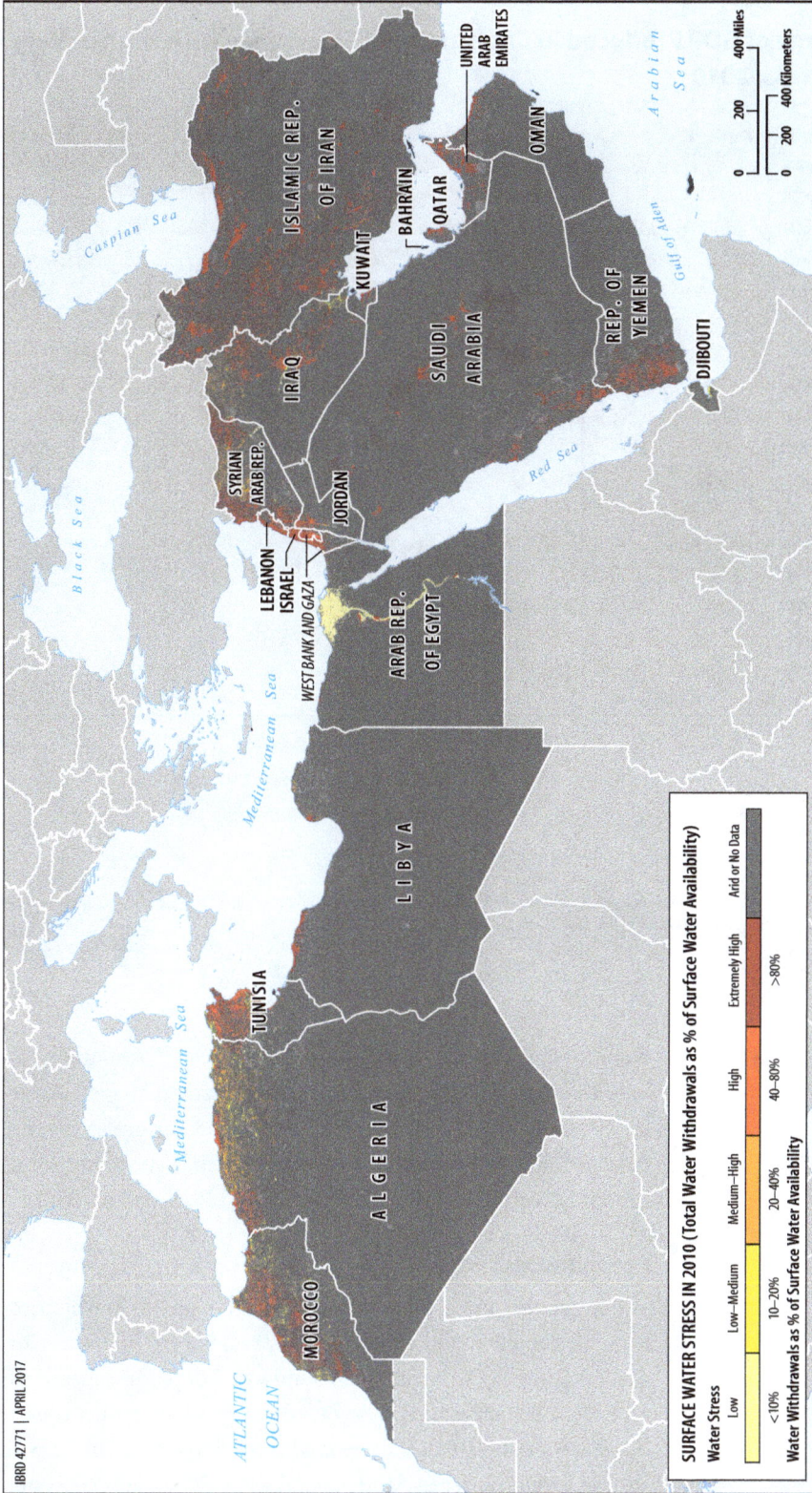

SURFACE WATER STRESS IN 2010 (Total Water Withdrawals as % of Surface Water Availability)

Water Stress

Low	Low–Medium	Medium–High	High	Extremely High	Arid or No Data
<10%	10–20%	20–40%	40–80%	>80%	

Water Withdrawals as % of Surface Water Availability

Source: Analysis and calculations based on World Resources Institute Aqueduct™ data.

Note: Water stress is estimated using administrative units for each country from the Global Database of Administrative Areas. Population data are from the PBL Netherlands Environmental Assessment Agency (Klein Goldewijk, Beusen, and Jansen 2010). This calculation does not account for seasonal variability in water availability or for upstream developments that may cause shortages in downstream countries.

FIGURE 2.2

Percentage of GDP Produced in Countries and Economies with High or Very High Water Stress, 2010

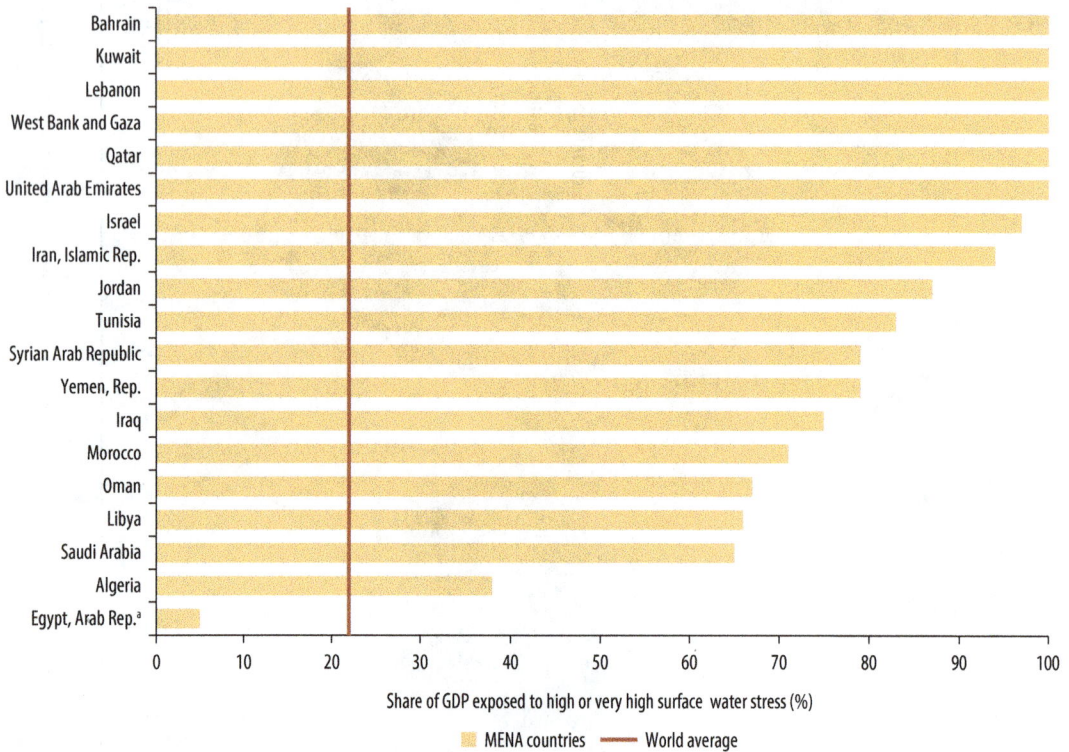

Share of GDP exposed to high or very high surface water stress (%)

MENA countries   ⎯⎯ World average

Source: Analysis and calculations based on World Resources Institute Aqueduct™ data.
Note: Areas where water withdrawals are 40 percent or more of surface water supplies are considered to have high or very high stress. This calculation does not account for seasonal variability in water availability, nor for upstream developments that may cause shortages in downstream countries. World average value from Veolia Water and IFRI (2011). No data were available for Djibouti.
a. Values appear low for the Arab Republic of Egypt, in part because the calculation does not take into account seasonal variability or upstream usage on the Nile River.

from rainfall, it is commonly regarded as a "free" resource. It is accessible only to plants and therefore cannot be directly managed. Agriculture and ecosystems are the only two competing uses for green water. Compared to blue water, the opportunity costs of using green water for agricultural production are far lower (Falkenmark and Rockström 2006).

Groundwater Stress

Every country and economy in the region has areas in which groundwater is being depleted, and groundwater stress is very high in many countries and economies. To quantify groundwater depletion in the Middle East and North Africa, the groundwater footprint index was used (Gleeson et al. 2012). The *groundwater footprint* is the area required to sustain groundwater use and groundwater-dependent ecosystem services.

FIGURE 2.3

GDP in Areas with High or Very High Surface Water Stress, by Country and Economy, 2010

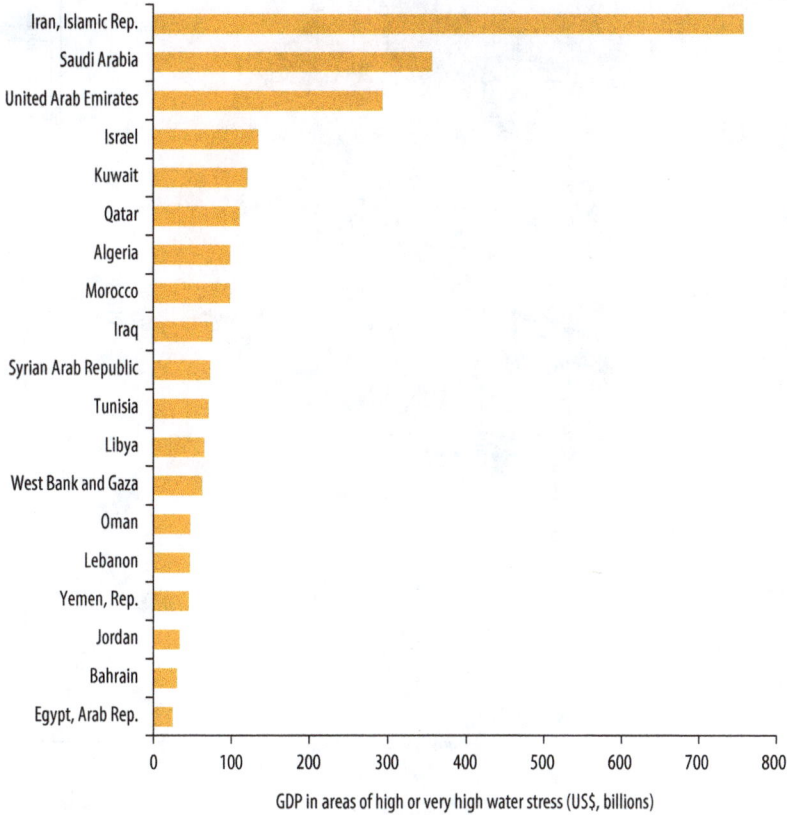

Source: Analysis and calculations based on World Resources Institute Aqueduct™ data.
Note: Areas where water withdrawals are 40 percent or more of surface water supplies are considered to have high or very high stress. GDP is measured in terms of purchasing power parity (PPP) and is in constant 2010 U.S. dollars.

It is essentially a water balance of groundwater recharge and groundwater use (including ecosystem use) estimated for an area of interest. Comparing the groundwater footprint with the actual aquifer area allows groundwater stress over a specific region to be quantified. When the ratio of the groundwater footprint to the aquifer area is greater than 1, then groundwater is being overabstracted and fossil aquifers are being depleted. A groundwater stress level greater than 1 means that more water is being withdrawn than recharged. The average groundwater stress for the Middle East and North Africa region, for 1990–2010, aggregated to local administrative units, is shown in map 2.4. The levels of average groundwater stress are medium to extremely high in the Mashreq and Gulf countries.

With a few exceptions, these already-high rates of groundwater abstraction are increasing across the region. In most areas in the Middle

MAP 2.3

Share of GDP in Areas of Surface Water Stress, Middle East and North Africa, 2010

IBRD 42770 | APRIL 2017

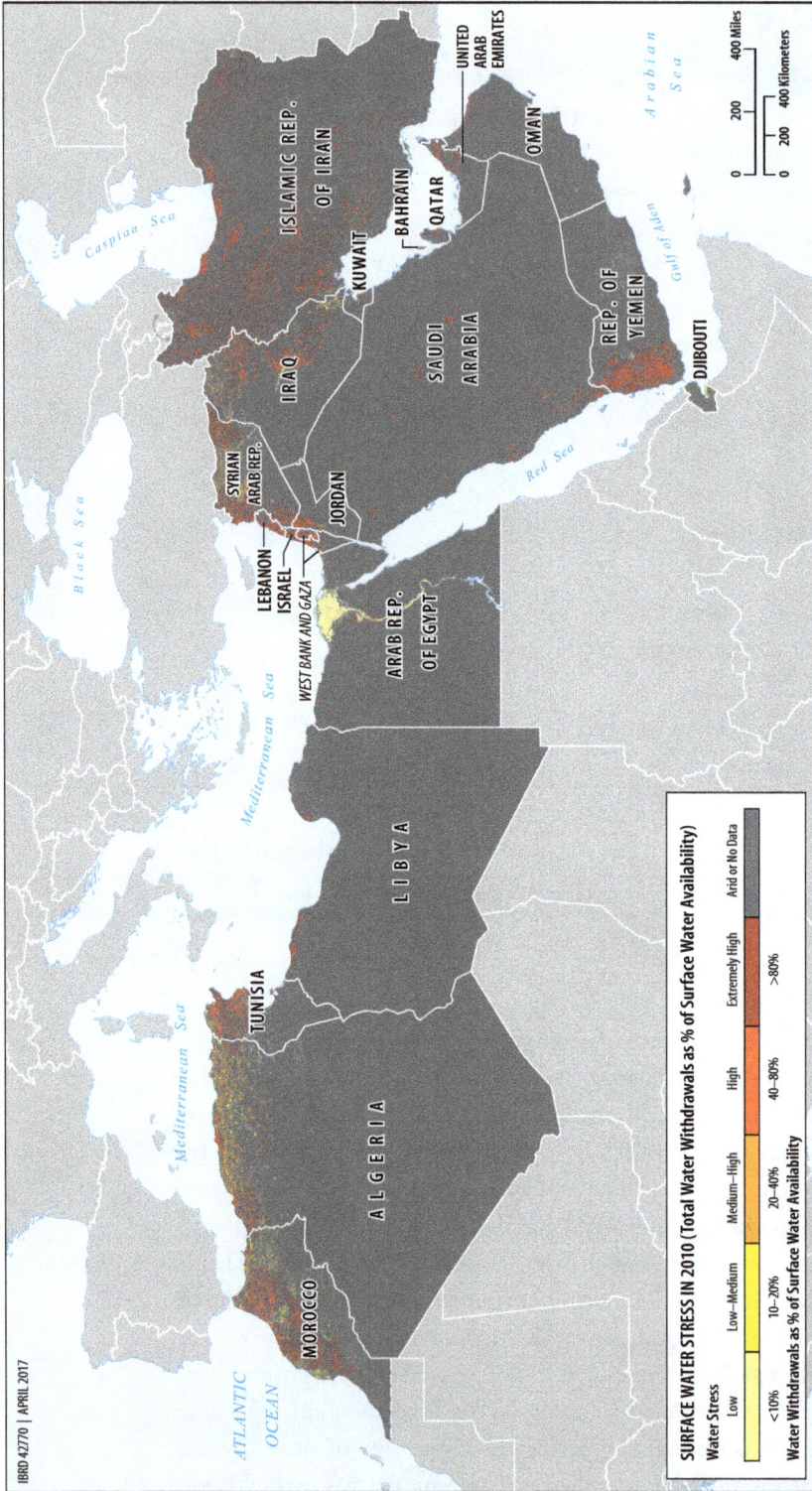

SURFACE WATER STRESS IN 2010 (Total Water Withdrawals as % of Surface Water Availability)

Water Stress					
Low	Low–Medium	Medium–High	High	Extremely High	Arid or No Data
<10%	10–20%	20–40%	40–80%	>80%	

Water Withdrawals as % of Surface Water Availability

Source: Analysis and calculations based on World Resources Institute Aqueduct™ data.

Note: Water stress is estimated using administrative units for each country from the Global Database of Administrative Areas. GDP data are from the PBL Netherlands Environmental Assessment Agency (Klein Goldewijk, Beusen, and Jansen 2010). This calculation does not account for seasonal variability in water availability or for upstream developments that may cause shortages in downstream countries.

FIGURE 2.4

Surface Water Year-to-Year Variability and Surface Water Stress, by Country and Economy

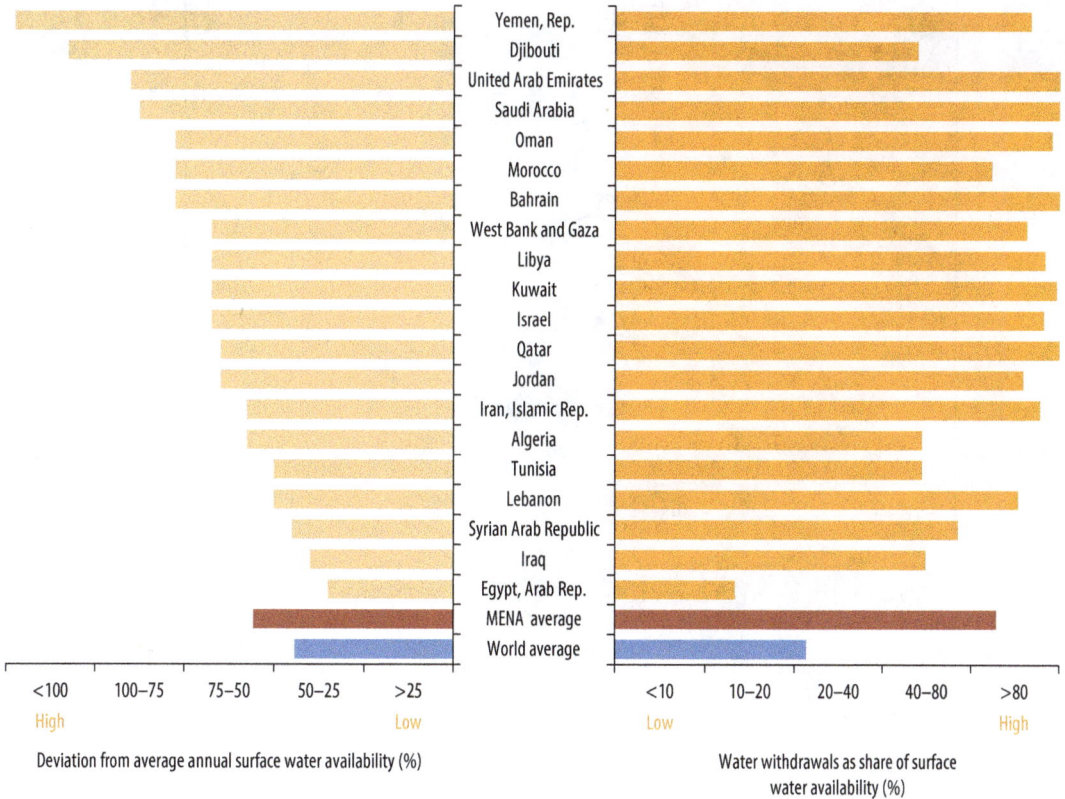

Yemen, Rep.	
Djibouti	
United Arab Emirates	
Saudi Arabia	
Oman	
Morocco	
Bahrain	
West Bank and Gaza	
Libya	
Kuwait	
Israel	
Qatar	
Jordan	
Iran, Islamic Rep.	
Algeria	
Tunisia	
Lebanon	
Syrian Arab Republic	
Iraq	
Egypt, Arab Rep.	
MENA average	
World average	

Left axis: <100 / 100–75 / 75–50 / 50–25 / >25 — High to Low
Deviation from average annual surface water availability (%)

Right axis: <10 / 10–20 / 20–40 / 40–80 / >80 — Low to High
Water withdrawals as share of surface water availability (%)

Source: World Resources Institute Aqueduct database (Gassert et al. 2014).
Note: MENA = Middle East and North Africa.

East and North Africa, groundwater stress increased between 1990 and 2010, as shown in map 2.5. Many factors are responsible for this increase in groundwater stress, including agricultural expansion and increased access to technology (such as tube well pumps in the Republic of Yemen), which have led to rapid increases in water use (Ward 2015), but also overall decreases in groundwater recharge because of changes in rainfall patterns. The decline in groundwater stress in the Mesopotamian marshes in southern Iraq may be ascribed to decreasing use because of population displacement. The decrease in groundwater stress in the Nile Delta may be due to an increase in groundwater recharge artificially induced by human activities and irrigation. The groundwater stress data shown in map 2.4 and map 2.5 allow for a first-level analysis of trends in groundwater consumption in the Middle East and North Africa.

MAP 2.4

Average Groundwater Stress, Middle East and North Africa, 1990–2010

IBRD 42772 | APRIL 2017

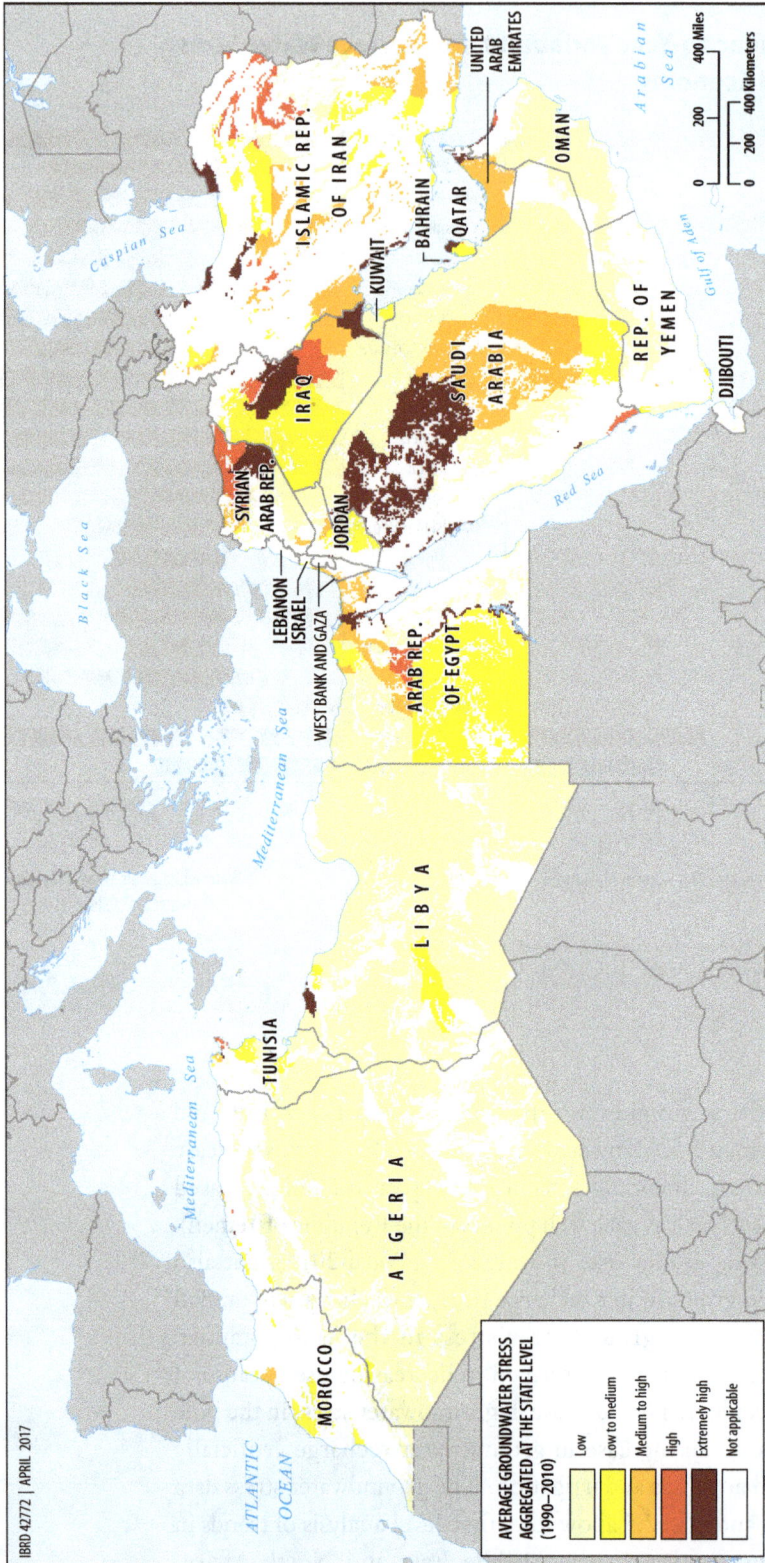

**AVERAGE GROUNDWATER STRESS
AGGREGATED AT THE STATE LEVEL
(1990–2010)**

- Low
- Low to medium
- Medium to high
- High
- Extremely high
- Not applicable

Source: Analysis and calculations from geospatial datasets developed by Stichting Deltares in cooperation with the University of Utrecht in the Netherlands. Permission granted by Stichting Deltares and the University of Utrecht; permission required for re-use.

Note: Groundwater stress is estimated as ABS/(RCH-fxRCH), where ABS is groundwater abstraction estimated with the PCR-GLOBWB model, RCH is groundwater recharge simulated by PCR-GLOBWB, and f is the fraction of RCH reserved to meet environmental flows. Groundwater stress is estimated using long-term averages to control for the effects of interannual variability. State levels correspond to the administrative units for each country in the Global Database of Administrative Areas.

IBRD 42773 | APRIL 2017

MAP 2.5

Change in Renewable Groundwater Stress, Middle East and North Africa, 1990–2010

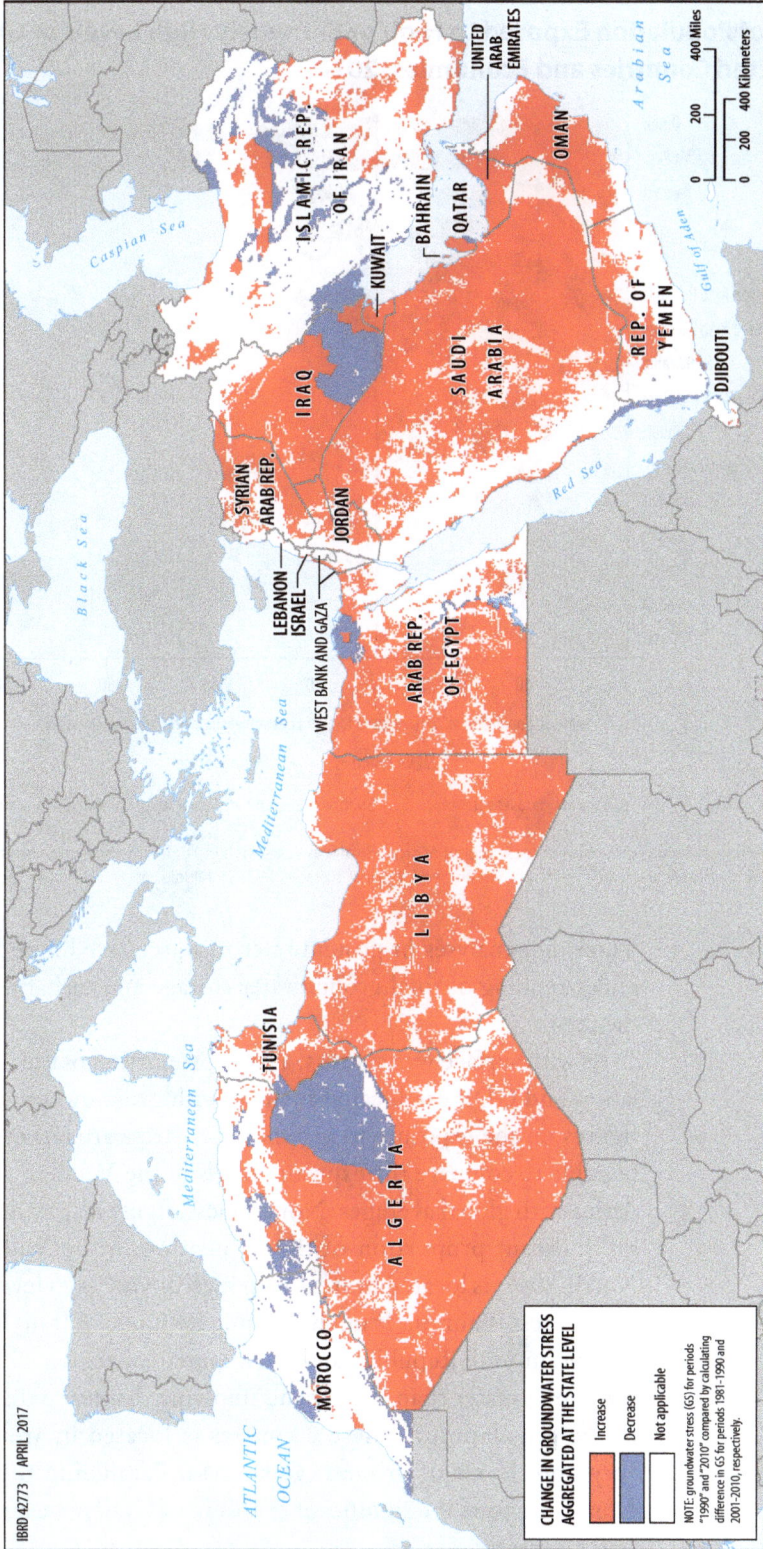

CHANGE IN GROUNDWATER STRESS AGGREGATED AT THE STATE LEVEL

- Increase
- Decrease
- Not applicable

NOTE: groundwater stress (GS) for periods "1990" and "2010" compared by calculating difference in GS for periods 1981–1990 and 2001–2010, respectively.

Source: Analysis and calculations from geospatial datasets developed by Stichting Deltares in cooperation with the University of Utrecht in the Netherlands. Permission granted by Stichting Deltares and the University of Utrecht; permission required for re-use.

Note: Groundwater stress is estimated as ABS/(RCH-f×RCH), where ABS is groundwater abstraction estimated with the PCR-GLOBWB model, RCH is groundwater recharge simulated by PCR-GLOBWB, and f is the fraction of RCH reserved to meet environmental flows. State levels correspond to the administrative units for each country in the Global Database of Administrative Areas.

FIGURE 2.5

Percentage of Population Exposed to High or Extremely High Levels of Groundwater Stress, Selected Countries and Economies, 2010

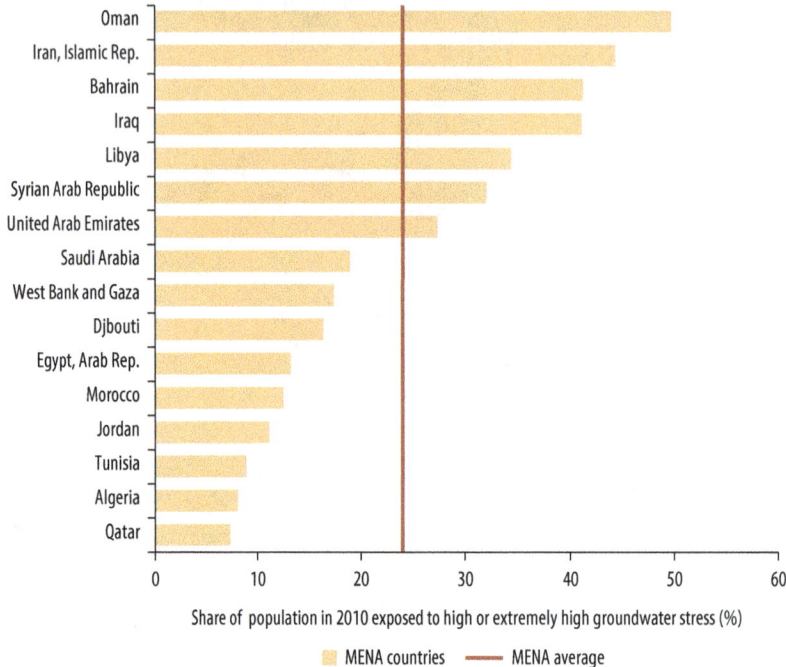

Share of population in 2010 exposed to high or extremely high groundwater stress (%)

▢ MENA countries   ━━ MENA average

Source: Analysis and calculations from geospatial datasets developed by Stichting Deltares in cooperation with the University of Utrecht in the Netherlands.
Note: High and extremely high levels of groundwater stress imply that groundwater use exceeds by 10 times (or more) groundwater recharge. No data were available for Israel, Kuwait, Lebanon, the Republic of Yemen, and for global averages. MENA = Middle East and North Africa.

Thorough analyses of groundwater resources are limited by a lack of understanding of total groundwater storage and recharge processes in the region.

As with surface water stress, a large proportion of the region's population and GDP are located in areas with groundwater stress. Global figures on the exposure to groundwater stress are lacking, so it is not possible to compare the exposure levels of the Middle East and North Africa with global averages. Nonetheless, figures 2.5 and 2.6 show that a significant proportion of the population in the Middle East and North Africa is located in areas with high or very high levels of groundwater stress. Bahrain, Iraq, the Islamic Republic of Iran, Libya, Oman, the Syrian Arab Republic, and the Republic of Yemen all have levels of exposure greater than 30 percent, implying that more than one-fourth of the population in these countries is located in areas of high or very high levels of groundwater stress. Paralleling these numbers, figure 2.6 shows the significant exposure of GDP per capita to groundwater stress.

FIGURE 2.6

Percentage of GDP per Capita in Areas of High or Extremely High Levels of Groundwater Stress, by Country and Economy, 2010

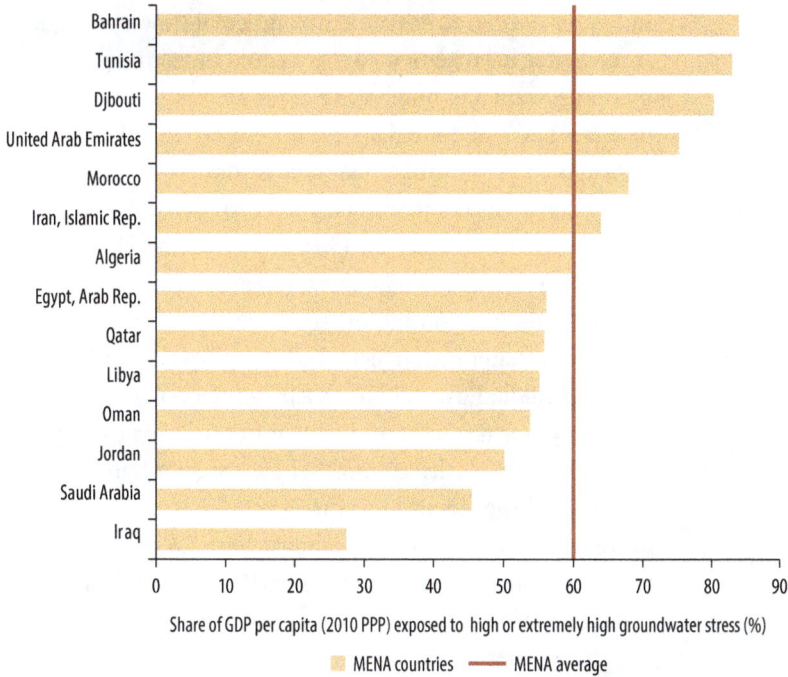

Share of GDP per capita (2010 PPP) exposed to high or extremely high groundwater stress (%)

MENA countries ——— MENA average

Source: Analysis and calculations from geospatial datasets developed by Stichting Deltares in cooperation with the University of Utrecht in the Netherlands.
Note: High and extremely high levels of groundwater stress imply that groundwater use exceeds by 10 times or more groundwater recharge. No data were available for Israel, Kuwait, Lebanon, Syria, and the Republic of Yemen and for global averages. MENA = Middle East and North Africa; PPP = purchasing power parity.

Groundwater resources are particularly vulnerable to water quality issues, and the deteriorating quality of groundwater contributes to water stress (Jasechko et al. 2017). Some of the major causes of deteriorating groundwater quality in the region are inadequate wastewater treatment, discharge of untreated industrial sewage, and leakage from unregulated dumping of solid waste. Gaza's coastal aquifer, for example, is being contaminated by inadequate treatment of sewage, excessive application of fertilizers, industrial pollution, and excessive groundwater pumping, which is causing the intrusion of brackish or salt water (Almasri 2008).

Sustainability

The limited levels of renewable water resources and increasing demand have led to the unsustainable use of surface and groundwater resources in many parts of the Middle East and North Africa. Unsustainable water use, or *overexploitation*, occurs when water withdrawals tap into nonrenewable water resources or when water is abstracted at a rate faster than it is replenished in the natural environment. In the case of groundwater, this amounts to abstracting more than the natural groundwater recharge or abstracting from fossil aquifers. For surface water, this means consuming the water needed to sustain environmental flows and aquatic ecosystems. If the water balance of a country could be compared to a bank account, then unsustainable water use is equivalent to withdrawing money faster than it is being deposited. As countries draw this "water account" down by unsustainably exploiting renewable resources, they need to at least ensure that other assets come into play that can produce water (desalination) or save water (reduce leakage). This report uses the Blue Water Sustainability Index (B1WSI) to estimate this water account (that is, the sustainability of human water use, considering the renewability and degradation of surface and groundwater resources) (Wada and Bierkens 2014).

The Middle East and North Africa region is a global hotspot of unsustainable water use. Unsustainable water use—or the overspending of the water account—is driven mostly by increasing human water use for agriculture and the expansion of irrigated areas, and to a lesser extent by a decrease in surface water availability. Map 2.6 shows the B1WSI by country and economy estimated for 2010. The BlWSI is a dimensionless quantity that ranges from 0 to 1. The index expresses the portion of water use that is met unsustainably by groundwater abstractions that exceed recharge, as well as by surface water abstractions that compromise environmental flow requirements. A BlWSI value of 0.5 means that 50 percent of a country's or economy's water consumption is met by unsustainable abstraction. BlWSI data show that, on average, 30 percent of the water consumption in the Middle East and North Africa is supplied from unsustainable water resources, with hotspots in the Gulf countries, the eastern Maghreb, and the Mashreq.

Surface water bodies in the Middle East and North Africa are overexploited, with surface water overabstraction compromising 20–50 percent of environmental flow requirements in some countries. In the Jordan River Basin, withdrawals in excess of natural surface water replenishment have significantly reduced flows (Comair et al. 2013) and degraded the ecological status of the river (EcoPeace 2015). Map 2.7 shows that in countries largely dependent on surface water—such as the Arab Republic of Egypt, Iraq, and Syria—between 20 percent and 50 percent of surface water abstraction compromises environmental flow requirements. In the Tigris-Euphrates River system, rapid and uncoordinated development and exploitation involving the three riparian countries (Turkey, Syria, and Iraq) has altered the river's flow regime, causing as much as 40–45 percent decrease in flows to the downstream river reaches in Iraq (Shamout Nouar 2015). These reductions have had catastrophic

MAP 2.6

Blue Water Sustainability Index, Middle East and North Africa, 2010

IBRD 42779 | APRIL 2017

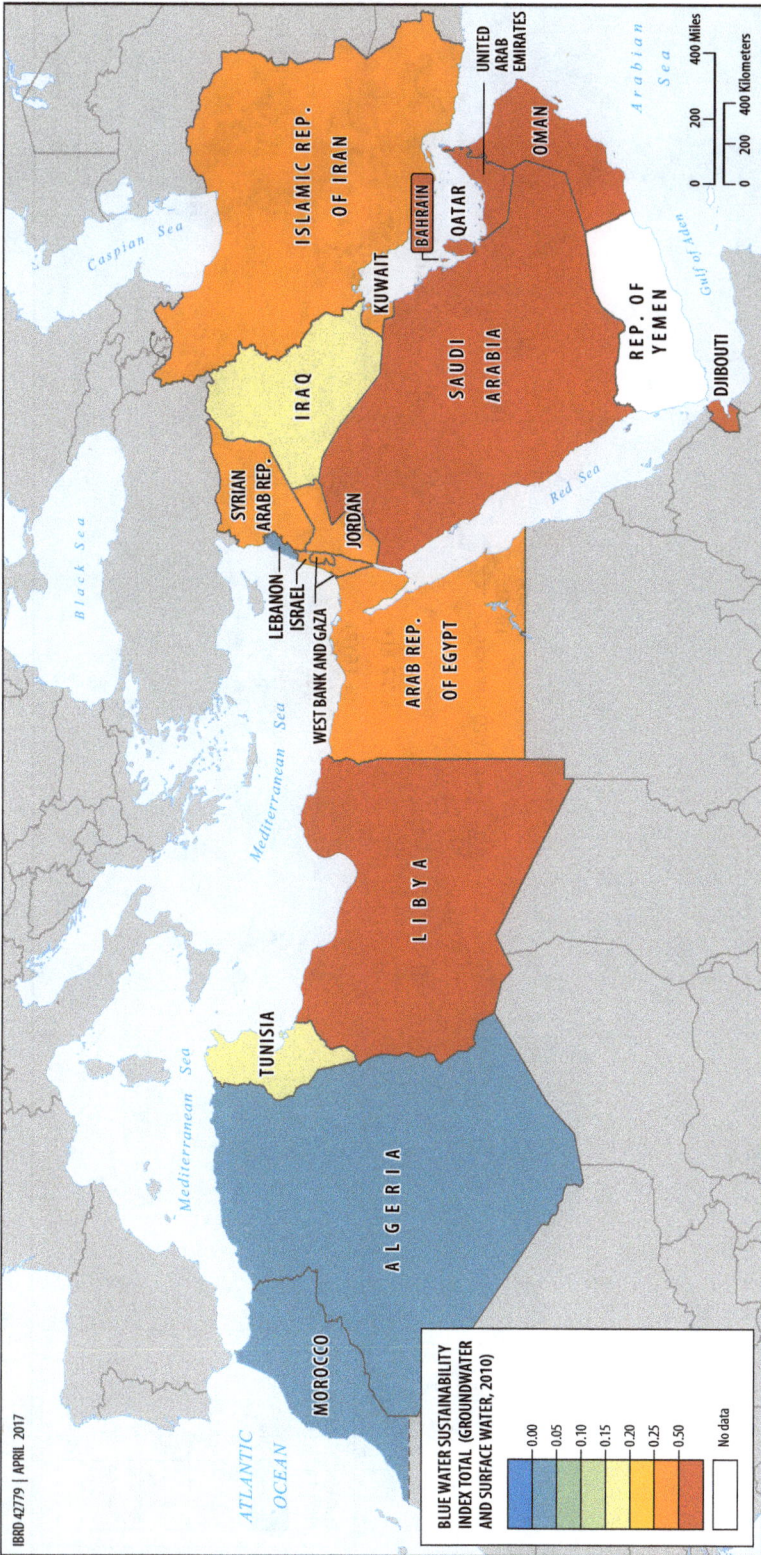

BLUE WATER SUSTAINABILITY INDEX TOTAL (GROUNDWATER AND SURFACE WATER, 2010)

- 0.00
- 0.05
- 0.10
- 0.15
- 0.20
- 0.25
- 0.50
- No data

Source: Analysis and calculations from geospatial datasets developed by the University of Utrecht.

Note: The Blue Water Sustainability Index (BWSI) is a dimensionless quantity ranging from 0 to 1 that expresses the portion of consumptive water use that is met from nonsustainable water sources. Blue = sustainable; red = unsustainable. Nonsustainable surface water use is estimated as the amount of environmental flow requirements not satisfied due to surface water overabstraction. Nonsustainable groundwater use is estimated as the difference between groundwater abstraction and natural groundwater recharge plus recharge from irrigation return flows.

MAP 2.7

Surface Water Blue Water Sustainability Index, Middle East and North Africa, 2010

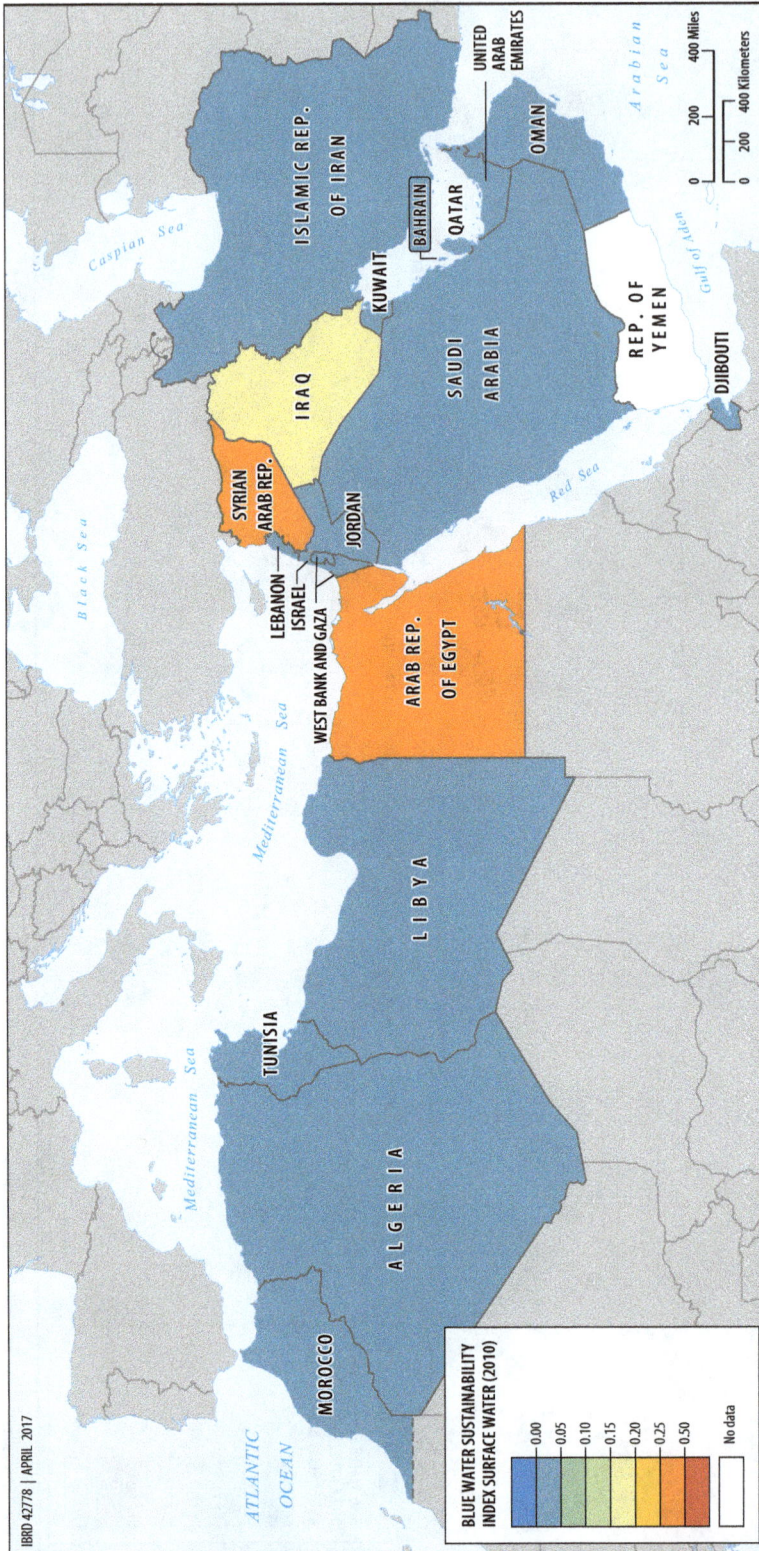

IBRD 42778 | APRIL 2017

BLUE WATER SUSTAINABILITY
INDEX SURFACE WATER (2010)

0.00　0.05　0.10　0.15　0.20　0.25　0.50　No data

Source: Analysis and calculations from geospatial datasets developed by the University of Utrecht.

Note: The Blue Water Sustainability Index (BIWSI) is a dimensionless quantity ranging from 0 to 1 that expresses the portion of consumptive water use that is met from nonsustainable water sources. Blue = sustainable; red = unsustainable. The index measures the portion of environmental flow requirements that is not satisfied due to local surface water consumptive use. Environmental flows are set equal to the monthly surface water flow exceeded 90 percent of the time under natural conditions. The model simulations include the impact of upstream water consumption on downstream flow. Regarding the aggregation methods, low values of the surface water Blue Water Sustainability Index may be observed in areas where there is high localized overabstraction, such as the Jordan River.

impacts on ecosystems and livelihoods in the lower reaches of the Tigris-Euphrates River system (Fawzi et al. 2016).

Groundwater overabstraction is also widespread in the Middle East and North Africa, especially in the Gulf countries, where 50 percent of groundwater consumption is unsustainable. The map of the BlWSI for groundwater (map 2.8) shows how in Libya, Jordan, the Islamic Republic of Iran, and the Gulf countries, groundwater abstraction exceeds natural recharge rates by at least 25 percent. Ongoing groundwater overabstraction may reach a critical point where fossil (nonrenewable) aquifers are depleted and where renewable aquifers are abstracted, to the extent that groundwater levels fall too deep to make abstraction economically feasible. It is difficult to predict when aquifers may become compromised, given the large uncertainties in total groundwater storage (Richey et al. 2015). Yet this uncertainty should not delay the development of groundwater management plans; rather, it should be a call for action to consider groundwater resources as a carefully managed part of a long-term water management strategy.

This regional picture of groundwater depletion is confirmed by many local studies, which report dramatic overexploitation of aquifers across the Middle East and North Africa region. Studies of the Paleogene and Cretaceous aquifers in Syria (Stadler et al. 2012), the Amman Zarqa Basin in Jordan (Al-Zyoud et al. 2015; Goode et al. 2013), and the Nubian Aquifer in Libya and Egypt all find evidence of overexploitation of groundwater resources.[2] The FAO estimates that groundwater abstraction in Libya is about eight times annual renewable groundwater resources, making Libya a hotspot of unsustainable water use that depends heavily on fossil, nonrenewable groundwater resources.[3] According to a 2013 study by the United States Geological Survey that preceded the influx of Syrian refugees, the portion of water potential extractable from Jordanian aquifers could decline by 30 percent to 40 percent by 2030 on average, with wells running dry altogether in some locations (Goode et al. 2013). As groundwater levels decline, abstraction becomes more energy intensive, increasing the costs of pumping. Salinity levels in groundwater also increase. When aquifers are close to depletion, high salinity levels may render the water unsuitable for human consumption.

Unsustainable water consumption has increased in the Maghreb and Mashreq since the 1970s (map 2.9). In the Gulf countries, the portion of water use that is unsustainable has increased only slightly or not at all. This trend partly reflects the phasing out of agricultural policies relying on fossil aquifers to supply irrigation districts and the increasing contribution of nonconventional water supplies. Although unsustainable water use in these countries seems to be slowing down, some of them also have

MAP 2.8

Groundwater Blue Water Sustainability Index, Middle East and North Africa, 2010

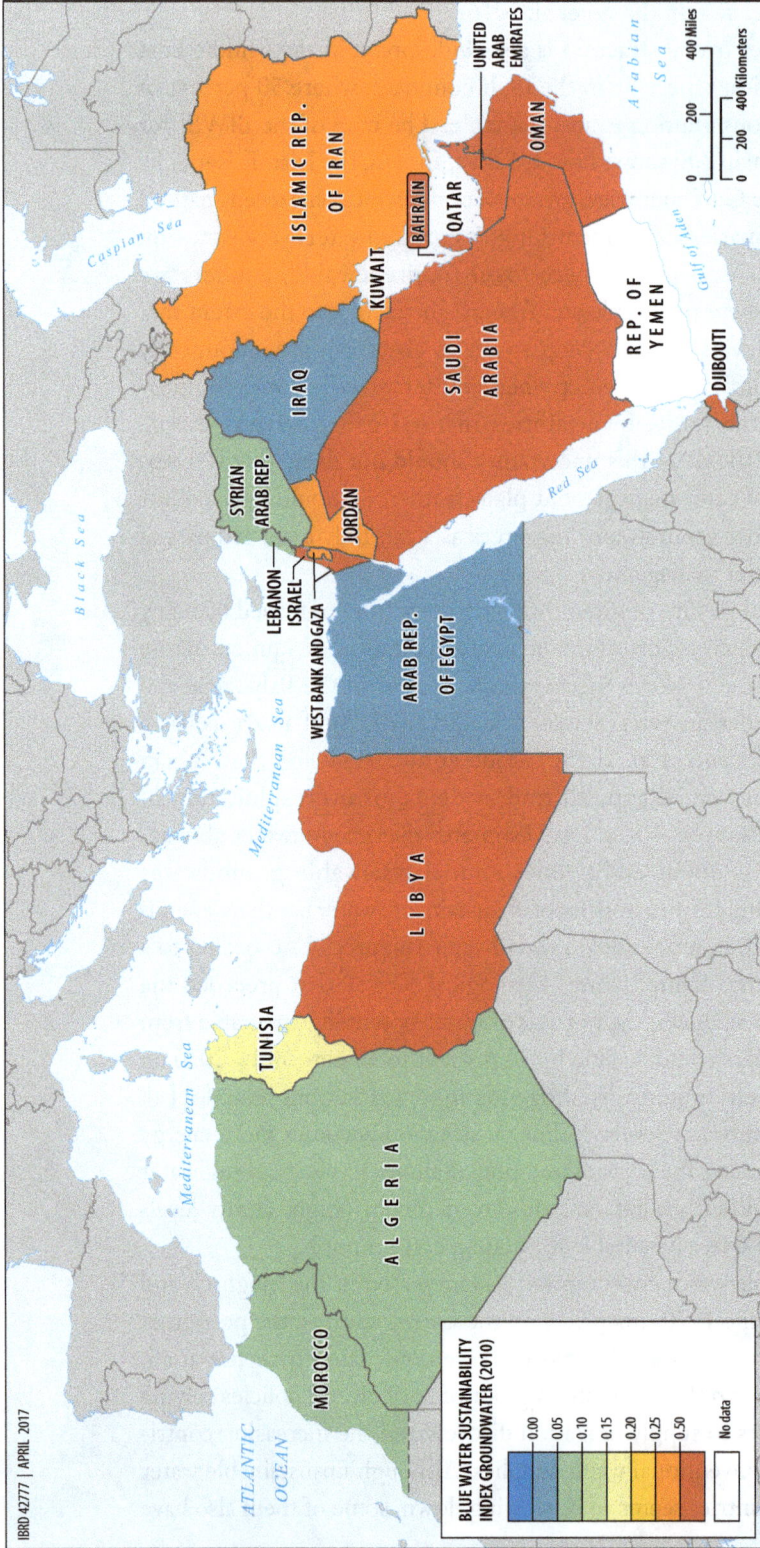

IBRD 42777 | APRIL 2017

BLUE WATER SUSTAINABILITY INDEX GROUNDWATER (2010)

- 0.00
- 0.05
- 0.10
- 0.15
- 0.20
- 0.25
- 0.50
- No data

Source: Analysis and calculations from geospatial datasets developed by the University of Utrecht.

Note: The Blue Water Sustainability Index (BWSI) is a dimensionless quantity ranging from 0 to 1 that expresses the portion of consumptive water use that is met from nonsustainable water sources. Blue = sustainable; red = unsustainable. The index measures the difference between groundwater abstraction and natural groundwater recharge plus additional recharge from irrigation return flows averaged for each country in the Middle East and North Africa. Aggregation may result in some areas of localized unsustainable groundwater abstraction not being represented by the country/economy-wide estimation.

MAP 2.9

Change in Blue Water Sustainability Indicator, Middle East and North Africa, 1970–2010

IBRD 42780 | APRIL 2017

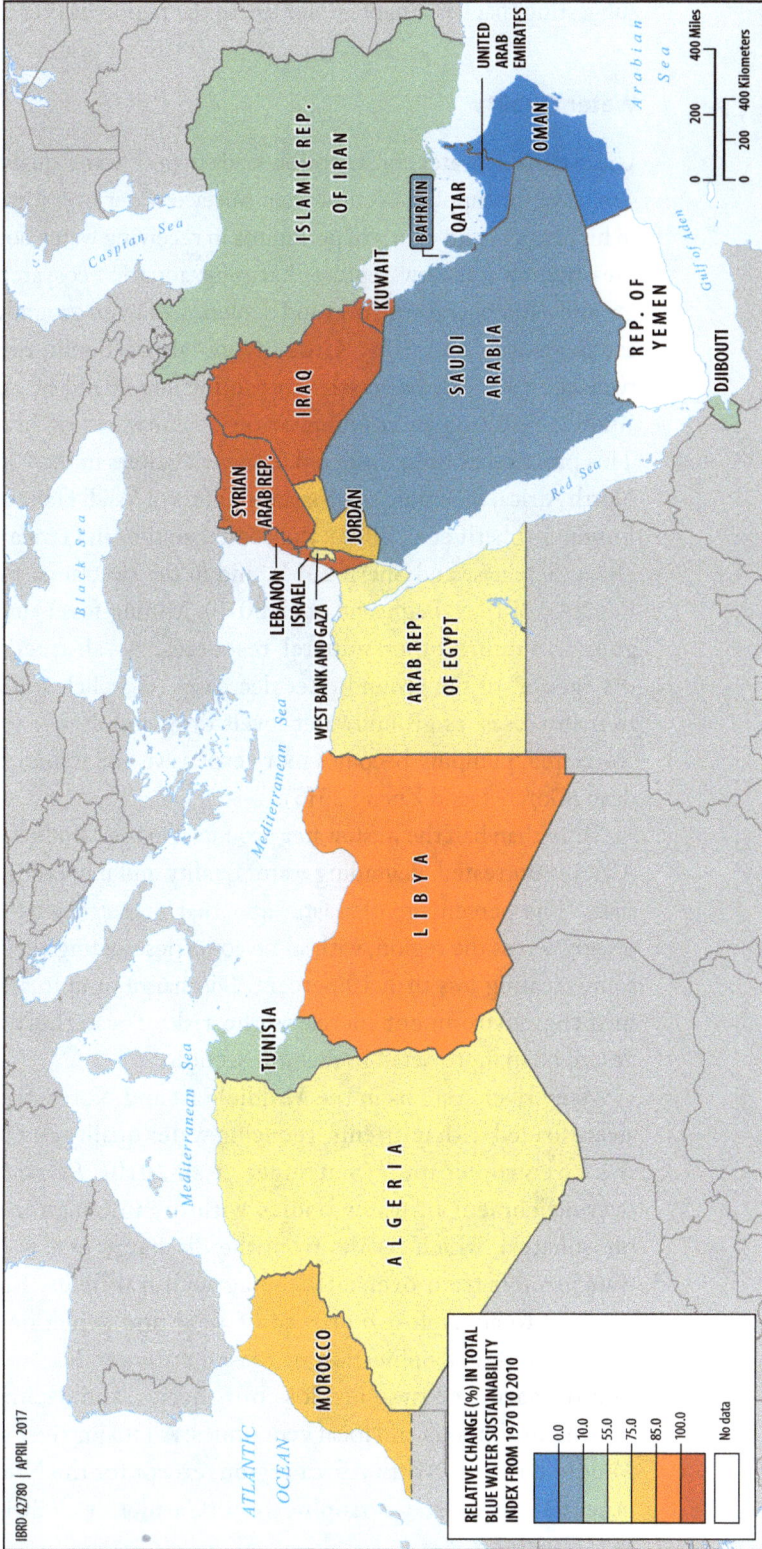

ATLANTIC OCEAN

Mediterranean Sea

MOROCCO

ALGERIA

TUNISIA

LIBYA

ARAB REP. OF EGYPT

Black Sea

Caspian Sea

ISLAMIC REP. OF IRAN

SYRIAN ARAB REP.

LEBANON
ISRAEL
WEST BANK AND GAZA

JORDAN

IRAQ

KUWAIT

BAHRAIN

QATAR

UNITED ARAB EMIRATES

OMAN

SAUDI ARABIA

Red Sea

Arabian Sea

Gulf of Aden

REP. OF YEMEN

DJIBOUTI

400 Miles
400 Kilometers
0 200 400
0 200

RELATIVE CHANGE (%) IN TOTAL BLUE WATER SUSTAINABILITY INDEX FROM 1970 TO 2010

0.0
10.0
55.0
75.0
85.0
100.0

No data

Source: Analysis and calculations from geospatial datasets developed by the University of Utrecht.

Note: The Blue Water Sustainability Index (BIWSI) is a dimensionless quantity ranging from 0 to 1 that expresses the portion of consumptive water use that is met from nonsustainable water sources. Blue = small or no increase in unsustainable water use; red = increase in unsustainable water use.

the greatest absolute levels of unsustainable abstraction (map 2.6), suggesting that sustainable water use in the region has yet to be achieved.

Water Quality

Unsustainable water consumption leads to poor water quality, which constrains water supplies even further. Surface water overabstraction results in higher concentrations of pollutants in receiving water bodies and modifies the natural flow regime, harming aquatic ecosystems. Similarly, groundwater overabstraction and depletion of fossil groundwater reserves can degrade water quality. Groundwater abstraction in excess of natural recharge rates can cause saltwater to intrude inland or upward into an aquifer, resulting in contamination by saltwater or brackish water.[4] This process has been observed in many aquifers in the Middle East and North Africa, including the coastal aquifers of Wadi Ham in United Arab Emirates (Sherif et al. 2012), the coastal aquifer in Gaza and in the Nile Delta (Sefelnasr and Sherif 2014), and in the central part of the Islamic Republic of Iran (Baghvand et al. 2010). Mining fossil aquifers is analogous to mining other mineral resources. As abstraction increases, the "grade" of the groundwater decreases (Gorelick and Zheng 2015). In many cases, as groundwater levels drop and deeper groundwater is abstracted, pumping becomes more expensive and water quality tends to drop (Gorelick and Zheng 2015).

More than half the wastewater produced in the Middle East and North Africa is untreated, degrading water quality and increasing public health risks. The percentage of wastewater that undergoes treatment differs greatly across the region, with some countries treating all wastewater and some treating less than 10 percent. Discharge of untreated wastewater into the environment increases the risk of waterborne diseases, as described in more detail in the next section.

Many river systems in the Middle East and North Africa are excessively loaded with nutrients, reducing water quality and increasing the risk of eutrophication (Seitzinger et al. 2010). *Eutrophication* is the overenrichment of water bodies with organic matter (nitrates and phosphates), which results from the discharge of sewage and storm water runoff from overfertilized agricultural fields. Eutrophication can lead to an explosive growth of algae and depletion of oxygen in waters. High eutrophication in coastal areas can lead to the degradation of marine ecosystems, loss of fisheries, and decline of tourism, hurting livelihoods and local economies. All major river systems in the Middle East and North Africa region, except for the Nile, have a high potential for coastal eutrophication (Garnier et al. 2010; Seitzinger et al. 2010).

Unsustainable water consumption and pollution are major threats to freshwater and marine ecosystems in the Middle East and North Africa. The International Union for Conservation of Nature (IUCN) estimates that on the Arabian Peninsula alone, 17 percent of freshwater species are threatened with extinction (García et al. 2015). The semi-enclosed nature of the Gulf also means that discharged untreated wastewater accumulates in a "pollutant trap," threatening marine ecosystems and human activities and livelihoods that rely on marine resources (Van Lavieren et al. 2011).

The cost of poor water quality in the Middle East and North Africa ranges from 0.5 percent to 2.5 percent of GDP every year (World Bank 2007). These impacts range from health damage due to the spread of waterborne diseases to the loss of ecosystem services and fisheries due to pollution of fresh and marine water bodies. Deteriorating water quality also increases the costs of providing water services. Polluted water sources generate large costs for water service providers, forcing them to switch supplies or invest in additional treatment. Costs at the household level can also be high if members are incapacitated by illness or are required to use their time to care for the ill, impeding income-generating activities and school attendance. Risks and long-term expenses may be elevated for households that are especially vulnerable to low quality water because of poverty, location, or a lack of information.

Formal water quality monitoring programs, legislation, enforcement, and regional partnerships are needed to improve water quality and protect aquatic ecosystems. Very little legislation currently covers the protection of freshwater and marine ecosystems from unsustainable abstraction and pollution (Van Lavieren et al. 2011). Existing models of regional cooperation for pollution control and ecosystem management, such as the Regional Organization for the Protection of the Marine Environment, need to be expanded to ensure that water quality monitoring and management become priorities in the economic agendas of governments in the Middle East and North Africa.

Water Use and Productivity

Water Withdrawals by Sector and by Source

Information on water withdrawals is essential to understand the human drivers of water stress and develop potential solutions. Despite its importance, information on water withdrawals is sparse and is not regularly collected in many countries in the Middle East and North Africa. Most data on water withdrawals are aggregated to the country level and lack the temporal and spatial resolution required to understand important characteristics of water use, such as trends, frequency, and timing of shortages and times of peak use. This report uses data on water withdrawals from

the Food and Agriculture Organization's AQUASTAT and the WRI's
Aqueduct databases to estimate indicative water use by sector and by
source of water. These data should be interpreted with caution, however,
because they come from different sources and are estimated over different
periods of time.

Water withdrawals can be divided into agricultural, industrial, and
domestic use, with agriculture accounting for the overwhelming share of
water withdrawals globally and in the Middle East and North Africa.
Globally, agriculture accounts for about 70 percent of water withdrawals
(FAO 2015). The proportion of agricultural water withdrawals is even
higher in the Middle East and North Africa region (about 80 percent),
where arid climatic conditions characterized by high evapotranspiration
and infiltration rates mean that little moisture is available in the soil,
which makes irrigation essential to crop growth. As figure 2.7 shows,

FIGURE 2.7

Water Withdrawals, by Sector, and by Country and Economy

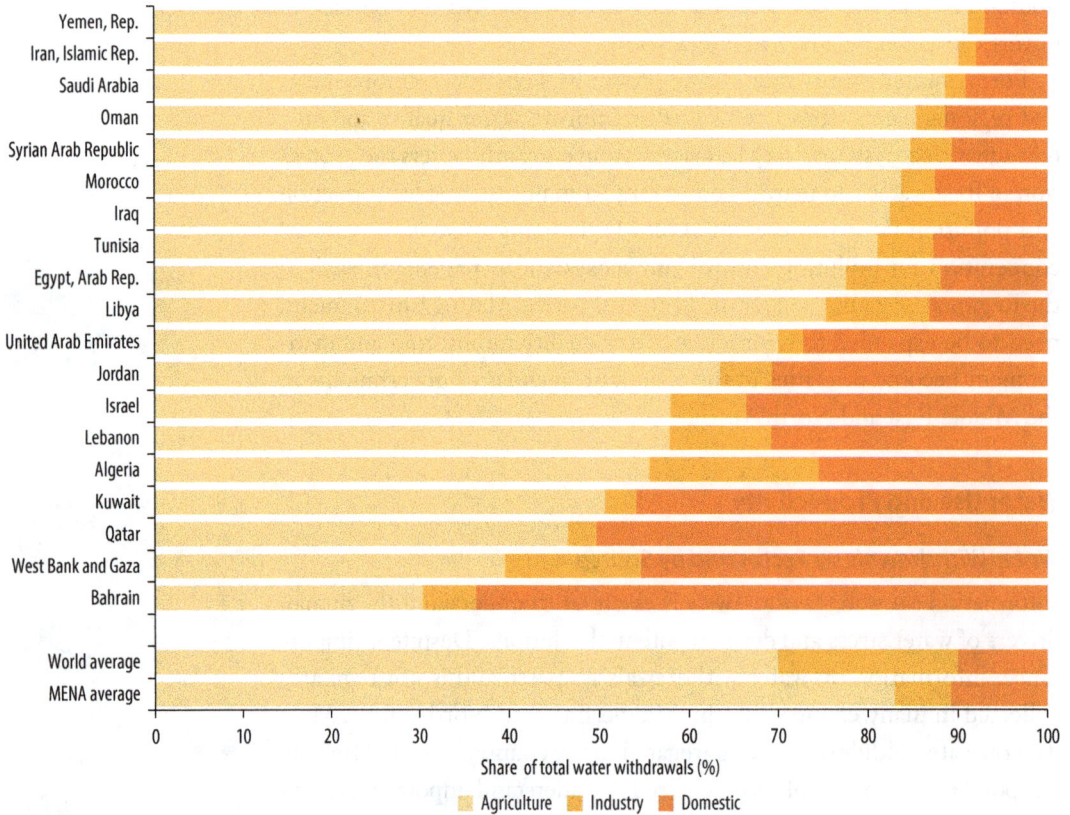

Source: World Bank, using data from FAO AQUASTAT (database).
Note: MENA = Middle East and North Africa.

irrigated agriculture is responsible for around 90 percent of all annual water withdrawals in Syria, Oman, Saudi Arabia, the Islamic Republic of Iran, and the Republic of Yemen. The volumes of water withdrawn for agriculture in different parts of the Middle East and North Africa are shown in map 2.10. The areas surrounding the Nile and the Tigris-Euphrates river systems stand out as having the largest volumes of agricultural water withdrawals. Levels of agricultural water use are also high in the irrigated areas in the western part of the Islamic Republic of Iran.

Groundwater withdrawals play a central role in meeting irrigation water demand. The demand for agricultural water for irrigation varies seasonally and tends to increase during the dry season, when surface water resources are scarcest. Groundwater is especially important for irrigated agriculture because of its availability on demand and its ability to act as storage, buffering the year-to-year and month-to-month variability that affects surface waters. Pumping groundwater allows farmers to continue irrigating during a drought, thus serving as a reliable supply source for agriculture—and hence income—in arid areas. However, intensive and unregulated groundwater pumping for agriculture can lead to a severe depletion of aquifers and potentially irreversible environmental damages and externalities (OECD 2015).

The Middle East and North Africa wastes a high portion of its water resources in losses along the food supply chain. The region has the highest per capita freshwater resources losses in food supply chain in the world (Kummu et al. 2012). Some Middle East and North Africa countries lose between 80 and 177 cubic meters per capita per year of freshwater resources (renewable and nonrenewable) from field to fork (Kummu et al. 2012). Agricultural losses, processing losses, and losses at the distribution and consumption stages are all responsible for this waste. At the consumption stage alone, FAO estimates that food waste in the Middle East and North Africa is 32 percent (FAO 2011). In the area of water-intensive fruit and vegetables, this proportion increases to around 60 percent. Improving the efficiency of the food supply chain could contribute to overall reductions in agricultural water use, as well as increasing food and energy security.

Municipal water withdrawals, which globally represent a relatively small share of water use (10 percent), account for a very large share of water use in some Middle Eastern and North African countries and economies. Projected population growth and migration to urban centers are increasing the demand for municipal water across the region (Tropp and Jägerskog 2006). In the Gulf states and in West Bank and Gaza, municipal water withdrawals account for almost half of all withdrawals (figure 2.7). In the Gulf states, a large portion of municipal water demand is supplied via desalination. Map 2.11 shows how municipal and industrial water

MAP 2.10

Agricultural Water Withdrawals from Freshwater Resources, Middle East and North Africa

IBRD 42774 | APRIL 2017

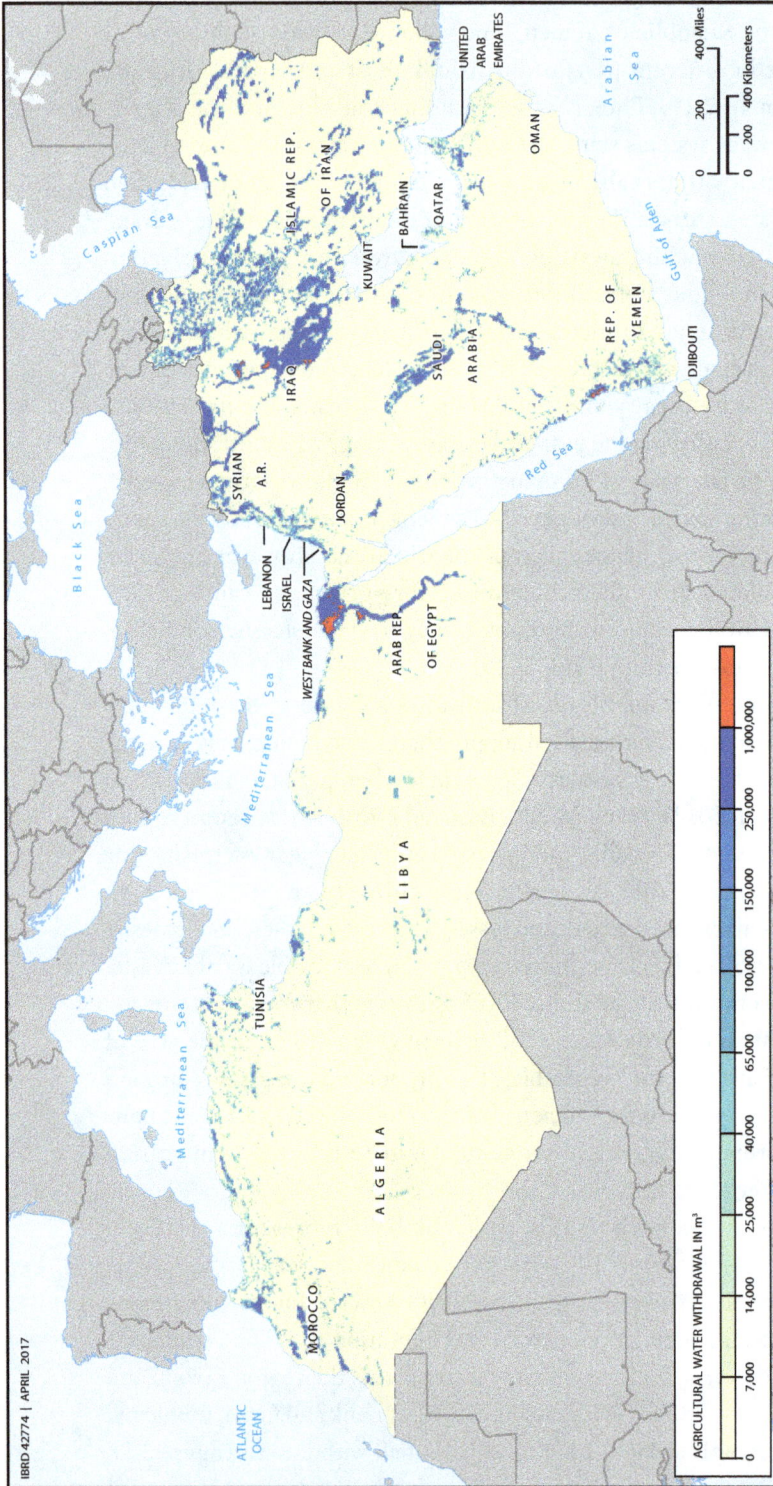

AGRICULTURAL WATER WITHDRAWAL IN m³

0   7,000   14,000   25,000   40,000   65,000   100,000   150,000   250,000   1,000,000

Source: Analysis and calculations based on World Resources Institute Aqueduct™ data.

MAP 2.11

Domestic and Industrial Water Withdrawals from Freshwater Resources, Middle East and North Africa

IBRD 42775 | APRIL 2017

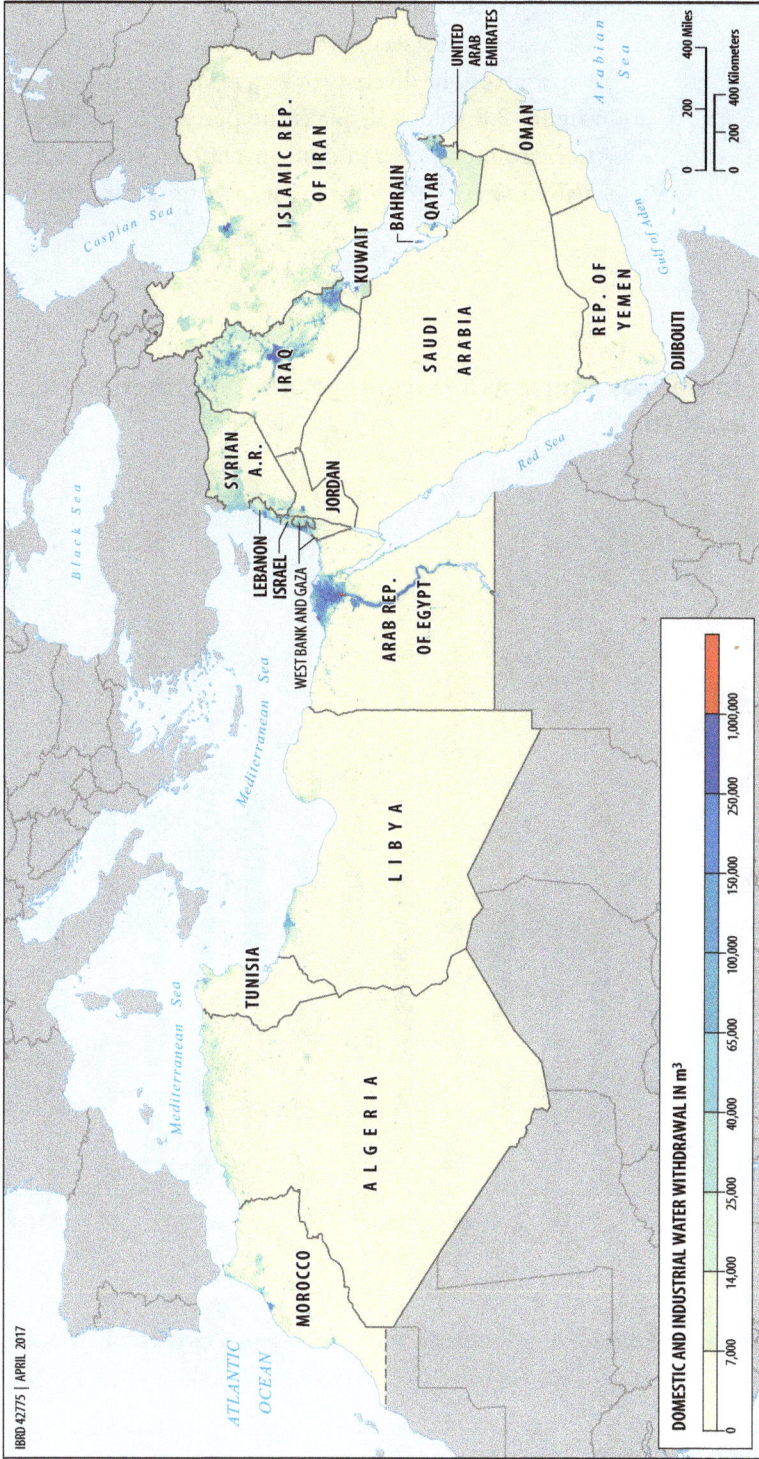

DOMESTIC AND INDUSTRIAL WATER WITHDRAWAL IN m³

| 0 | 7,000 | 14,000 | 25,000 | 40,000 | 65,000 | 100,000 | 150,000 | 250,000 | 1,000,000 |

Source: Analysis and calculations based on World Resources Institute Aqueduct™ data.

withdrawals are considerably lower than agricultural withdrawals in absolute terms. Across most of the region, withdrawals for the municipal and industrial sectors do not exceed 25,000 m³ per year.

Assessing water security requires an understanding of water withdrawals by source. The diversity of water supply sources in the region is shown in figure 2.8, which displays the percent of withdrawals from surface water, groundwater, and nonconventional water supplies. *Surface water withdrawals* refer to the amount of water abstracted from surface water

FIGURE 2.8

Water Withdrawals, by Source as a Percentage of Total Withdrawals, and by Country and Economy, 2010

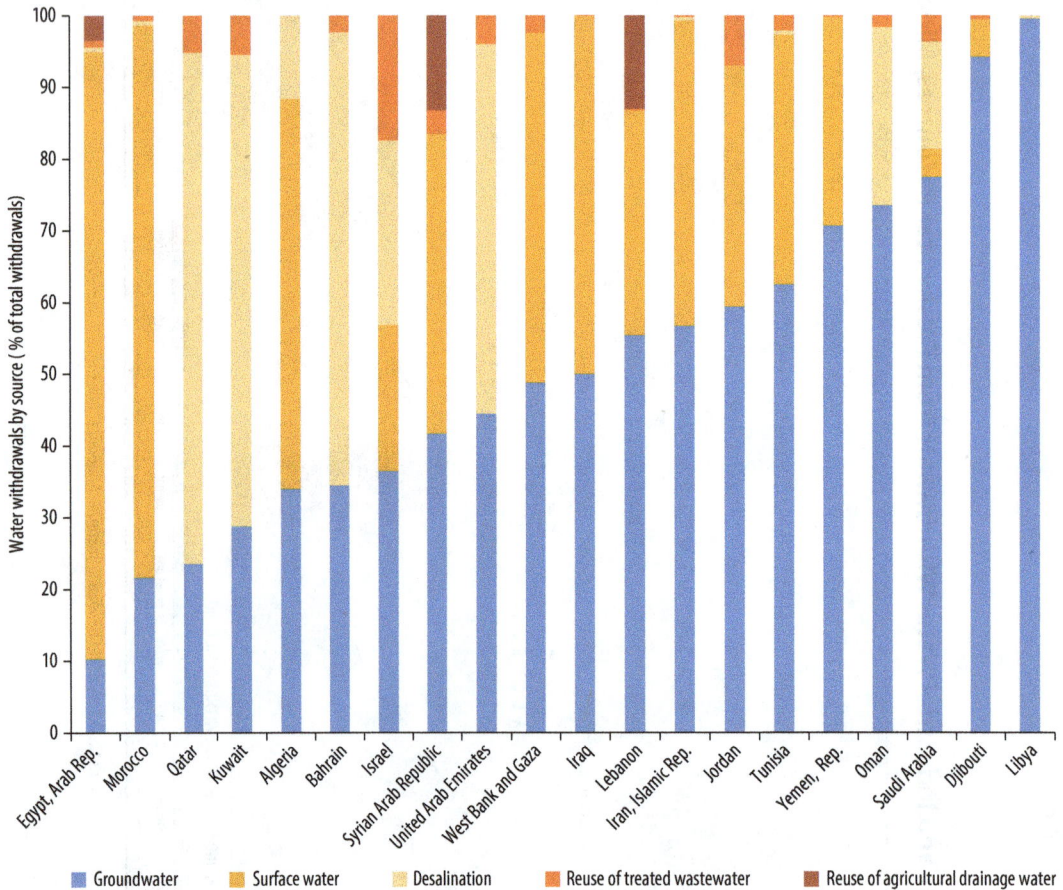

Groundwater | Surface water | Desalination | Reuse of treated wastewater | Reuse of agricultural drainage water

Sources: World Bank calculations. Data on desalination capacity are from Global Water Intelligence 2016. Data on all other categories are from FAO AQUASTAT.

Note: For Iraq, Syria, and West Bank and Gaza, the breakdown between surface and groundwater withdrawals was not available and withdrawals were split equally between the two categories. In absolute terms, Egypt has the largest volume of reuse of agricultural drainage water, while Saudi Arabia has the largest desalination capacity in the region. Caution should be used in comparing data on annual freshwater withdrawals, which are subject to variations in collection and estimation methods.

bodies, including rivers, lakes, and reservoirs. *Groundwater withdrawals* refer to the amount of water abstracted from aquifers, including nonrenewable groundwater abstraction from fossil aquifers, commonly referred to as groundwater mining. *Nonconventional water* is defined as the total water withdrawals from desalinated water, treated wastewater, and agricultural drainage water.[5]

Sources of water supply vary greatly across the Middle East and North Africa region, with the Maghreb countries generally using more surface water, while the Mashreq and Gulf states rely more heavily on groundwater and nonconventional sources. For example, Saudi Arabia uses desalination as its primary source for municipal water, while Egypt relies almost entirely on surface water. The percentages given in figure 2.8 also show the importance of groundwater as a major supply source in the region. For instance, Djibouti, Libya, and Oman rely almost entirely on groundwater supplies.

Water Productivity

The productivity of water matters everywhere, but particularly under conditions of scarcity. In the Middle East and North Africa, where the majority of water is used for agriculture, agricultural water productivity is a priority. Broadly defined, *agricultural water productivity* means growing more food and gaining more benefits with less water.[6] This definition can be broadened to assess the wider productivity of economies in terms of economic output per volume of water used by the economy.[7] This is referred to as *total water productivity* and is shown in figure 2.9 for Middle Eastern and North African countries and economies (except for Syria and the Republic of Yemen). This indicator measures the water intensity of the economy. It can be useful in monitoring how a given economy uses water over time. An increase in the indicator over time would capture the reallocation of water to more economically productive sectors of the economy.

There are striking differences in total water productivity across the region, which features some of the most water-productive as well as some of the least productive countries in the world. Water productivity in the Gulf states and Israel is much higher than the rest of the world, underscoring these countries' endeavors to make every drop count, but also their economic systems largely based on high-value services and nonrenewable natural resources. Other countries and economies—such as Jordan, Lebanon, West Bank and Gaza, and Algeria—have higher levels of total water productivity than the average middle-income country. Other countries—such as Egypt, the Islamic Republic of Iran, and Iraq—have levels of water productivity that are below the average for middle-income economies.

FIGURE 2.9

Total Water Productivity, Selected Countries and Economies

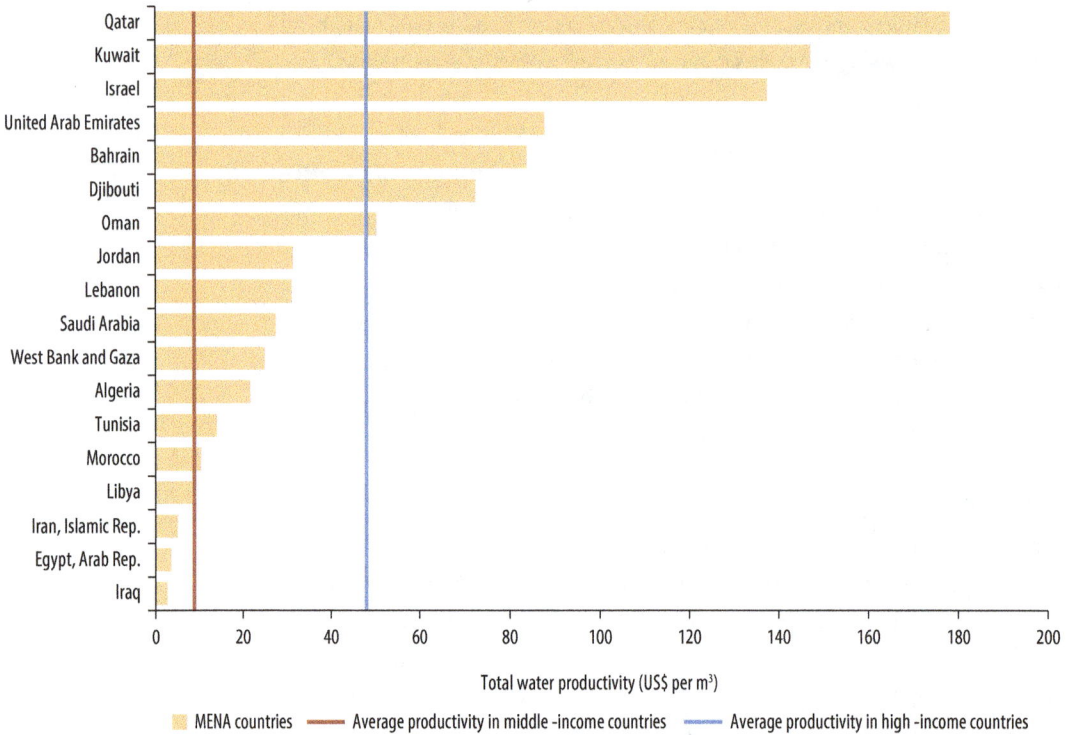

Total water productivity (US$ per m³)

■ MENA countries   ▬ Average productivity in middle -income countries   ▬ Average productivity in high -income countries

Source: Data for Syria and the Republic of Yemen are missing. Data estimated as the ratio of constant 2010 $ GDP (from World Bank GDP estimates) over cubic meters of total water withdrawals from FAO AQUASTAT database.
Note: Water withdrawals also include water withdrawn from nonconventional supply sources, such as desalination and wastewater reuse. Given the different economic structure of each country, these indicators should be used carefully, taking into account a country's sectorial activities and natural resource endowments. MENA = Middle East and North Africa; m³ = cubic meters.

Water productivity also differs significantly by sector, with the lowest productivity in agriculture. One recent global study using accounting-based measures of water productivity suggests that domestic water uses produced twice the value of agricultural water, and that industrial uses produced three times the value (Aylward et al. 2010). Agricultural water productivity—defined as agricultural GDP divided by freshwater withdrawals for agriculture—for selected Middle Eastern and North African countries and economies is shown in figure 2.10; and industrial water productivity is shown in figure 2.11. Agricultural water productivity ranges from a fraction of a cent to $12 per cubic meter of water withdrawn. Industrial water productivity ranges from a fraction of a cent to $4,000 per cubic meter.

FIGURE 2.10

Agricultural Water Productivity, by Country and Economy, 2012

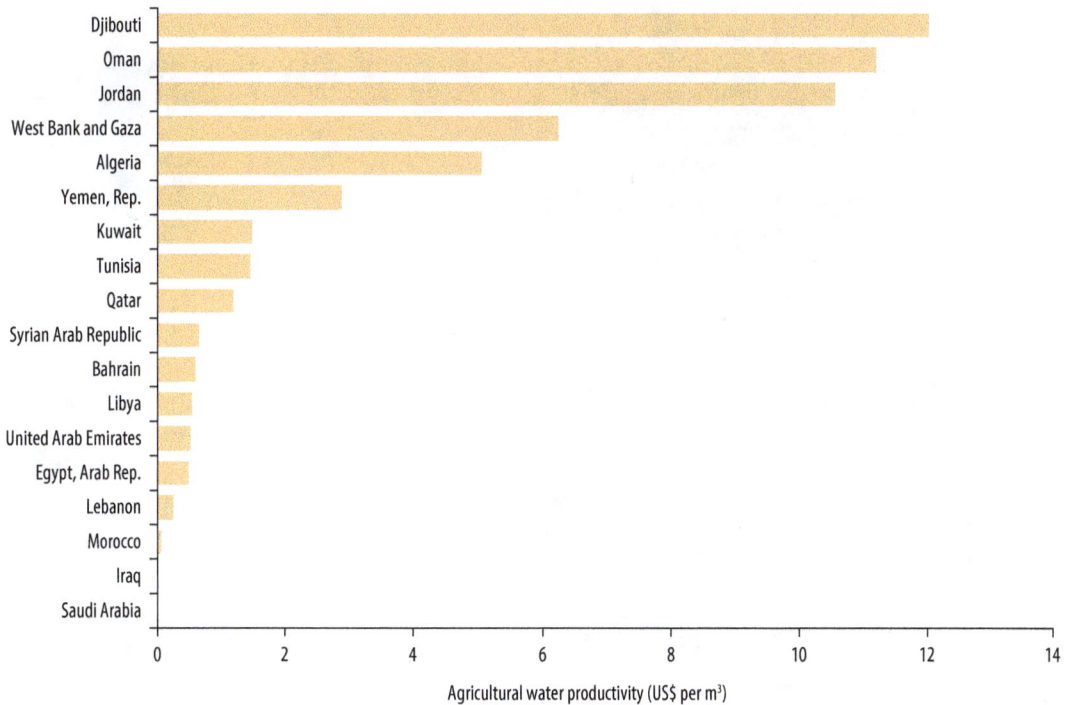

Source: Data are based on estimates provided in AWC (2012, table 79).
Note: Agricultural water productivity is an indication of economic output from the agricultural sector (irrigated and rainfed agriculture and livestock) per unit of water resources withdrawn. These indicators should be used cautiously, taking into account the fact that each country estimates and reports water withdrawals differently. m³ = cubic meters.

A number of caveats apply to data on agricultural productivity. For instance, GDP data come from different years and inflate agriculture's contribution by combining data on irrigated and rainfed systems. Data on agricultural withdrawals are also uncertain because they ignore recent changes in the area equipped for irrigation.[8] Furthermore, these indicators must be used cautiously because they capture different economic circumstances and are not built on water-crop production functions but on macro-level data based on GDP estimates. Box 2.1 describes how Earth observation technology is improving agricultural water management and understanding rates of agricultural water consumption. These advances can inform policies targeted at increasing agricultural water productivity (for instance, by giving information on how best to time water supplies).

FIGURE 2.11

Industrial Water Productivity, Selected Countries and Economies, 2012

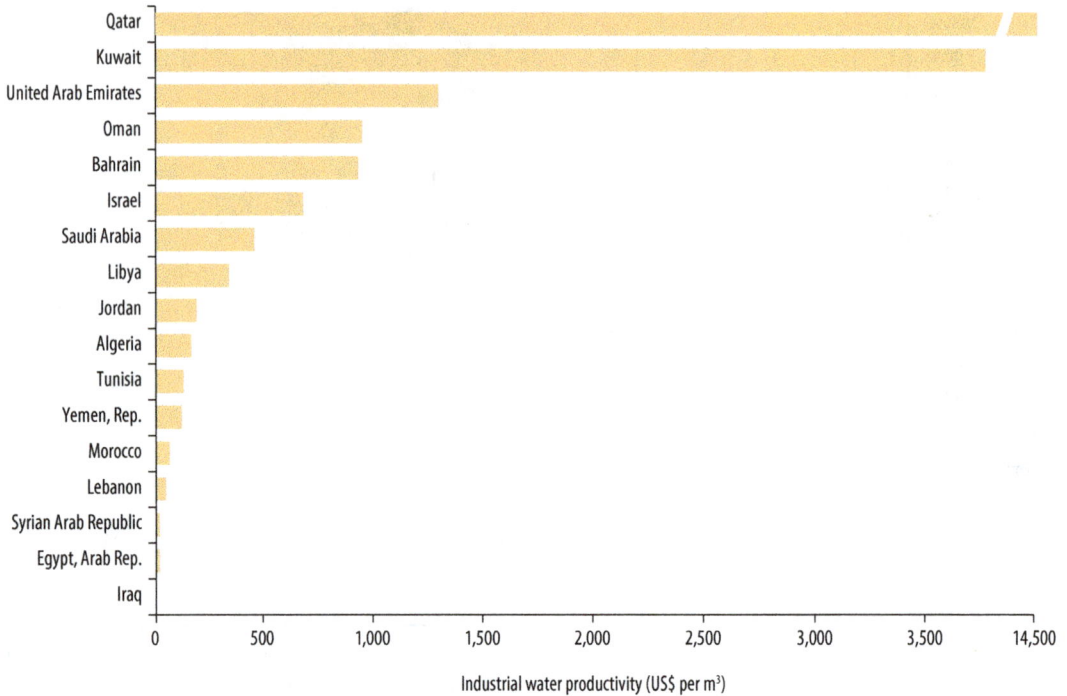

Industrial water productivity (US$ per m³)

Sources: Data are based on estimates provided in AWC (2012, table 79).
Note: Industrial water productivity is an indication of economic output from the industrial sector per unit of water resources consumed. Data for Israel were generated using data on industrial GDP from the *CIA World Factbook* and industrial water withdrawals from FAO AQUASTAT. These indicators should be used cautiously, taking into account the fact that each country estimates and reports water withdrawals differently. m³ = cubic meters.

Balancing Supply and Demand: Overcoming Physical Water Scarcity

Balancing water supply and demand is central to water security. Where demand outstrips supply, there are essentially three nonexclusive strategies that can be pursued to strengthen water security:

Strategy 1: Use (or lose) less water, to reduce demand.
   Methods: Demand management strategies (productivity enhancements, leakage control).
Strategy 2: Reallocate water, to realign demand.
   Methods: Market-based tools and regulations (pricing and permitting, subsidy reform, environmental protection).
Strategy 3: Provide (or create) more water, to meet demand.
   Methods: Supply-side responses (storage and transfers schemes, non-conventional water).

BOX 2.1

Earth Observation for Agricultural Water Management

Sustainably managing water in agriculture requires information on a range of variables, including rates of water withdrawals and water use by different types of crops. Earth observation is an appropriate tool for estimating some of these variables. Monitoring of evapotranspiration allows for the estimation of the ratio of agricultural produce to the amount of water use by a crop, which is a key indicator of the efficiency of agricultural water use. Earth observation can also be used to monitor rates of irrigation water use by combining high-resolution data on evapotranspiration with information on the location and size of irrigated crops.

Many global and regional initiatives are now under way to exploit the potential for recent advances in Earth observation sciences to contribute to sustainable agricultural water management. For instance, the Food and Agricultural Organization (FAO) of the United Nations is developing a publicly accessible, real-time database (Water Productivity Open-access Portal, or WaPOR) to monitor and report agricultural water productivity over the Middle East and North Africa using Earth observation.

Source: García et al. 2016.

Strategy 1. Using or Losing Less Water

The most cost-effective way to address water scarcity is managing and reducing water use. Placing a value or price on water to signal its extreme scarcity and promote its conservation is the first step to reducing water use in the Middle East and North Africa.[9] Undervaluing or underpricing water, particularly where governance and regulation arrangements are weak, creates incentives for the overexploitation and depletion of water resources. Beyond signaling water scarcity, *water pricing*—meaning a fee to cover the costs of service provision—is essential to provide financial resources for water resources protection, infrastructure maintenance, and service delivery.

Within a river basin, reductions in water use and increases in water productivity may be achieved by accounting for water use, depletion, and productivity at the basin scale (Ward and Pulido-Velazquez 2008). At the level of municipal and industrial water use, measures include reducing leakage and monitoring *nonrevenue water* (water that is produced and "lost" before it reaches the customer), metering water, reducing pressure in piped distribution, and controlling consumption by charging water service fees and encouraging changes in water use (behavior change) (SWIM-SM 2013).

A range of factors make it difficult to tackle nonrevenue water in the Middle East and North Africa, including lack of meters, poor data quality, lack of trained staff, infrastructure in disrepair, and illegal connections (Ardakanian and Martin-Bordes 2010). Some attempts have been made to reduce nonrevenue water in the region, but they need to be scaled up. For instance, pressure management and training staff members who deal with network operations has helped reduce water losses by up to 40 percent in Ain Al Basha in Jordan (GIZ 2014, 206). In Fez, Morocco, the installation of pressure-reducing valves and pipe network modeling led to a 10 percent reduction in the system's losses over an eight-year period, and a full recovery of the initial installation and investments in modeling (SWIM-SM 2013).

Decreasing water use will also entail changing people's understanding of and attitudes about the value of water. Encouraging signs are emerging with respect to water issues and overconsumption. A recent survey of the region's population by the Arab Forum for Environment and Development has shown high levels of awareness around excessive water consumption, with over 75 percent of the survey's respondents acknowledging that the region's levels of individual water use rank among the highest in the world (Saab 2015).[10] In other parts of the Middle East and North Africa, citizens have increasingly voiced their concerns with respect to water overexploitation using social media, highlighting increasing societal consciousness around the value of water and the impacts of its mismanagement (Madani 2014).

Reductions in agricultural water withdrawals can reduce water stress in the region, yet more far-reaching actions are needed to cope with chronic scarcity. Reducing agricultural withdrawals in the Middle East and North Africa by 30 percent would reduce water stress on economic activities in those areas worth $68 billion, corresponding to 2.5 percent of regional GDP. Reducing agricultural demand by 30 percent would reduce the water stress for about 9 million people across the region, about 3 percent of the current exposed population.[11] These relatively small impacts also demonstrate how reductions in agricultural water use may not be sufficient to reduce water stress and that water scarcity is here to stay (World Bank 2016). Making better use of green water could also help reduce blue water agricultural use.

Strategy 2. Reallocating Water

Addressing water scarcity by reducing agricultural water use could enable water to be allocated to other sectors. In several Middle Eastern and North African countries, domestic and industrial water use is a small fraction of agricultural water use. A small decrease in agricultural water use could go a long way toward generating surplus water for a growing municipal and industrial demand in some Middle Eastern and North African countries and economies. These reductions could be achieved by encouraging reductions in the number of irrigation applications or area irrigated or by promoting switches to crops that consume less water (Scheierling, Young, and Cardon 2006). Actual decisions on reallocation among sectors would have to be based on basin-scale water accounting and considerations of the social, economic, and environmental value of water, and associated distributional impacts on communities and households within the basin.

Projected increases in municipal demand could be met by reductions in agricultural water use. As the population in the Middle East and North Africa continues to grow, the municipal water demand will increase, straining an already-scarce water resource. Given that in most Middle Eastern and North African countries, water resources are already fully allocated (that is, there is no excess water supply), reducing agricultural water use can help meet growing municipal water demand. In most Middle Eastern and North African countries, outside the Gulf Cooperation Council (GCC) (except Saudi Arabia), the projected increases in domestic demand amount to less than 20 percent of current agricultural water use, as shown in figure 2.12. This means that if agricultural water use could be reduced by 20 percent by 2030, these countries would be able to meet their projected increases of municipal water demand without having to augment water supplies. These reductions could be achieved by improving accounting of water use at the basin level to identify opportunities for saving water or by switching to crops that use less water. In areas where water use is already high and projected to increase because of population growth or migration, the potential for reductions in agricultural use to meet projected municipal demand is smaller.

Reducing water use and reallocating water can have significant distributional effects. The degree to which poor and vulnerable households would benefit from reductions in agricultural water use needs to be quantified to inform policies. Similarly, the unintended consequences of reallocation (including loss of livelihoods) need to be accounted for when planning water allocation among sectors.

Strategy 3. Augmenting Supplies

To address water scarcity and variability, Middle Eastern and North African countries and economies have also invested in technologies and infrastructure to store water and augment supply. Investments initially focused on capturing and storing storm water. As a result, the region has the world's highest proportion of freshwater stored in surface water reservoirs as a percentage of total freshwater availability (World Bank 2007). About 85 percent of total surface freshwater resources in the Middle East

FIGURE 2.12

Domestic Water Demand as a Share of Agricultural Water Demand by 2030, by Country and Economy

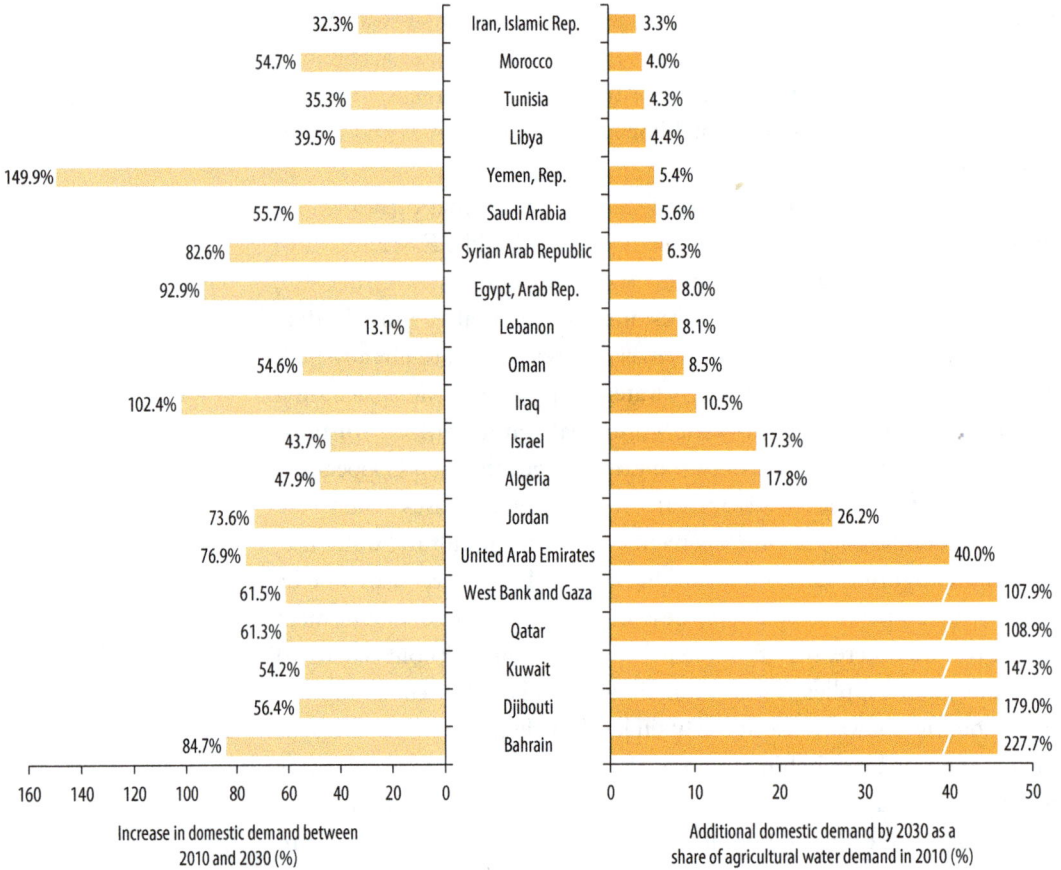

Country	Increase in domestic demand between 2010 and 2030 (%)	Additional domestic demand by 2030 as a share of agricultural water demand in 2010 (%)
Iran, Islamic Rep.	32.3%	3.3%
Morocco	54.7%	4.0%
Tunisia	35.3%	4.3%
Libya	39.5%	4.4%
Yemen, Rep.	149.9%	5.4%
Saudi Arabia	55.7%	5.6%
Syrian Arab Republic	82.6%	6.3%
Egypt, Arab Rep.	92.9%	8.0%
Lebanon	13.1%	8.1%
Oman	54.6%	8.5%
Iraq	102.4%	10.5%
Israel	43.7%	17.3%
Algeria	47.9%	17.8%
Jordan	73.6%	26.2%
United Arab Emirates	76.9%	40.0%
West Bank and Gaza	61.5%	107.9%
Qatar	61.3%	108.9%
Kuwait	54.2%	147.3%
Djibouti	56.4%	179.0%
Bahrain	84.7%	227.7%

Source: Analysis and calculations based on World Resources Institute Aqueduct™ data.
Note: In most countries, the projected increases in domestic demand by 2030 are less than 20 percent of current agricultural demand, underscoring the potential benefits of water saving in agriculture as a mechanism to "free" water for other sectors. Increase in domestic demand is projected for a "middle-of-the-road" scenario under shared economic pathways SSP2 that is comparable to a business-as-usual scenario of socioeconomic development (moderate urbanization and population increases, same water use intensities) (O'Neill et al. 2015). Agricultural demand is kept constant at 2010 levels.

and North Africa are stored in reservoirs, compared to a global average of 10 percent.

While the region has a very high percentage of water stored in reservoirs as a proportion of its scarce surface water resources, it has very low absolute volumes of water stored in dams on a per capita basis (figure 2.13). This situation is mostly due to the very scarce surface water resource availability, the limited availability of sites for surface water storage, and increasing environmental concerns. Countries with low levels of surface water storage per capita have a high vulnerability

FIGURE 2.13

Surface Water Stored in Dams per Capita, Selected Countries and Economies

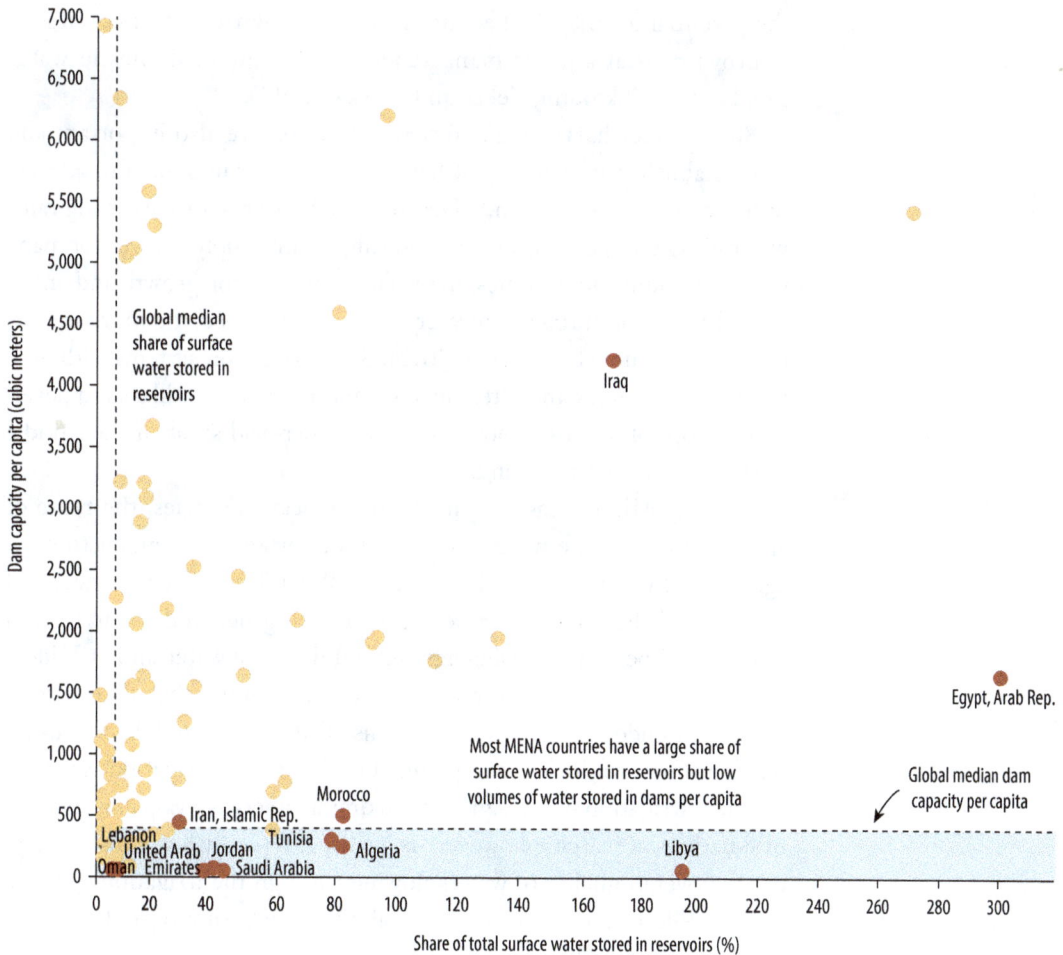

Source: World Bank, using data from FAO AQUASTAT (database).
Note: No data were available for Djibouti, Israel, Qatar, or West Bank and Gaza.

to supply disruptions and hydrological variability. To increase supply security, countries in the region are increasingly relying on aquifers to store water.

The intentional storage and treatment of water in aquifers (*managed aquifer recharge*) helps secure supplies and reduce evaporative losses. It also improves water quality because particulate and microbial materials present in the water are removed or diluted by interaction with native groundwater and aquifer materials (Gale 2005). In the Islamic Republic of Iran, managed aquifer recharge schemes based on floodwater spreading are able to store more than 80 percent of flood waters

(Esfandiari-Baiat and Rahbar 2005). Similarly, in Jordan, limestone aquifers are used to store water in Madaba (UNESCO 2014). In other Middle
East and North Africa countries, such as Oman, research has highlighted
the potential for managed aquifer recharge using treated wastewater to
improve coastal aquifer management and augment domestic water
supplies (Al-Maktoumi, Zekri, and El Rawy 2016).

Storm water harvesting and spate irrigation are also important and
well-established measures that have been used for millennia to address
water scarcity in the region.[12] Decentralized systems for harvesting rainwater using tanks and cisterns provide important supply sources for many
urban and rural communities. In the face of population growth and ongoing urbanization, urban rainwater harvesting will become more important in the future (Lange et al. 2012). Spate irrigation systems, although
technically complex and often uneconomic at scale, are still a valid development option for rural populations in hyper-arid areas of the Middle
East and North Africa (Van Steenbergen 2010).

In many Middle Eastern and North African countries, the reuse of
agricultural drainage water provides an important supplement to meet
agricultural water demand. Egypt reuses about 3 billion cubic meters of
agricultural drainage water per year, reducing demand for irrigation
water by 20 percent. Reusing agricultural drainage water allows Middle
Eastern and North African countries to use more water than their natural
freshwater endowment. Water that runs off from irrigated fields is cana-
lized in drainage ditches and pumped back into the irrigation canals to
augment irrigation water. Agricultural drainage acts as a valuable addition
in situations of scarcity; however, its quality is typically low, thus decreasing the overall quality of waters flowing through the irrigation systems.
On the Nile Delta, higher levels of salinity have been reported in drainage water (Barnes 2014).

More recently, nonconventional water supply resources, such as desalination and water recycling, have been deployed at scale to augment supply and thus meet demand from multiple sectors. Desalination and water
recycling offer the potential for highly reliable water supplies independent of the effects of climate change. These technologies are appealing
because they provide a "drought-proof" supply source, essentially allowing countries to break free from natural physical water scarcity. Figure 2.14
shows the percentage of water use supplied by nonconventional water
supply sources for each country and economy in the Middle East and
North Africa. This percentage is compared to GDP per capita to show
how investment in nonconventional water supply resources has taken
place mostly in the wealthy and oil-rich countries in the Gulf, where
revenues from oil exports were reinvested in enhancing water supply.

FIGURE 2.14

Nonconventional Water Supply and GDP per Capita, by Country and Economy

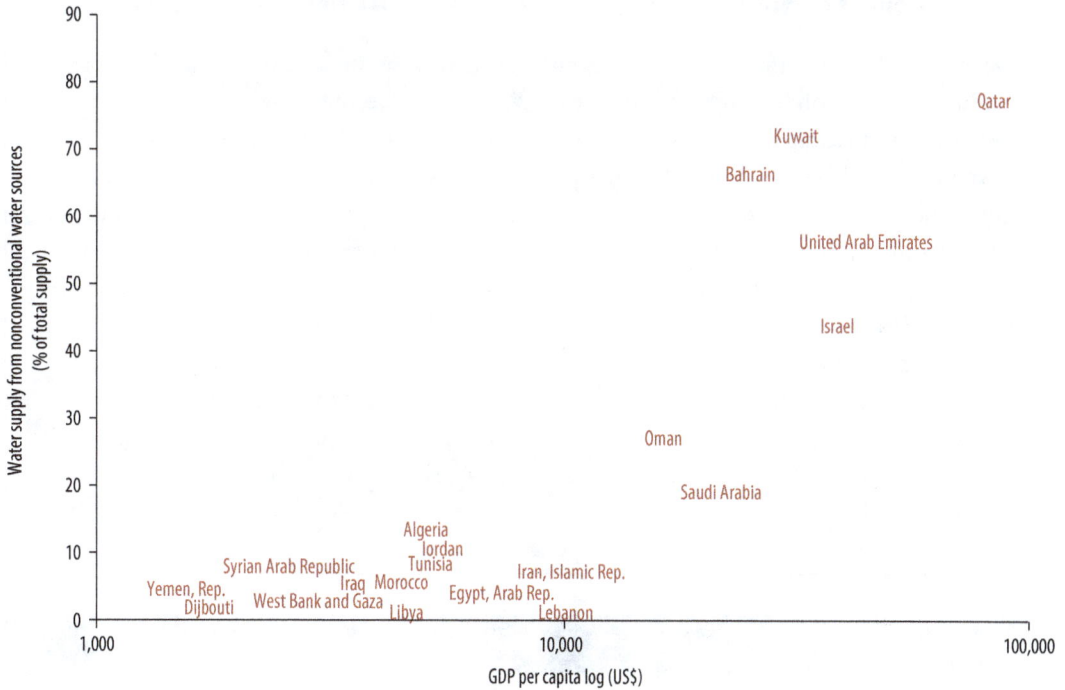

Sources: World Bank, using data from FAO AQUASTAT (database).
Note: Data on water supply from nonconventional water sources include desalination and treated wastewater reuse. Country-level data from FAO AQUASTAT come from different years and therefore should be interpreted with caution. GDP per capita is expressed in current U.S. dollars and was obtained from World Bank national accounts data.

Production costs of desalinated water have been falling as new technologies are being adopted (box 2.2) (Ghaffour, Missimer, and Amy 2013). Recent advances in membrane technology are making desalination an increasingly viable alternative to traditional freshwater resources (box 2.3). However, in addition to the costs of desalination technologies, costs per cubic meter of water delivered depend on a range of factors, such as salinity levels, energy prices, and water subsidies. Approximately half the costs of desalination consist of energy costs, which, given the volatility of the energy market, adds considerable challenges to the future of desalination relying on nonrenewable fossil fuels in the Middle East and North Africa (World Bank 2012). Furthermore, desalination costs and feasibility depend on the quality of seawater at the intakes. Excessive brine discharge or a lack of wastewater treatment complicate desalination processes, increasing costs and forcing plants to shut down occasionally.

Making better use of green water can help reduce pressure on other water (blue water) being used in agricultural production. Most of the

BOX 2.2

The Economics of Nonconventional Water: Trends in Desalination Costs

Technological improvements, system integration, and competition have helped reduce the costs of desalination in the last 20 years. Current prices have reached $0.53/m³ for large-scale seawater reverse osmosis plants in certain locations. Prices have decreased significantly for two of the most commercial desalination processes (multistage flash distillation and seawater reverse osmosis, or SWRO).

Although desalination is more expensive than the conventional treatment of freshwater, recent decreases in the cost of desalination, using reverse osmosis, mean that desalination is now a viable alternative to traditional freshwater resources requiring treatment in some contexts. Comparing the cost trends for different raw waters treated by reverse osmosis, Ghaffour, Missimer, and Amy (2013) found that the cost of desalination and reuse is approaching the cost of traditional freshwater treatment. Unless renewable energy sources are used, these trends may reverse, depending on increases in conventional energy (fossil fuels) prices.

Source: Ghaffour, Missimer, and Amy 2013.

BOX 2.3

Will Advances in Membrane Technology Solve Water Scarcity?

Membrane- and nanomaterials-based water treatment technologies can play an important role in water purification and desalination. These technologies produce water of superior quality, are less sensitive to fluctuations in the quality of the water fed into the system, and have a much smaller energy and environmental footprint compared to conventional desalination and water purification technologies. In addition, membrane-based technologies are inherently more energy efficient than thermal approaches. For example, membrane-based reverse osmosis (RO) technology uses as little as one-fifth the energy required for seawater desalination by thermal desalination technologies.

Next-generation, highly selective desalination membranes will represent an important advance. Enhanced membrane selectivity will play a significant role in improving water quality and eliminating the need for additional separation stages—for example, lowering boric acid concentration in seawater desalination to acceptable levels for agriculture—thereby reducing energy usage and the cost of desalination.

Despite these major efforts, recent improvements in water purification and desalination membranes have been marginal because of inherent material limitations, low fouling resistance of membrane materials, and lack of molecular-level design, among other factors.

Source: Werber, Osuji, and Elimelech 2016.

water used for agricultural production in the region is green water. Incorporating aspects pertaining to the management of green water into agricultural practices could increase agricultural yields.

Despite having half the world's desalination capacity, some Middle Eastern and North African countries and economies have invested very little in research and development (R&D), with most plants employing foreign technology (UNDP 2013). This lack of investment in R&D can be ascribed to a variety of reasons, including a lack of private sector participation in desalination (World Bank 2005) and low energy prices, which do not provide an incentive to pilot new technologies (Bushnak 2010), especially desalination technologies based on renewable energy. Recent public-private partnerships have shown the opportunities for the private sector to contribute to the development of nonconventional water supplies and the uptake of technologies (see box 2.4).

Renewable energy desalination is a promising alternative to desalination based on fossil fuel energy sources. It can help reduce greenhouse gas emissions from desalination and can increase water security by decoupling water production from fossil fuels, including in situations, such as those affected by fragility and conflict, when fuel supply and access can be irregular.[13] The potential for renewable energy desalination technologies in the Middle East and North Africa has been recognized (AWC 2014; World Bank 2012) and shown to be a technically feasible solution (MENA NWC 2015).

Desalination offers a potential strategy to alleviate water scarcity, yet it is capital and energy intensive both to produce and to transport, making it an expensive solution for many countries in the region. Desalination needs to be concentrated along coasts. This adds considerable costs because some major demand centers are located away from the coast, requiring the water to be conveyed for long distances. This expensive requirement, coupled with the price per cubic meter, has made desalination uneconomic in many places at the scales required to meet agricultural irrigation water demand. Furthermore, maintenance and power supply needs can make it an extremely complicated option to implement, even in areas facing extreme scarcity where desalination has been determined to be necessary, like Gaza.

The environmental impacts of brine disposal on marine ecosystems and greenhouse gas emissions present additional challenges to the widespread implementation of this technology. When seawater is desalinated, it produces a brine waste product that is higher in salinity and hotter than seawater. This brine is generally released back into the sea. While some plants report that salinity levels and temperatures within a few hundred meters of their outfalls are equivalent to the surrounding waters, it is unclear what the environmental impact may be over time, in specific marine environments, and as desalination plants proliferate (box 2.5). These impacts will in

BOX 2.4

Leveraging the Private Sector's Help with Public-Private Partnerships to Develop Nonconventional Water Supplies and Wastewater Treatment Plants

Several types of public-private partnerships have been implemented in the Middle East and North Africa region. In the area of nonconventional water supplies, build-operate-transfer (BOT) and design-build-operate (DBO) projects have been piloted in the Middle East and North Africa to develop wastewater treatment and desalination facilities. BOT and DBO schemes allow countries to select the lowest combined capital and operational expenditures over the life of the project, instead of just the lowest capital and operational expenditures, as is typically done under traditional construction contracts. BOT and DBO projects usually require significant design and construction as well as long-term operations for new-build (greenfield) projects or projects involving significant refurbishment and extension (brownfield). Partnering with the private sector through BOT and DBO allows the public sector to deal better with complex technologies, including their operation and maintenance, as well as selecting

technological options, and reducing the risk of cost overrun and delays.

BOT contracts have been widely used in the region to develop water supplies, especially via desalination plants. In Algeria alone, 13 BOT contracts have been put in place for desalination. The Gulf countries have a long experience in BOTs for securing water supplies. In Jordan, BOTs have been used to improve water supply for the city of Amman via the Disi-Amman water conveyor project and are going to be used for the planned Aqaba desalination plant as part of the Red-Dead Sea Project.

The New Cairo Wastewater Treatment Plant is an example of how public-private partnerships using BOT modalities have been employed to develop wastewater treatment capacity in the region. In this case, the International Finance Corporation's role as transaction adviser was essential to provide comfort to potential investors and design a contract that included the necessary guarantees for the project to be bankable.

Source: Philippe Marin, World Bank.

part depend on the characteristics of the water bodies into which the brine is discharged and the concentration of desalination plants.

Recycled water is another potential nonconventional supply source that is generally more cost-effective and less energy intensive than desalination. However, its implementation remains in the early stages in the Middle East and North Africa. Not all wastewater undergoes treatment; and of the wastewater that is treated, the majority is discharged unused into the sea. The discharge of treated wastewater into the sea wastes a useful supply source, and with it, part of the expenses of wastewater treatment (figure 2.15). At present, a proportion of the treated wastewater is

BOX 2.5

The Impact of Brine Discharge on Marine Environments and Desalination Processes

Brine discharge from desalination plants can significantly degrade the water and salt mass balances of receiving water bodies. In the Arabian Gulf, brine discharge from desalination plants is estimated to have increased ambient seawater salinity by about 20 percent. This can have a long-term negative impact on the environment and on the desalination process itself.

Negative environmental impacts can occur where brine is discharged close to vulnerable aquatic ecosystems. Such ecosystems include shallow seas with little circulation and abundant marine biodiversity. Open-sea and high-energy marine environments tend to be less sensitive to changes in salt mass balances because the waters mix more quickly.

Brine discharge can also have detrimental effects on the desalination process itself. The salinity concentrations of Red Sea and Arabian Gulf waters have increased due to desalination. As a result, desalination plants produce less potable water for the same amount of energy input. This raises the cost of desalination.

Sources: Bashitialshaeer, Persson, and Aljaradin 2011; and Dawoud and Al Mulla 2012.

FIGURE 2.15

Percentage of Collected Wastewater That Is Untreated, Treated, and Reused in Irrigation

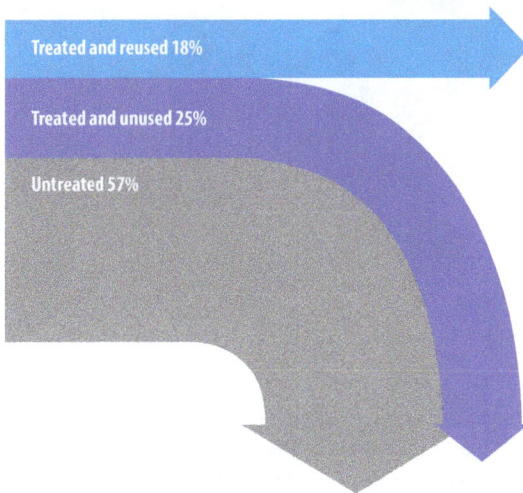

Treated and reused 18%

Treated and unused 25%

Untreated 57%

Source: World Bank, using data from FAO AQUASTAT (database).
Note: The figure was generated by summing country-level data on wastewater treated and reused from FAO AQUASTAT. Country-level data are based on estimates provided by the governments and are subject to variations in estimation methods and year of collection.

recycled in agricultural systems or is injected in coastal aquifers to prevent saltwater intrusion. Some of the untreated wastewater is often diluted and used by urban and peri-urban farmers to irrigate crops and orchards, posing health hazards if not managed or applied properly (Hussain et al. 2002). Statistics on wastewater production, treatment, and recycling should be interpreted with caution because they are self-reported by country government officials and experts. Data on annual volumes of wastewater are collected using a range of methods and are often subject to assumptions that limit the accuracy of some of these data (Mateo-Sagasta and Salian 2012).

There are significant opportunities for recycled water to meet increasing water demand in the Middle East and North Africa, and successful examples exist in the region. Figure 2.16 compares the percent of municipal wastewater that undergoes treatment and the percent of total water withdrawals met by recycled water. This may be a missed opportunity to respond to landscape or agricultural demand at a relatively low cost.

FIGURE 2.16

Comparing Reuse of Treated Wastewater and Percentage of Wastewater That Undergoes Treatment, by Country or Economy

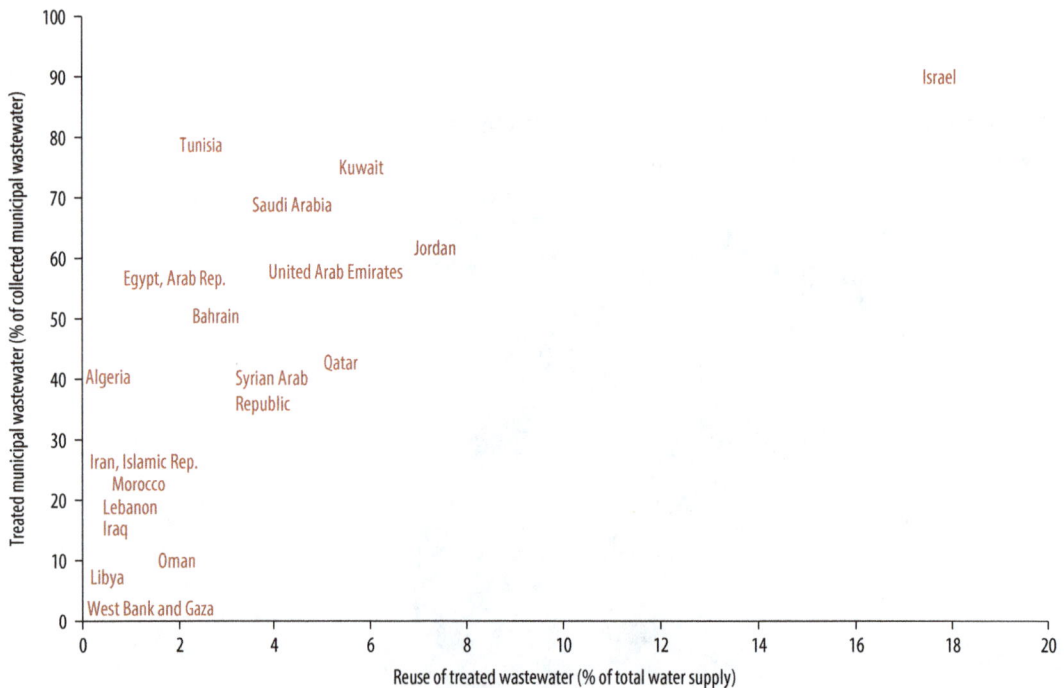

Source: World Bank, using data from FAO AQUASTAT (database).
Note: Data on wastewater produced, treated, and reused in the Middle East and North Africa sourced from FAO AQUASTAT. Country-level data are based on estimates provided by the governments and are subject to variations in estimation methods and year of collection. No data were available for Djibouti and the Republic of Yemen.

Studies from the region also underscore the economic feasibility of managed aquifer recharge using treated wastewater as a potential supply source (Zekri et al. 2014). Positive experiences in Jordan (As-Samra) and Tunisia (Souhil Wadi) show that wastewater can be safely recycled for use in irrigation and managed aquifer recharge.

Water recycling is often considered uneconomic because transportation from treatment plants to agricultural users is costly, but there are many alternative uses for recycled water. To date, these spatial concerns have discouraged water planning decisions to recycle water in megacities, which could provide a potential source of water for arid irrigation areas. However, within large cities, there may also be nonpotable uses for recycled water. In Southern California, for instance, treated wastewater is used for municipal landscapes and industrial uses. It is also injected into coastal barrier wells to guard against salt water intrusion.

In most places, the main barrier to water recycling is social acceptability. Additional concerns include the uncertain impacts on surface and groundwater quality and health risks, the lack of economic analysis to back up reuse proposals and highlight benefits (such as savings in fertilizer, and the value of sanitation improvements), and the high cost of wastewater treatment and conveyance if compared to the low price of irrigation water (World Bank and Arab Water Council 2011). Experts have also highlighted constraints related to the lack of legal frameworks and their weak enforcement, as well as wider institutional issues resulting from the large number of agencies involved in wastewater management (Bazza 2003; Jeuland 2015). In most countries, at least five ministries are involved in the management of wastewater resources. Thus, institutional frameworks for interagency collaboration are an essential element to ensure the long-term success of water recycling. Creating an additional layer of complexity, cultural and religious tradition in some communities can hinder water recycling initiatives.

Water recycling should be considered as a potential supply source in the Middle East and North Africa alongside other options and within an overarching policy designed to ensure water quality, address water scarcity, and improve the status of water bodies. Where wastewater is already treated to high standards or where investments in wastewater treatment are being planned, recycling should be considered as part of integrated water management strategies to meet known demand (Kfouri, Mantovani, and Jeuland 2009). Full cost recovery is unlikely unless recycling is considered as part of broader wastewater treatment and collection projects and unless the financial model for recycling includes payments from consumers or beneficiaries (Kfouri, Mantovani, and Jeuland 2009). In Israel, for example, the cost of wastewater treatment is charged to the municipal water users who consume fresh, nonrecycled water and produce the wastewater that is being treated (an application of the polluter pays principle). This financing structure acts as a cross-subsidy that provides an incentive to industry, farmers, and other users of nonpotable water to utilize the subsidized recycled water. Research on the benefits and risks of treated wastewater recycling in agriculture in Oman shows that farmers were able to halt trends in groundwater depletion, keeping it as a strategic supply source during droughts. At the same time, farmers were able to save money because they lowered fertilizer needs when they applied treated wastewater to their crops (MENA NWC 2015).

Strengthening Planning to Preserve Adequate Water Resources

The trend of groundwater and surface water overexploitation calls for enhanced water management strategies focused on achieving long-term sustainable water use. Sustainable water management does not aim to restore water resources to their status before abstraction, as this may be financially and technically unfeasible. *Sustainable water management* entails transparently and clearly defining an objective of resource utilization as part of a long-term, strategic, and adaptive water management plan that relies on nonrenewable resources while working toward securing renewable or nonconventional supplies and improving efficiency of use. As shown in figure 2.17, this objective may be gradual recovery, but it may be general stabilization or even orderly depletion.

FIGURE 2.17

Freshwater Resources Availability under Three Water Resource Management Strategies

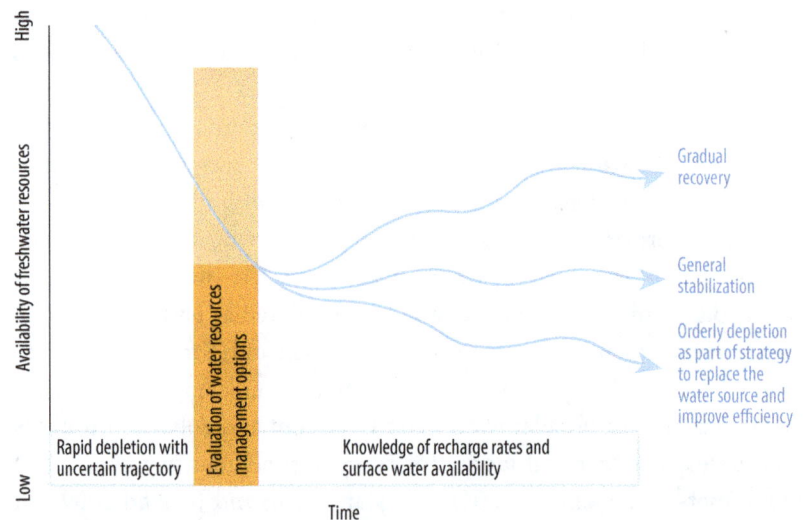

Source: Adapted from Marcel Kuper, CIRAD (Centre de coopération internationale en recherche agronomique pour le développement).

Surface and groundwater must be managed conjunctively. Groundwater depletion leads to reductions in surface water flows, and excessive abstraction of surface waters also impairs groundwater recharge (Famiglietti 2015). Planned *conjunctive use* of surface and groundwater consists of combining the use of both sources of water to minimize negative impacts and optimize the supply/demand balance. It can prevent resource depletion and enhance water productivity. To succeed, it requires basic institutional arrangements for groundwater management (Foster et al. 2010). Some of these arrangements are starting to emerge in some Middle Eastern and North African countries and economies.

Designing a long-term water use strategy is particularly relevant in the context of groundwater systems. Using groundwater sustainably requires understanding and monitoring recharge and abstraction so that a long-term groundwater management strategy can be adopted. This strategy may aim to recover the depth of the water table before abstraction; achieve a general stabilization of the water table depth; or, in extreme cases, lead to a controlled lowering of the water table depth in light of gradual improvements in water use efficiency and productivity, of the development of alternative supply options (such as artificial recharge using treated wastewater), or of emergency water resources needs. The Ash'Sharqiyah Sands in Oman are an example of using non-renewable groundwater as a strategic reserve to respond to drought conditions.[14]

Capitalizing on Regional Experiences: The Role of Research and Development

The constraints posed by water have forced many Middle East and North Africa countries to pursue innovative technologies and mechanisms for water resources management for millennia. Several institutional measures as well as technological advances have been developed to manage variations and imbalances in supply and demand. Box 2.6 presents an example of how R&D is helping the United Arab Emirates to balance water supplies and demand over the long term.

Recent advances in mobile and sensor technologies have supported irrigation decisions. Sensors provide real-time information on plants' water needs and responses to environmental factors (soil moisture, humidity) (MENA NWC 2015). Research centers and agricultural businesses in Jordan, Oman, and the United Arab Emirates, among others, have been testing and deploying electronic sensors to measure green water content and plant transpiration to assess water status and support farmers' decisions on water application and conservation decisions (ICBA 2015).

BOX 2.6

Diversifying Water Supplies in the United Arab Emirates

The United Arab Emirates has invested in a diversified portfolio of options to balance the supply and demand for water over the long term. Options that are being currently implemented or considered include:

1. Investing in research and development (R&D) for cloud seeding. The country has had a cloud seeding program since the early 1990s. The program is expected to play a significant role in increasing the amount of rain in the United Arab Emirates. In 2015, $5 million was invested in the R&D to make cloud seeding more efficient and effective.

2. Adopting new technologies for desalination. The United Arab Emirates has historically depended on thermal desalination technologies. With the increasing cost of fuel and the introduction of clean energy to the power generation mix, the need for nonthermal desalination technologies such as reverse osmosis and forward osmosis has increased. The United Arab Emirates is investing and employing these technologies to increase the efficiency of desalination and to reduce the energy required. Furthermore, investments are being made in the R&D of new technologies such as low-cost nanomaterials.

3. Using solar direct or indirect desalination.

4. Exploring air-to-water technologies. The United Arab Emirates is also exploring ways of extracting water from humid ambient air.

5. Injecting treated and desalinated water into aquifers as strategic reserves. Injection of desalinated or treated water in the aquifer is allowing the United Arab Emirates to ensure a strategic water supply reserve.

6. Exploring the economic feasibility of using spring water within the Gulf.

7. Exploring the feasibility of locating desalination plants outside the Gulf. This would reduce the environmental impacts of brine discharge on the waters of the Gulf.

8. Encouraging R&D to recycle water used during oil production. Most oil production uses significant quantities of water. The United Arab Emirates is exploring ways to recycle this water in different agricultural uses, as done in Oman, where water from oil fields is used to irrigate sugarcane.

9. Increase the usage of treated water. The United Arab Emirates aims to reuse treated wastewater in agriculture, industry, and energy production.

10. New technologies for agriculture that save water. Hydroponics (a method that grows plants without soil, using mineral solutions dissolved in water to deliver nutrients to plants) is being tested to reduce the amount of water used for irrigation and preserve groundwater resources.

11. Building storage. The United Arab Emirates is also investing in dams to protect areas in close proximity to surface water bodies and to harvest rainfall.

Source: Matar Hamed Al Neyadi, Undersecretary of the Ministry of Energy, United Arab Emirates.

Resource mapping and assessment initiatives are also improving water management in the region. The United Arab Emirates, in partnership with the International Center for Biosaline Agriculture, has developed soil maps based on detailed surveys. The maps are being used to better assess soil moisture conditions and the potential for agricultural water management improvements. Research teams from Oman, Morocco, and Qatar are using radar technologies to locate and map desert aquifers. In addition to mapping the depth of the water table, the ability of radar to monitor water freshness is being explored to understand potential seawater intrusion that can degrade water quality (MENA NWC 2015).

Advances in the collection and use of information to support evidence-based water resources planning are also occurring in the Middle East and North Africa. In 2016, Qatar published its first water statistics report, which presents a comprehensive overview of water resources and uses in Qatar. By looking at trends in water use, wastewater generation and treatment, as well as water quality, the report is a crucial element for monitoring water's contribution to Qatar's National Vision 2030 (MDPS 2016).

Many types of technological measures can enable successful supply and demand management, given the diversity of environmental, economic, and sociopolitical characteristics in the Middle East and North Africa. In view of these differences, it is essential to integrate these technological and management advances with appropriate institutional measures that address the underlying drivers of policy effectiveness. In areas where knowledge, skills, or technologies might be lacking in one country, they might exist in another country. This also emphasizes the potential for R&D to foster regional collaboration and information sharing.

Summary: Sustainability, Efficiency, and Innovation

Highly variable hydrology, increasing and inefficient water use, and the overexploitation of scarce resources mean that 61 percent of the Middle East and North Africa's population lives in areas with high or very high water stress, compared to 36 percent in the rest of the world. GDP exposure to water stress is also higher in the Middle East and North Africa, with about 71 percent of the region's economic activities being produced in areas of high or extremely high water stress, compared to a global average of 22 percent.

More water than is available on a renewable basis is being used in the Middle East and North Africa. In some countries, more than half of water use is unsustainable, as shown in figure 2.18. Unsustainable water use is

FIGURE 2.18

Sustainability of Water Withdrawals, by Source as a Percentage of Total Withdrawals, and by Country and Economy

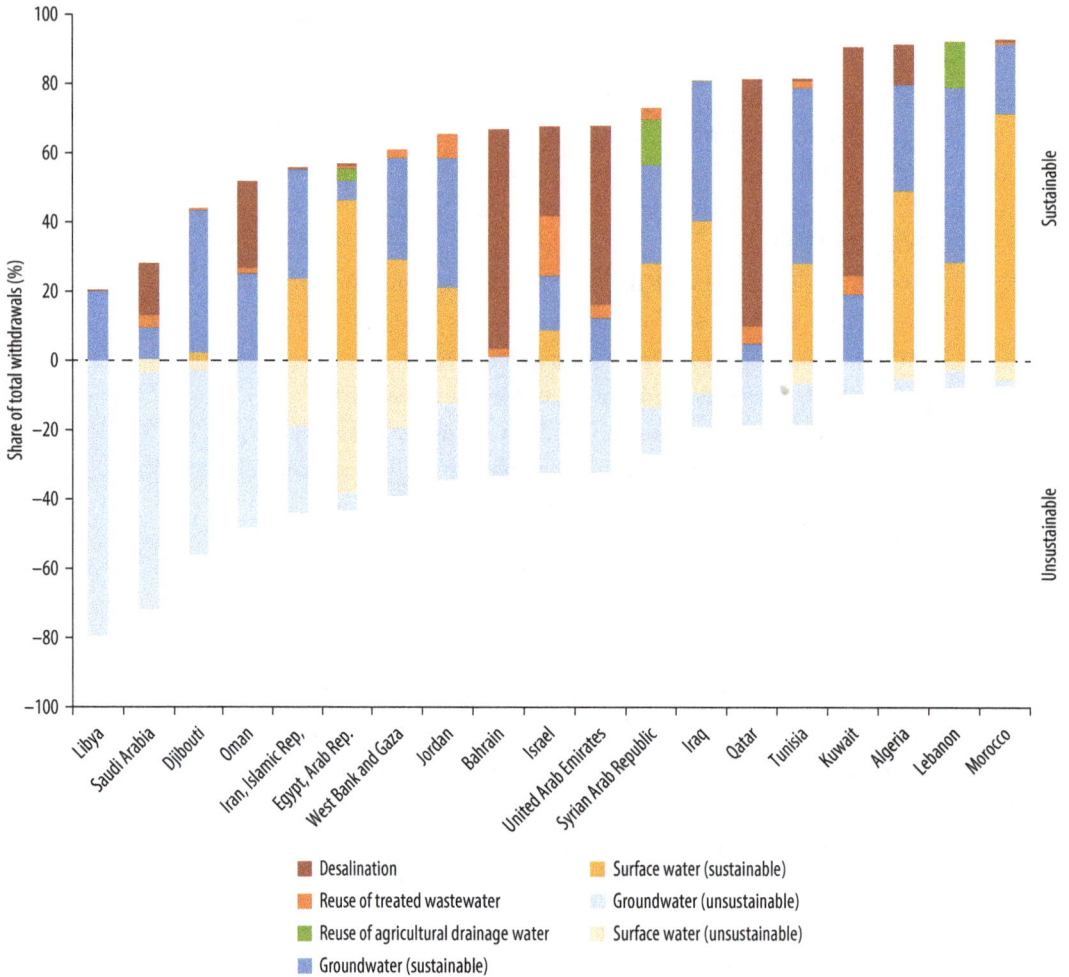

Sources: World Bank calculations. Data on desalination capacity come from Global Water Intelligence 2016. Data on all other categories are from the FAO AQUASTAT database.

Note: Negative values imply unsustainable water withdrawals. The percentage of unsustainable groundwater and surface water withdrawals was estimated for this study using the Blue Water Sustainability Index. No data were available for the Republic of Yemen on sustainability of water use. Caution should be used in comparing data on annual freshwater withdrawals, which are subject to variations in collection and estimation methods. For Iraq, Syria, and West Bank and Gaza, the breakdown between surface and groundwater withdrawals was not available, and withdrawals were split equally between the two categories. In absolute terms, Egypt has the largest volume of reuse of agricultural drainage water and Saudi Arabia the largest desalination capacity in the region.

projected to increase in the future, calling for a combination of interventions including efficiency improvements, smart allocation, and nonconventional water supply sources.

Understanding and reducing water use, especially in the agricultural sector, is essential to address water scarcity and resource overexploitation. Agriculture accounts for nearly 80 percent of water use in the Middle East and North Africa, and this water is often not used efficiently. Modest gains in agricultural water productivity, improved water use accounting at the basin scale, and policies promoting crops that use low amounts of water or reductions in irrigated areas could potentially save large volumes of water. Reductions in agricultural water use could be used to reduce unsustainable water consumption and meet the increasing demand from municipal and industrial water users. However, reforms can have unintended consequences. For example, more efficient irrigation technology can lead farmers to select more water-intensive crops, and changes in crops can affect livelihoods along the supply chain. Winners and losers, and distributional impacts, should be analyzed before implementing reforms.

The region has some of the most water-productive countries in the world, as well as some of the least productive. This highlights the potential for regional learning and exchange, though this must be done with sensitivity to the range of circumstances (for example, with regard to conflict and fragility), as well as wealth and public resources.

To reduce unsustainable water withdrawals, desalination and water recycling offer the potential to increase water supplies independent of climatic conditions. More than 50 percent of the world's desalination capacity is in the Middle East and North Africa, and this proportion is projected to increase. However, as the proportion of water demand met by desalination increases, so too do the complexities of this supply source related to salinity levels at plant intakes and energy price volatility. There are significant opportunities for recycled water to meet increasing water demand in the region, but there are also challenges related to factors such as financing, low demand for recycled water, and the lack of economic analysis of water recycling and treatment options.

The lack of strategic water resources management depletes national assets and limits progress toward water security. Managing water resources strategically entails integrating a diverse set of options to secure supplies with options that target water use. To reduce unsustainable water use, surface and groundwater must be managed conjunctively. As shown in figure 2.18, some countries in the region have made progress in diversifying supply sources in the face of hydrological variability, while some others still rely mostly on single sources.

Diversified solutions lead to greater resilience to systemic shocks—be they climatic or economic. This starts with "closing the water resources loop" rather than thinking of water usage as "once through the system" and with employing different water supply sources (see figure 2.18). Examples of diversification include optimizing local surface water as well as groundwater storage; developing nonconventional water resources, such as desalination, recycling, and recharge; reducing leakage; and promoting conservation.

Water governance issues—in particular, the failure to create incentives that signal extreme water scarcity and promote water conservation—are the common denominator of water resources management in the Middle East and North Africa. Excessive consumption and resource depletion are the predictable consequences of undervalued water, weak governance arrangements, and inadequate enforcement. The lack of legal frameworks and poor institutional coordination also prevent the region from exploiting recent advances in wastewater treatment and recycling technologies.

Delivering Water Services

Water services play a fundamental role in maintaining a stable social contract and sustaining human health and economic activities. *Water services* encompass safe water and sanitation; reliable supply delivery to agricultural, industrial, and domestic users; and financially sustainable utilities capable of keeping the cost of service low and of ensuring basic services for all inhabitants. Living conditions, business and industrial activities, and irrigation all benefit from reliable, affordable, and sustainable water services. Water services delivery can also benefit communities of refugees and internally displaced persons when designed to alleviate human suffering and promote return to places of origin.

Access to water supply and sanitation services in the Middle Eastern and North African countries and economies has improved significantly, and most countries have met their Millennium Development Goals (MDG) water and sanitation targets. Data collected as part of the MDGs have yielded country-wide information on access to improved sources of water supply and sanitation. Within a country, however, the situation on the ground may vary from location to location and household to household—depending, for example, on damage to infrastructure because of recent conflicts, large differences between urban and rural contexts, or the strained socioeconomic conditions of marginalized communities. Therefore, to understand local needs and requirements for investment, more disaggregated analysis of access to water supply and sanitation services characteristics is required.

Access is essential, but it is only one aspect of water services. To fully assess the status of water services in the Middle East and North Africa and to build a more comprehensive picture, other aspects must also be considered (Zawahri, Sowers, and Weinthal 2011). These aspects include the quality of the water delivered—recognizing that different sectors may require different levels of water quality, the reliability of the water supply, and the financial sustainability of water services. All these factors were not included in the MDG targets, meaning that statistics on access do not necessarily provide information on the quality and type of water services that different members of society receive.

Sustainable Development Goal 6 (SDG 6) provides an opportunity to move beyond access metrics to provide more representative measures of water services. For instance, SDG 6.2 places great emphasis on ensuring quality of access to sanitation and hygiene for vulnerable groups, especially women and girls. SDG 6 also promotes improved principles of water management, encouraging integrated water resources management (see box 1.1). The broader set of targets, and IAEG (Inter-Agency and Expert Group) SDG indicators,[15] under SDG 6 means that future assessments of water services will help build a more complete picture of water security in the Middle East and North Africa. At present, data to quantify country-wide elements of water services and distributional effects are incomplete.

This report builds on prior data collection efforts to sketch out, as comprehensively as possible, a picture of water services at the national scale. Although there is considerable subnational variation in the provision of water services in most Middle Eastern and North African countries (Brixi, Lust, and Woolcock 2015), national statistics allow for an initial assessment to be carried out. Large data gaps remain, highlighting the potential for improved data gathering to inform future policies and benchmarking of water services in the region. These multiple dimensions of water services are discussed next.

Progress in Access to Water Supply and Sanitation

The Middle East and North Africa region has made good progress toward meeting targets for access to water supply and sanitation. Across the region, access to improved water supply sources has increased since 1990, and so has access to improved sanitation. However, UNICEF and World Health Organization (WHO) data suggest that progress on water and sanitation has barely kept up with population growth, especially in urban areas (UNICEF and WHO 2015a, 17). Population growth and urbanization will place unplanned burdens on water supply and sanitation facilities, potentially outpacing recent gains in coverage. The growth of megacities may contribute to localized centers of extremely high water demand where water scarcity will concentrate, leading to competition with water currently used in agriculture (Tropp and Jägerskog 2006).

Despite significant progress, substantial improvements are still needed (UNICEF and WHO 2015b). In some countries and economies, access rates are still low. In the Republic of Yemen, Libya, and West Bank and Gaza, less than 80 percent of the population has access to safe drinking water (figure 2.19). In Djibouti, the Republic of Yemen, Morocco, Libya, and Iraq, 50 percent to 30 percent of the population still lacks access to adequate sanitation (figure 2.20). While some countries such as Morocco have made some progress, they remain several steps away from achieving universal access. Algeria is the only country in the Middle East and North Africa that has made no progress toward universal access, with the percentage of population with improved water sources actually decreasing since the World Health Organization and UNICEF's Joint Monitoring Programme was launched (see box 2.7) (UNICEF and WHO 2015b). Extending coverage to rural areas has proven to be particularly challenging (see figures 2.19 and 2.20), indicating that rural populations are particularly disadvantaged and populations in these areas face greatest

FIGURE 2.19

Percentage of Population with Access to Safe Drinking Water, by Country and Economy

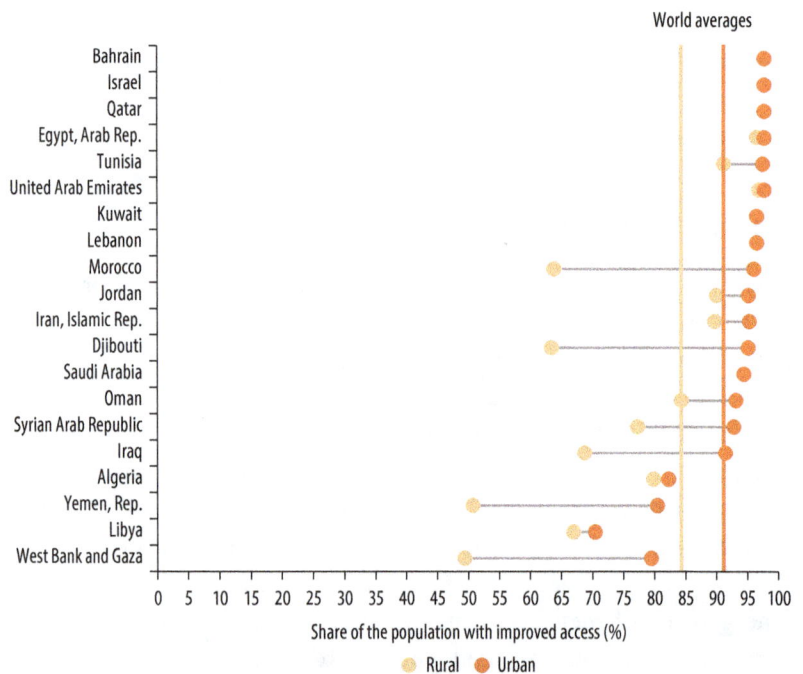

Sources: ACWUA 2015; and WHO/UNICEF Joint Monitoring Programme for Water Supply and Sanitation.
Note: An improved drinking-water source is defined as one that, by nature of its construction or through active intervention, is protected from outside contamination, in particular from contamination with fecal matter. Data for Libya, Syria, and the Republic of Yemen are from 2000.

FIGURE 2.20

Percentage of Population with Access to Improved Sanitation, by Country and Economy

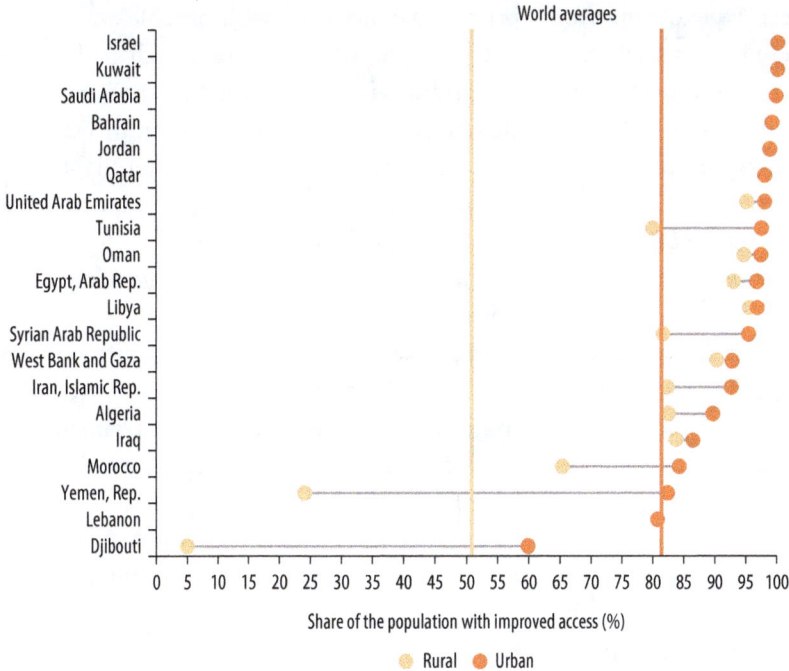

Sources: ACWUA 2015; Water Supply and Sanitation Services in the Arab Region (MDG+ initiative); WHO/UNICEF Joint Monitoring Programme for Water Supply and Sanitation.
Note: For MDG monitoring, an improved sanitation facility is defined as one that hygienically separates human excreta from human contact. Data for Libya, Syria, and the Republic of Yemen are from 2000.

BOX 2.7

What Does It Mean to Have Access to Water?

All people have some access to water; they cannot live without it. The global statistics on access to water actually refer to access to improved water services. The WHO/UNICEF (World Health Organization / United Nation Children's Fund) Joint Monitoring Programme (JMP) publishes coverage statistics for two definitions of improved water services. The first is the simplest and most straightforward: "a piped water connection on the premises." This definition includes both yard taps (outdoor plumbing only) and piped water delivered inside the house (indoor plumbing). The second is "an improved water source that by the nature of its construction, adequately protects the source from outside contamination, in particular with fecal matter." The JMP classifies all of the following as improved sources: piped into dwelling, plot or yard; public tap/standpipe; tube well/borehole; protected dug well;

(continued on next page)

BOX 2.7 *Continued*

protected spring; and rainwater collection. "Piped into the dwelling, plot, or yard" (the first item) is one of the six types of improved sources, so the first definition is a subset of the second definition: that is, reported coverage using the second definition will always be higher than reported coverage using the first definition.

Both indicators of coverage can be misleading. First, a piped water connection on the premises is counted as an improved source in both JMP definitions, but there is no assurance that the quality of water delivered to the household is potable. A piped connection that delivered unreliable, poor-quality water is still counted as an "improved source." Similarly, for the second definition, water from the other types of improved sources may be contaminated, and the household will still be counted as having an improved source.

Second, water sources considered by the JMP to be "unimproved" may, in fact, provide a household with potable water. For example, water vendors (both tanker trucks and distributing vendors) and bottled water are counted as "unimproved sources," even though they may reliably supply a household with sufficient quantities of safe (high-quality) water.

Third, both indicators of coverage implicitly assume that a household uses only one source for its drinking water. This is often not true. Households may collect drinking water from both improved and unimproved sources, even if their "improved" water source is a piped water connection on the premises.

Despite these limitations, the JMP data on improved water coverage are the best available, and they are used here to examine water supply and sanitation access statistics in the Middle East and North Africa.

Source: Dale Whittington, University of North Carolina at Chapel Hill.

---

risks to health and well-being from a lack of access to safe drinking water and sanitation facilities.

Conflicts challenge progress toward universal access. Water supply and sanitation facilities are often targeted during conflicts (ICRC 2015). Damaged and destroyed facilities place urban and rural populations at risk of waterborne diseases and significantly hamper recovery, economic opportunity, and livelihoods. In 2015, Iraq's outdated and damaged water and sewage systems were blamed for a cholera outbreak that spread to 17 Iraqi governorates (WHO 2015). The World Health Organization expects the rate of waterborne infections in Iraq to increase as a result of the conflict situation.[16] In the Republic of Yemen, Oxfam warned that conflict and fuel shortages caused 3 million people to lose access to drinking water, increasing the total number of Yemenis without access to at least 16 million.[17] Between 2011 and 2013, access to water supply services in Syria declined by 70 percent as a result of conflict (UN-Water 2015).

And in Gaza, only 10 percent of the population has access to potable water because of groundwater depletion and contamination, which is compounded by movement and access restrictions that hinder infrastructure development.

Aggregate statistics on improved supply and sanitation often hide local realities and geographic disparities, where unsafe drinking water and a lack of sanitation in certain locations can still cause broad public health risks. For instance, many improved sanitation facilities, such as sewage treatment plants and septic tanks, often malfunction, resulting in overflows and contamination of surface and groundwater bodies (Al-Ansari 2013). Assessments of water services need to go beyond statistics of access to the level of improved water and sanitation facilities. In particular, these statistics overlook aspects related to the human and economic impacts of inadequate access and the reliability and quality of the service to different users, as well as its affordability. These dimensions of water services are discussed next.

Human and Economic Impacts of Inadequate Water Supply and Sanitation

Inadequate water supply and sanitation cause diseases and deaths, impair child development, and reduce human welfare. Data from the World Health Organization show that mortality due to unsafe water, sanitation, and a lack of hygiene in the Middle East and North Africa is lower than in Sub-Saharan Africa and South Asia. However, as shown in figure 2.21, some countries in the Middle East and North Africa still have high mortality rates compared to regional and global averages, suggesting that many obstacles remain to reducing mortality due to inadequate water services.

Lack of access to water services still poses a significant public health risk in some countries in the Middle East and North Africa, where diarrheal diseases are responsible for 5–15 percent of deaths among children under the age of 5. Diarrheal diseases are still a leading killer of young children in some parts of the Middle East and North Africa, especially in conflict-affected Syria, as shown in figure 2.22. Improving water services could also prevent child deaths due to diarrheal diseases in Morocco, Algeria, Egypt, the Republic of Yemen, and Iraq. In turn, these high rates of disease burden health systems; and household caretakers, who are often female, find themselves constrained from participating productively in the economy.

Inadequate water supply and sanitation also have a severe economic impact, costing the region about $21 billion a year. Country-level data

FIGURE 2.21

Mortality Rate Attributed to Exposure to Inadequate Water Supply and Sanitation and Lack of Hygiene, by Country and Economy, 2012

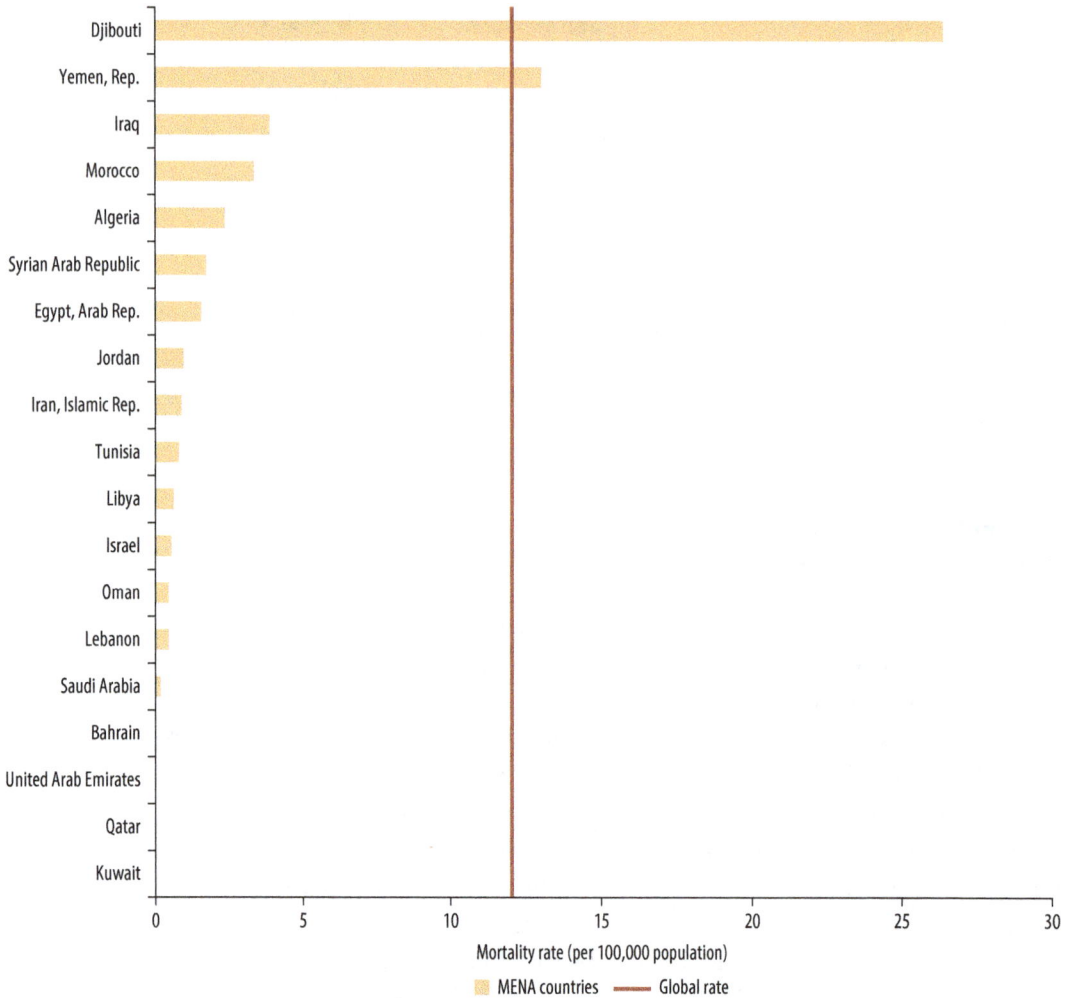

Mortality rate (per 100,000 population)

MENA countries ▬▬▬ Global rate

Source: World Health Organization, 2012 Global Health Observatory Data (http://www.who.int/gho/phe/water_sanitation/burden/en/).
Note: No data are available for West Bank and Gaza.

on the economic losses are shown in figure 2.23. These estimates include the value of time savings that would result if improved water and sanitation facilities were closer to home. The estimated economic costs include health care costs, lost productive time due to being sick, and premature mortality.[18] The economic impact is greatest in Libya, the Republic of Yemen, Iraq, and West Bank and Gaza. These statistics cannot be disaggregated by gender, so they tell only part of the story. At the household level, women bear most of the burden of inadequate

FIGURE 2.22

Percentage of Deaths among Children under Age 5 Attributable to Diarrhea, by Country, 2015

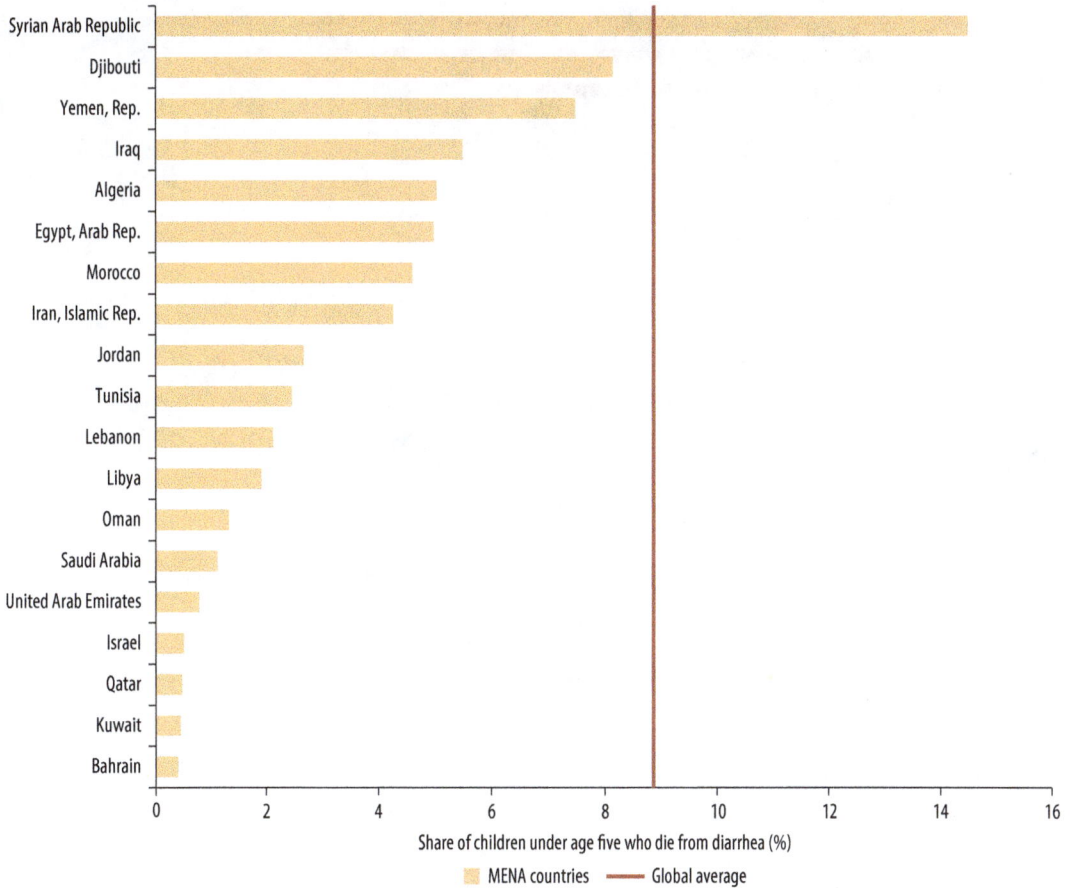

Source: WHO and Maternal and Child Epidemiology Estimation Group (http://data.unicef.org/topic/child-health/diarrhoeal-disease/).
Note: No data available for West Bank and Gaza.

water supply and sanitation. Box 2.8 discusses the strains on water, sanitation, and hygiene that large influxes of refugees have caused in some parts of the region.

Irrigation Water Service Delivery

Irrigation water service delivery is also an important dimension of water security. Being able to supply the right amount of water to a crop at the right time, when it needs it most, increases yield per unit of water delivered (that is, increases productivity). The timing, amount, and reliability of water delivery to fields all influence yield (Molden et al. 2007).

FIGURE 2.23

Economic Losses from Inadequate Water Supply and Sanitation, by Country and Economy, 2010

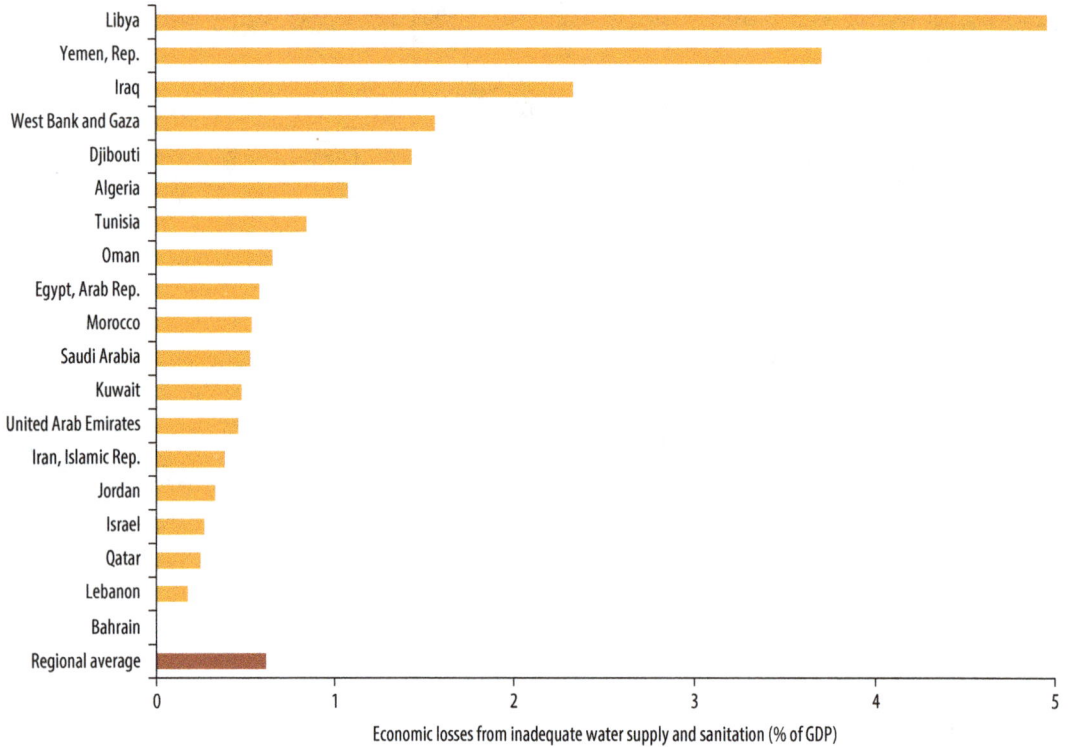

Economic losses from inadequate water supply and sanitation (% of GDP)

Sources: Hutton 2013; and Sadoff et al. 2015.
Note: No data are available for the Syrian Arab Republic.

Greater flexibility in the timing of delivery and reliability of irrigation water delivery give farmers greater freedom in terms of the timing of planting and harvest and can play an important role in influencing investment decisions.

Improving water service delivery to irrigation systems increases agricultural production by 1–8 percent, depending on the type of crop and location.[19] If all the available water allocated to agriculture in the Middle East and North Africa could be stored and delivered efficiently to irrigated agriculture, agricultural production would increase and variability in production of some commodities would decrease. Maize (corn) production would increase by 8.4 percent at the regional level, mostly driven by large gains of the top regional producers, the Islamic Republic of Iran and Egypt. Rice production would increase by about 5 percent. Wheat production would

BOX 2.8

The Water, Sanitation, and Hygiene Situation in Refugee Camps and Host Communities

Armed conflict in the Syrian Arab Republic, Iraq, the Republic of Yemen, and Libya has had devastating consequences, forcefully displacing millions of people. The influx of refugees and internally displaced persons can exacerbate demographic pressures on limited water resources, and if not well managed, can lead to social tensions and increased fragility within refugee communities and between refugees and host communities. Innovative technologies are being implemented to address water challenges in refugee settlement areas, including camps, yet many issues remain. In particular, the risks of sexual and gender-based violence remain, especially among women and girls accessing sanitation and cooking facilities and water points, which may lack adequate lighting. Gender segregation of these facilities is a key consideration in the effort to prevent sexual and gender-based violence in refugee settlements.

The Za'atari refugee camp in northern Jordan, which now hosts more than 80,000 people, is one of the largest refugee camps in the world. Since the camp opened, wastewater has been transported by trucks to a treatment plant about 45 kilometers away from the camp, costing UNICEF approximately $3.6 million per year. The economic burden led to the introduction of new Mobile Wastewater Treatment Units, which are expected to reduce costs to $700,000 per year. The new Wastewater Treatment Units comprise a trickling filter and a membrane bioreactor. Plans are also under way to use the treated water for the irrigation of alfalfa and other crops.

Whether they live inside or outside of camps, refugees place an unplanned burden on water resources and services in host communities. In Lebanon, where most Syrian refugees reside in existing communities, the Ministry of Environment estimates that domestic water demand increased by 43–70 million cubic meters per year. This corresponds to an increase in national water demand of 8–12 percent. The increase in water demand is exacerbating current stresses on water resources, especially groundwater. On a similar scale, the influx of refugees has led to an 8–14 percent increase in wastewater volumes generated in Lebanon.

Sources: MOE/EU/UNDP 2014; UNFPA and UNHCR 2015; and UNICEF 2015.

---

increase by about 1.5 percent at the regional level, and by as much as 4 percent by the top regional wheat producer, Egypt. By reducing variability in agricultural production, improved irrigation service delivery would also reduce food prices, benefiting consumers around the world.

Improving the way in which water is stored and delivered to irrigation water users could lead to an estimated $10 billion welfare gain, amounting to about 0.5 percent of regional GDP, according to the International Food Policy Research Institute's IMPACT model (Rosegrant et al. 2008). These gains come from standard measures of producers' surplus (improved water services and availability) and consumers' surplus (reduced food prices). In addition, half the gains would be in the form of spillover effects to the nonagricultural sector. These welfare gains are shown in figure 2.24. Countries and economies that could reap the greatest relative benefits by improving irrigation water service delivery are West Bank and Gaza, the Islamic Republic of Iran,

FIGURE 2.24

Welfare Change as a Result of Improved Irrigation Water Service Delivery, Selected Countries and Economies

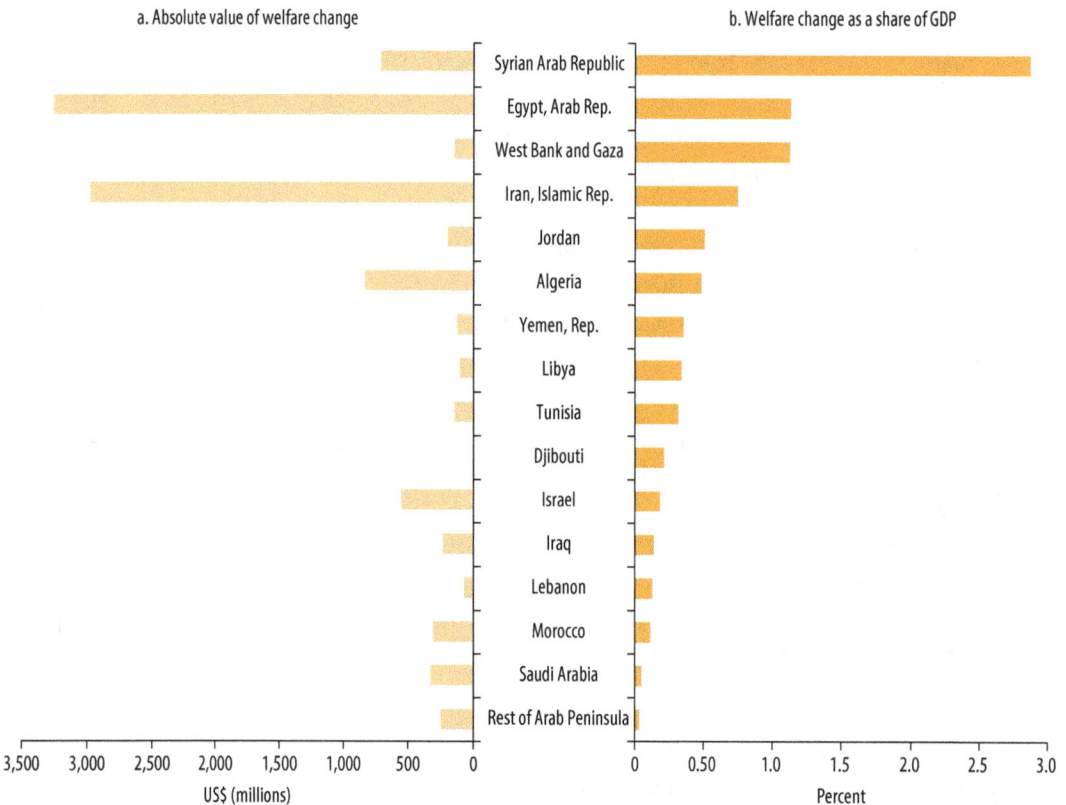

a. Absolute value of welfare change

b. Welfare change as a share of GDP

US$ (millions)

Percent

Source: International Food Policy Research Institute.

Note: Absolute value of welfare change is shown on the left, and welfare change as a share of GDP (from 2015) on the right. Values were generated with IFPRI's IMPACT model, assuming improvements in water storage and delivery capacity that maximize water available for agriculture. Welfare gains are calculated from measures of consumer and producer surplus (reduced food prices for consumers and increased water availability for producers) and spillover effects from agriculture to the rest of the economy. Irrigation areas and irrigation methods remain unchanged in the simulation. Rest of Arab Peninsula includes Bahrain, Kuwait, Oman, Qatar, and United Arab Emirates.

Egypt, and Syria. In absolute terms, the biggest welfare benefits would be reaped in Egypt and the Islamic Republic of Iran, where irrigated agriculture is a fundamental component of the economy. In this scenario, irrigation area and irrigation methods are fixed, meaning that the production and welfare gains are a function only of improvements in irrigation water service delivery (for instance, water storage and delivery capacity) that maximize use of all available water. The design of those investments could be further improved by more extensive analysis of the distribution of benefits of any improvement within these countries.

Municipal Service Levels, Reliability, and Quality

Progress in access to supply and sanitation needs to be paired with steps to improve and sustain the quality of water services. A range of factors determine the quality of water services, including continuity of supply, drinking water quality, and level of treatment of wastewater. These characteristics are difficult to quantify because they depend on the service provider (the utility or private suppliers), the characteristics of the water resources, and the water quality standards of the country. This report attempts to present water services data on drinking water quality and continuity of supply in some Middle Eastern and North African countries. The analysis is based on recent data reported by single countries and economies to the Arab Countries Water Utilities Association (ACWUA 2015).

The level of disinfection of the supply source is used as an indicator of good drinking water quality. Figure 2.25 presents the percent of population whose supply was disinfected at the source, as reported to ACWUA by selected Middle Eastern and North African countries. Patterns of the characteristics of drinking water quality differ by country. However, in countries and economies affected by conflict and energy shortages, such as Iraq and West Bank and Gaza, the actual quality of the supply source may be considerably lower than the quality reported by the countries in figure 2.25 (box 2.9). For example, water treatment plants may be in place, but they may not be providing the services reported in the data set, perhaps due to war damage or a lack of energy and chemical supplies. Consequently, the reality on the ground may differ from statistics reported by ACWUA. Furthermore, country-level data are limited because they do not reveal which locations inside a country are affected by poor-quality and low-reliability water services.

Good service levels require rural and urban water supplies that function continuously over the long term and that are resilient to variations in the availability of water resources. To provide indication of

FIGURE 2.25

Reported Percentage of Urban Population Whose Water Supply Was Disinfected at the Source, Selected Countries and Economies, 2015

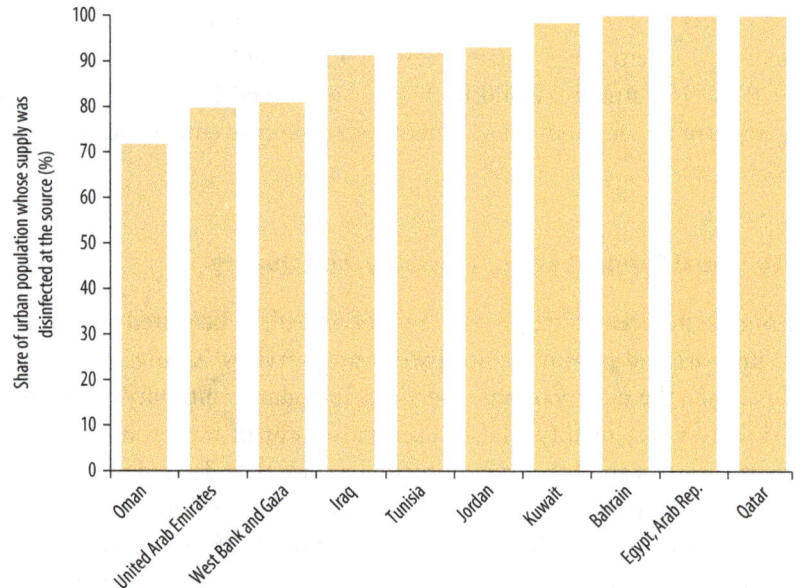

Source: ACWUA 2015.

service levels and reliability of water supply, countries report the percent of population with continuous daily urban water supply. In the GCC countries, all municipal water users have continuous daily supplies. Over 90 percent of the population in Tunisia and Egypt also has continuous daily supplies. In other countries and economies, such as Jordan and West Bank and Gaza, water users receive water only during a particular time of the day, and often with some irregularity in scheduled water deliveries, thus requiring storage facilities at the household level (ACWUA 2015).

The Value of Water, Subsidies, and Pricing

The Middle East and North Africa is the most water scarce region in the world, yet it also has the lowest water service fees and the highest proportion of GDP spent on public water subsidies. Water service fees in the Middle East and North Africa do not reflect the scarcity value of water or the cost of delivery, especially in the agricultural sector (AWC 2011). The region has also some of the lowest water service fees for irrigation water in the world (Berglöf and Devarajan 2015).

BOX 2.9

Gaza's Alarming Water Situation

Only 10 percent of Gaza's population has access to improved drinking water sources, compared to 90 percent in the West Bank and 85 percent in the Middle East and North Africa in general. Decades of conflict have resulted in extensive damage to water and wastewater systems and other infrastructure. The overall infrastructure sector incurred an estimated $900 million in damages between September 2000 and July 2003. About 25 percent of the total financial cost of the damage, or about $140 million, occurred in the water and wastewater sector. On the ground, this translated into broken water supply lines, destroyed water pumps and water wells, and damage to wastewater networks, wastewater pumps, treatment facilities, and other installations.

As the crisis deepened, the Palestinian Water Authority (PWA) and municipalities were unable to collect fees from an increasingly impoverished citizenry, reducing their ability to invest in the operation and maintenance of the system. Gaza's very high population density (it is the third most densely populated area in the world) and high rates of population growth challenge this fragile situation even more. Infiltration of raw wastewater into aquifers from densely populated areas and high water demand mean that Gaza faces both water quantity and quality challenges. At present, most people in Gaza must rely on expensive water from private vendors.

The Palestinian Water Authority's 2017–22 water strategy aims to develop nonconventional supply sources and implement water efficiency measures to reduce water losses in the system due to damaged infrastructure. The World Bank is supporting these activities with infrastructure projects aimed at augmenting water supplies with a desalination plant and improving water quality with wastewater treatment and reuse, alongside projects aimed at strengthening capacity in the Palestinian water sector.

Source: Adnan Ghoshesh, World Bank.

Water service fees in some cities in the Middle East and North Africa are seven to eight times lower than water service fees in other cities of the region and the world. Water bills in Riyadh, Cairo, Tehran, Algiers, and Tunis are several times lower than in Mexico City or Dar es Salaam, as shown in figure 2.26. These are also significantly lower than water bills in other large cities in the Middle East and North Africa, such as Rabat and Casablanca. In West Bank, Israel, United Arab Emirates, Oman, and Qatar, water service fees are closer to fees in other cities of the world.

Failure to properly price water services also undermines the financial sustainability of the water sector and contributes to unsustainable use.

FIGURE 2.26

Combined Water and Wastewater Service Fee per Cubic Meter, Selected Cities in the Middle East and North Africa and Other Regions, 2016

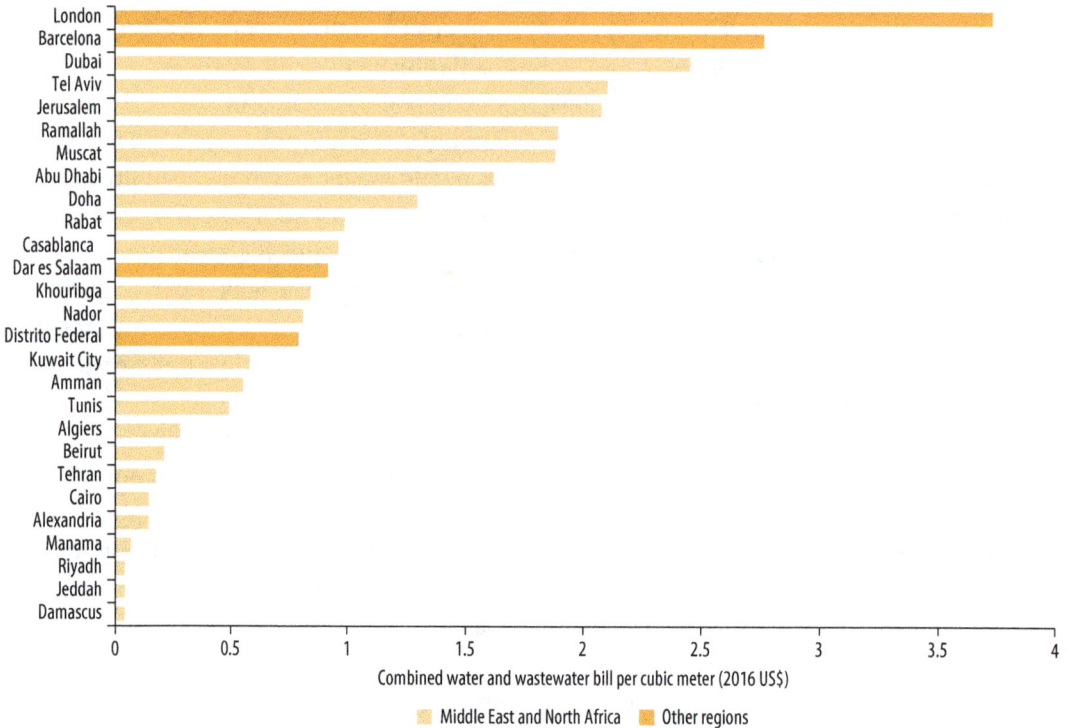

Combined water and wastewater bill per cubic meter (2016 US$)

■ Middle East and North Africa   ■ Other regions

Source: Global Water Intelligence, Global Water Tariff Survey 2016.
Note: Exchange rates as of July 1, 2016. Average household water use varies by household and by water utility, and here is assumed to be 15 cubic meters per month.

The average service costs are greater than average service fees in most Middle Eastern and North African countries and economies (ACWUA 2014, table 14), suggesting a lack of cost recovery, as shown in table 2.1. On average, the fee charged for water services in the region is about 35 percent of the cost of production for conventional sources. In the case of desalinated water, only 10 percent of costs are covered by fees (Gelil 2014). Cost recovery is essential to ensure the long-term sustainability of water services and appropriate levels of investment in the operation and maintenance of water delivery systems—not just in infrastructure but also in training staff. A lack of financial sustainability of service providers can also severely undermine a utility's capacity to treat wastewater, leading to deteriorating water quality and degradation of freshwater ecosystems.

The effects of water subsidies on the financial viability and performance of water services are well known. Subsidies are defined as the

TABLE 2.1

Average Service Cost and Service Fees, Selected Countries and Economies

Country/economy	Average service fee (per cubic meters)	Average service charge (per cubic meters)
Egypt, Arab Rep.	$0.0.11 (water)	$0.05 (water)
	$0.13 (wastewater)	$0.02 (wastewater)
Yemen, Rep.	$0.90 (water)	$0.50 (water)
	$0.02 (wastewater)	$0.30 (wastewater)
West Bank and Gaza	$1.40 (water)	$1.10 (water)
	$1.50 (wastewater)	— (wastewater)
Jordan	$2.40 (combined)	$1.40 (combined)

Source: ACWUA (2014, table 14).
Note: All values cover operations and maintenance costs, depreciation, and debt service. Jordan includes average charges for all sectors. West Bank and Gaza gives average values from 11 water and sanitation services utilities under the Palestinian Water Authority. — = not available.

FIGURE 2.27

Water Subsidies to Urban Water Utilities as a Percentage of Regional GDP, by Country Groups and World Regions

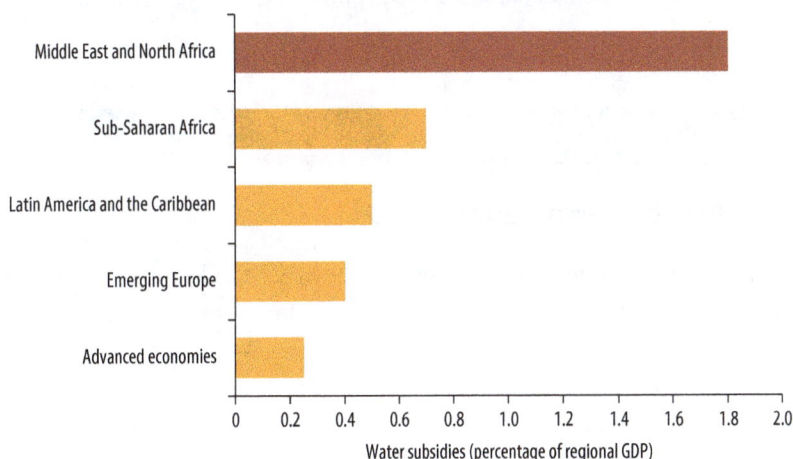

Source: Kochhar et al. 2015.
Note: Subsidies are defined as the difference between actual water charges for water users and a reference price that would cover all costs associated with supplying that water.

difference between actual water service fees for water users and a reference price that would cover all costs associated with supplying that water. The fiscal burden of subsidized water utilities is significant, and is estimated at 2 percent of regional GDP (Kochhar et al. 2015). This is the greatest proportion of GDP spent on public water subsidies (for domestic water supplies) of any other region in the world, as shown in figure 2.27.

Subsidizing water has at least three effects. First, it contributes to unsustainable water use. Subsidized or free water promotes wasteful use of water supplies, exacerbating physical water scarcity in the Middle East and North Africa (Berglöf and Devarajan 2015). In the agricultural sector, low water service fees enable farmers to grow water-intensive crops and discourage the adoption of water-saving irrigation technologies. Evidence shows that pricing of irrigation water services can lead to water savings (box 2.10). Furthermore, subsidies distort the prices of conventional water supply sources, effectively creating a barrier to the wider adoption of nonconventional water sources, such as recycled water (Jeuland 2015).

Subsidized water can hurt the poor. Wealthier areas can benefit more from subsidized water than poorer neighborhoods in some cases (Berglöf and Devarajan 2015). When richer communities are better served than poor ones, their per capita consumption is comparatively higher. In the worst case, poor households may be located in areas unserved by utilities, requiring residents to buy water of dubious quality from vendors in the informal sector at prices much higher than those paid by the rich. Even when the poor have access to piped water, because they use less water, they capture a smaller share of the benefits of the subsidies (Whittington et al. 2015). Available data for selected countries globally suggest that the

---

BOX 2.10

Effects of Water Service Fees on Agricultural Water Use

Understanding the effects of water service fees on savings and efficiency of water use is crucial to designing successful water reforms. Modest increases in water service fees might lead to significant water savings. Evidence from multiple studies suggest that higher service fees can result in lower water use in agriculture in the Middle East and North Africa (that is, the price elasticity is negative). For instance, Rosenberg, Howitt, and Lund (2008) found that in Jordan a 10 percent increase in the service fees resulted in a 1 percent reduction in water use in agriculture. In certain contexts, the current service fee may be so low that water use may not be reduced until a certain threshold is reached.

Water service fees can be tailored to provide a base allocation for a low initial fee and incremental allocations for higher fees. This approach guarantees farmers a base allocation, thus protecting their incomes, while presenting them with a higher fee for additional water use. By charging more for additional water use, this mechanism provides an incentive to farmers to use each additional unit of water more efficiently.

Source: Jarvis and Pétraud 2013.

poorest 20 percent of the population received less than 10 percent of subsidies incurred by public water utilities. In contrast, the richest 20 percent captured over 30 percent of the subsidies (Fuente et al. 2016). Lack of proper pricing of wastewater treatment services can also severely undermine the capacity of utilities to treat water. Treated water could potentially provide environmental and economic benefits for all types of households—rich and poor.

Service providers' dependence on government subsidies diminishes their customer orientation. As a result, utilities are more inclined to prioritize service improvements on the basis of political preference, with differing impacts regarding both service quality and inclusion (Berglöf and Devarajan 2015).

Experiences in the region show that removing subsidies is possible in a way that avoids disproportionate impacts on the poor and major social unrest (box 2.11). Indeed, the Middle East and North Africa region has

---

BOX 2.11

Is It Possible to Remove Subsidies? The Case of the Islamic Republic of Iran's Energy Subsidy Reform

The Islamic Republic of Iran was one of the first oil-exporting countries to implement drastic energy subsidy reforms. Its 2010 Targeted Subsidies Reform illustrates how the government has succeeded in initiating effective reforms and avoiding any serious public unrest.

The reform significantly reduced indirect subsidies to energy products and replaced them with across-the-board energy dividend transfers to the population. The price increases removed nearly $50–$60 billion in annual product subsidies, according to some estimates.

Key elements of the reforms that helped avoid serious problems at the outset of the changes included the simplicity of the compensatory scheme; a well-designed, broad public awareness campaign; the readiness of the banking system to facilitate massive cash transfers; and government policies that helped prevent dramatic increases in the inflation rate. Furthermore, the use of multitier tariffs on electricity, natural gas, and water played an important role in moderating the impact of the price increases on small, mostly poor users, and in accounting for regional disparities in the availability of different heating fuels.

In more recent years, the Iranian government has had difficulties in sustaining the reform because of inflationary pressures, currency depreciation, and institutional challenges. Nonetheless, the Iranian experience shows that subsidy reform in a complex economic and political context can achieve some success, even though it could not completely remove subsidies.

Sources: Guillame, Zytek, and Farzin 2011; Vagliasindi 2012; Verme 2016.

recently witnessed a surge in subsidies reform, especially in the energy sector (Verme 2016). These reforms, although they have not achieved complete removal of energy subsidies, are encouraging because they demonstrate the possibility of implementing large subsidy reforms in the region, even during a period of adverse economic and political conditions (Verme 2016).

The success and effectiveness of policies to remove subsidies will depend on the political economy context. Nonetheless, experiences in the region show that effective subsidy removal and pricing policies share common features, such as well-designed service fee structures that balance cost recovery and economic efficiency needs with equity and affordability (Vagliasindi 2012). Well-designed subsidy removal and pricing policies also include accurate targeting of price changes—as in Bahrain, which targets higher consumption users—and public campaigns explaining the reason for pricing changes and the availability of compensatory mechanisms.

Water service fee reforms are being successfully implemented in some countries in the Middle East and North Africa. In Qatar, the national water utility Kahramaa increased service fees for energy and water usage for expatriate, commercial, and industrial users, tiered according to consumption. In Bahrain, water service fees were increased for higher tiers of consumption and for commercial and industrial users. Similar reforms were also successfully implemented in the Emirate of Abu Dhabi and in Oman.

There are other ways to value water beyond service fee reforms. Consciousness around water can be changed with intensive media campaigns incentivizing water savings, as was done in Tunisia. Legal instruments to reduce wasteful water use have also been introduced in the GCC countries. In Qatar, for instance, wasteful uses of water are punishable by fines of up to $6,000.

Fiscal pressures may increasingly cause governments to revisit their pricing policies. Governments in the region recognize that the lack of financial sustainability in the water sector leads to poor water services and a subsequent deterioration of relationships between the government and citizens. Low service fees and inadequate operating funds result in declining levels of service and an inefficient use of water, which in turn make urban and rural water users unwilling to pay for poor services. For example, poor and unreliable water services can harm farmers' harvests and incomes. Perceptions that the government is not doing enough to ensure water services can erode the social contract, fueling grievances toward institutions and intensifying political instabilities. Achieving financial sustainability and recovering costs in water supply and wastewater improve the quality of water services, which in turn promotes a renewed social contract.

The challenges of making wastewater treatment financially sustainable are especially great. Wastewater treatment investments generally have high costs, but very low rates of return (Kfouri, Mantovani, and Jeuland 2009). For wastewater treatment to make sense (financially), it must be considered within a longer-term water management strategy that includes recycling treated wastewater and equitable service fees for wastewater disposal and treatment services. Improved economic analysis of the multiple benefits of wastewater treatment (protecting aquatic ecosystems, safeguarding amenities and tourist destinations, preventing the spread of waterborne diseases) will help countries in the Middle East and North Africa evaluate, case by case, the option of water recycling.

Confronting Governance, Financing, and Information Constraints in Water Service Delivery

Confronting the challenges of water service delivery ultimately requires addressing the challenges of water governance. Broadly interpreted, *water governance* is the process by which state institutions interact with citizens and nonstate institutions to ensure that water services are delivered (World Bank 2017). Nonstate institutions may be humanitarian agencies or firms in the private sector, whose importance in water service delivery varies depending on the context. In some countries in the Middle East and North Africa affected by conflict and fragility, nonstate institutions have become primary service providers.

The Middle East and North Africa region offers many successful examples of policies to improve the governance of water services. Yet institutional and governance constraints, such as low accountability or a lack of financial skills within the sector, still pose a barrier to progress toward improved service delivery. As evidence around the world shows, improvements in the governance of public services can take many forms (World Bank 2017). A diverse range of policies and paths can contribute to improvements in the governance of water services. Some of these are discussed in this section.

Decentralized governance has been recognized as a potential arrangement to address governance challenges in water services delivery. At their most effective, decentralized systems increase innovation and participation in water services. However, they only work when the correct incentives and well-defined assignments are in place (World Bank 2017). In Morocco, the decentralization of the operation and maintenance of irrigation water schemes to water users' associations has helped users define appropriate service levels, water charges, and water allocation (UNDP 2013).

Alongside decentralization, public-private partnerships for utilities have also been implemented in the Middle East and North Africa to tackle financial constraints in water service delivery. These public-private partnerships can be viewed as one of the tools available to governments for improving the performance and financial sustainability of the water sector. Public-private partnerships have been very active in the Middle East and North Africa region to support improvements in the efficiency and quality of service delivery. Public-private partnerships in the water utility space have mostly worked using management- and performance-based contracts. The advantage of this type of partnership is that the ownership of the assets remains in the hands of the public utility. The private operator becomes involved over short to medium time scales (5–7 years) in the operation and maintenance of municipal water and wastewater systems, where the public utility seeks specific improvements in service delivery and quality. Utility public-private partnerships can also be focused on reducing leakage in distribution networks and ensuring that these efficiency gains are maintained over time. In this case, the benefit of the partnership is that the public utility gains from reduced levels of nonrevenue water and the contractor benefits through performance-based fees linked to the volume of water saved.

The Middle East and North Africa has been the most active place in the world for public-private partnerships to improve water utility performance over the last six years. Across the region, almost 28 million people have been provided improved water services via utility public-private partnerships.

Information and monitoring systems are also essential to address governance challenges in service delivery. Information flows reduce institutional costs and promote more transparent operational performance and increased financial sustainability of service providers (Hope and Rouse 2013). Information and monitoring are key elements of any effective water service governance mechanism because they link policy reform with implementation in the water sector.

Monitoring of service provision—in terms of functionality, timely and adequate water supply, water quality, and water use management—is crucial to ensure that coverage indicators are giving a true picture of improved access (Ndaw 2015). On the one hand, effective and transparent monitoring allows users to see the quality of the services delivered and to rationalize and reduce water use. On the other hand, it allows institutions to track policy progress across a range of indicators related to water services. Each country will adapt those indicators and monitoring technologies that are best suited to its priorities and resources, but this will nonetheless provide a better understanding of common challenges and opportunities for improving water service delivery.

Integrating smart and mobile technologies in water service delivery has several potential benefits. First, mobile-based systems ensure rapid access to information and data sharing, creating a system of transparency and accountability. In turn, this strengthens public participation and voice, as well as promoting a more rational use of the resource. For instance, the Dubai Electricity and Water Authority is aiming to install smart meters across the entire United Arab Emirates to monitor actual consumption and promote reductions in water and electricity use (box 2.12).

The World Bank Water and Sanitation Program has found that integrating mobile technologies into service delivery also leads to better water supply and sanitation services for the underserved and poor (Ndaw 2015). This is because mobile technology is widespread and low cost, allowing the poorest communities in remote areas to contact service providers and, for instance, signal the need for maintenance

---

BOX 2.12

Smart Metering for Sustainable and Accountable Service Delivery: The Experience of the Dubai Electricity and Water Authority

Smart applications through smart meters and grids will provide various benefits and new applications to the customers of the Dubai Electricity and Water Authority (DEWA), including automatic and detailed readings (both current and historical) of water consumption. The data obtained through these readings will be available to customers to monitor actual consumption for a specific period of time to better rationalize consumption.

Smart meters will be able to send accumulated data via sophisticated means of communication to DEWA, while providing a full history of consumption and consumption processes to both DEWA and customers. Smart meters in residential, commercial, and industrial sectors allow DEWA to compare the production rate against the consumption of resources. This enables DEWA to identify and target losses due to nonrevenue water. DEWA has successfully implemented the first phase of the initiative, installing 200,000 smart meters by January 2016, and it expects to have installed over 1 million smart meters by 2020, covering the entire United Arab Emirates and replacing all mechanical and electromechanical meters.

Source: Dubai Electricity and Water Authority.

or repairs. Mobile technologies also give water users more transparent and up-to-date access to information on water availability, quality, and price.

Good use and integration of information and mobile technology greatly benefit service providers. Improved information flows via mobile technology allow water service providers to monitor in real time the functionality and state of water infrastructure and distribution systems and to monitor progress in key performance indicators. Evidence from different parts of the world shows that the introduction of mobile water payment options improved collection efficiency and increased utilities' revenues (Hope et al. 2012).

Summary

The Middle East and North Africa region has had among the best performance globally since 1990 in terms of increasing access to improved water supply and sanitation. Extending access to rural areas has been more challenging. Furthermore, access statistics often hide the reality on the ground, where access to water depends on a range of factors, including reliability (notably, some households classified as having access receive water only once a week), affordability, and social status. Following ongoing armed conflict in the region, access gains have been reversed as infrastructure has been damaged and capacity has been lost in institutions. In Syria, access to water supply services decreased by 70 percent between 2011 and 2013 (UN-Water 2015).

As the region moves toward the Sustainable Development Goals, new challenges are arising, especially in relation to improving the quality and reliability of water services. High operation and maintenance costs, low service fees, and high subsidies translate into weak financial sustainability for water services in the region. Poor households suffer from inadequate water services, which often force them to rely on informal vendors to meet their water requirements, often at higher costs. The provision of reliable and high-quality water supplies remains a challenge in many parts of the region, especially in densely populated informal settlements and in rural areas.

Water use incentives and a gradual removal of subsidies could be an important step to improve the quality of water services. Far from undermining the quality of water services for the poor, water service fees and subsidy reforms could potentially enable more inclusive and affordable water service delivery for the populations of the Middle East and North Africa. Moreover, because water subsidies are often disproportionately captured by wealthier populations, well-designed reform could help the poor.

More innovative mechanisms for providing water services should be explored. Integrated urban water resources management, combining traditional and new approaches, could help improve service delivery. For instance, on-site source separation may be an attractive solution to facilitate wastewater treatment in rapidly growing urban centers.[20] The private sector has been at the forefront in developing many innovations for augmenting water supplies and enhancing efficiency. There is scope to extend public-private partnerships to improve the quality of water services.

Improving water services could help strengthen the social contract between public institutions and citizens. When governments fail to provide adequate and inclusive water services, citizens' trust in these institutions can be undermined. Reversing this trend requires working toward better service quality, accountability of water service providers, and a clear understanding of citizens' expectations with respect to water services.

Better service quality also needs better data and monitoring. The lack of information and monitoring makes it difficult to obtain a comprehensive picture of the quality of water services, especially for agricultural and industrial users. The newly launched SDG 6 targets and associated indicators provide a tremendous opportunity to build a more evidence-based and comprehensive picture of the status of water services in the Middle East and North Africa.

Mitigating Water-Related Risks

Assessing water security means assessing the possibility that harmful water-related events will occur. This possibility can seldom be eliminated. Thus, gathering and evaluating evidence of risks related to water is a central component of any water security assessment. *Risk* is here intended in the broadest possible sense, as an uncertain event related to water with harmful consequences for single or multiple actors, from individuals to communities to aquatic ecosystems.

Understanding risks is essential for compiling a comprehensive picture of water security. Thinking about uncertain water-related events in terms of risks helps policy makers find responses that are proportionate to the risks they are facing. In the context of water security, risks may be the result of extreme hydroclimatic events, such as floods or droughts, or may be the result of sociopolitical conditions, such as transboundary water development, population displacement, or the unintended consequences of reforms associated with the water-energy-food nexus.

Water-related risks arise from hydroclimatic and sociopolitical factors that are highly specific to the context. In exploring risks in the Middle

East and North Africa region, it is important to pay particular attention
to how water-related risks affect efforts to reduce poverty and how they
may relate to conflict and violence in the region.

Climate Change

While population and economic growth will increase water demand,
climate change will be the primary driver for the most pronounced
changes in surface water stress across the region. Figure 2.28 shows how
climate change and socioeconomic change will influence surface water
stress in 2030, comparing change driven by climate change (right side of
the graph) and change driven by socioeconomic factors (left side of the
graph). These projections show that climate change will be the main
driver behind the most significant increases in water stress.

   Some of the biggest changes induced by climate change in surface
water stress will occur in countries already facing politically and

FIGURE 2.28

Future Drivers of Surface Water Stress in the Middle East and North Africa

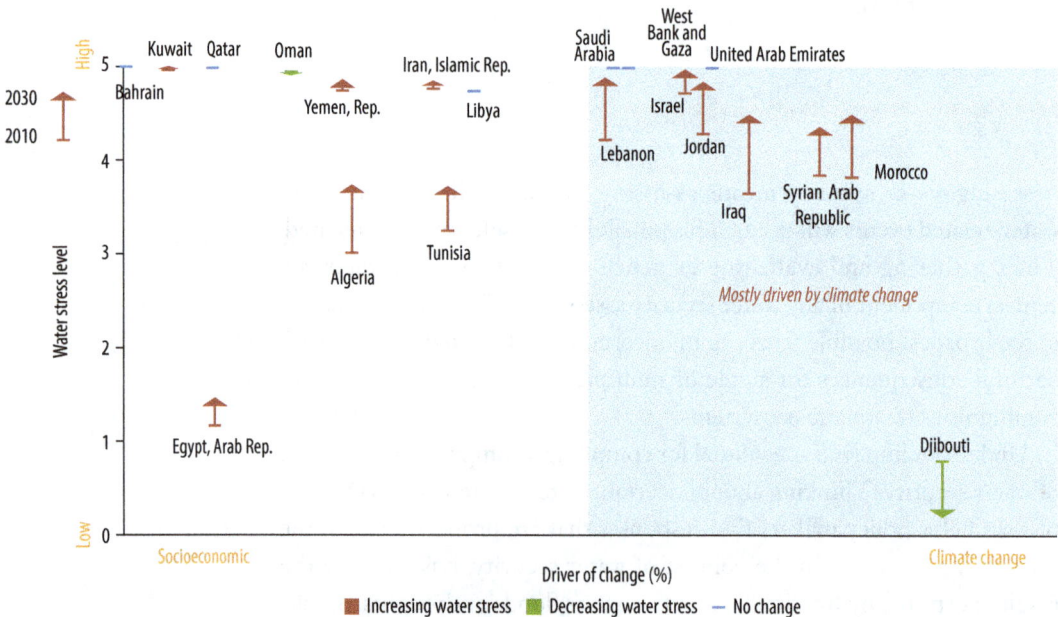

Source: Analysis and calculations based on World Resources Institute Aqueduct™ data.
Note: Water stress is quantified as the ratio of annual water withdrawals to average annual surface water availability under an RCP 8.5 (high emission
scenario) and SSP2 (business as usual for socioeconomic change). The position of each country along the horizontal dimension reflects the percentage
of change in water stress that is driven by climate change (right) or socioeconomic change (left). Future climate change is modeled using an ensemble
of climate models for a high-emission scenario (RCP 8.5). Socioeconomic change is modeled using a middle-of-the-road scenario, where future socioeconomic trajectories do not shift markedly from historical patterns (that is, a business-as-usual scenario for population growth and the economy)
(O'Neill et al. 2015). Estimates of surface water stress do not account for withdrawals from groundwater and nonconventional water supplies.

environmentally fragile situations. The projections in figure 2.28 suggest that Iraq, Lebanon, Jordan, Israel, Syria, and Morocco will all experience significant increases in surface water stress driven by climate change. On the other hand, socioeconomic change will drive increases in surface water stress in countries such as Algeria, Egypt, the Islamic Republic of Iran, and the Republic of Yemen. Climate change will also drive increases in the exposure to floods, as explained in the next section.

Climate change increases water stress through multiple mechanisms, including reductions in rainfall and increasing temperatures (IPCC 2014). Climate models project an increase in temperature (Verner 2012) and heat extremes in the Middle East and North Africa (Lelieveld et al. 2016). Increasing temperatures may lead to unprecedented heat waves, which would severely harm agricultural production and, in some cases, lead to extreme conditions intolerable to humans (Pal and Eltahir 2016). Temperature increases will lead to higher evapotranspiration rates and crop water requirements, potentially increasing the already-high water consumption of the agricultural sector (Verner 2012). Furthermore, increased variability and uncertainty about the timing and intensity of rainfall events pose risks for rainfed agriculture.

Climate change contributes to the rise of sea levels, increasing the risk of flooding and salinization in coastal areas of the Middle East and North Africa. Low-lying deltas, such as the Nile and the Shatt-al Arab, have been identified as at risk from the impacts of climate change (Tessler et al. 2015), as have low-lying coastal areas, such as Morocco's Mediterranean coastal zone (Snoussi, Ouchani, and Niazi 2008). In Alexandria, on the Nile Delta, average annual flood losses in 2050 might double compared to 2005 levels if the current standard of flood defense is maintained (Hallegatte et al. 2013). Sea-level rise also causes saltwater to intrude into freshwater aquifers. Coastal areas where groundwater is overexploited are particularly vulnerable to saltwater intrusion into aquifers, because excessive groundwater abstraction makes space for saltwater to flow into freshwater aquifers (Mabrouk et al. 2013).

Unmanaged water-related impacts of climate change will perpetuate poverty (Hallegatte et al. 2016). In the Middle East and North Africa, poorer populations are already more vulnerable to weather-related shocks (Wodon et al. 2014). A recent survey of five countries found that the bottom three quintiles report higher losses due to weather shocks than do the richer households in the upper two quintiles, as shown in table 2.2. At a macroeconomic scale, studies show that climate change could lead to declines in growth rates equivalent to 6–14 percent of the Middle East and North Africa's GDP by 2050 (World Bank 2016).

TABLE 2.2

Share of Population Reporting an Economic Impact Following a Weather Shock, Selected Countries and Economies, by Quintile
Percentage

| Type of impact | Quintile | | | | | |
	Q1 (poorest)	Q2	Q3	Q4	Q5 (richest)	All
Lost income	46	44	43	29	21	37
Lost crops	58	62	62	49	42	55
Lost livestock or cattle	24	25	30	23	15	23
Less fish caught	10	10	9	10	5	9

Source: Hallegatte et al. 2016.

Droughts

Droughts are a long-standing and recurrent challenge in the Middle East and North Africa and are different from the region's water scarcity (Kaniewski, Van Campo, and Weiss 2012). *A drought* is a natural hazard caused by large-scale climatic variability that cannot be prevented by water management decisions (Van Loon and Van Lanen 2013). *Water scarcity*, as described, is a long-term condition caused by the unsustainable use of water resources where demand consistently exceeds supply. Water management can mitigate or exacerbate the impacts of droughts on society and the economy, and water management policies can be put in place to address long-term water scarcity challenges. However, water management cannot prevent droughts from happening. Droughts can have far-reaching consequences, including the partial to total destruction of agricultural production and forced displacement of communities.

Projections from climate models almost uniformly point toward drying in the Middle East and North Africa, and suggest that the region will experience more severe and intense droughts (Dubrovský et al. 2014). Recent droughts have been exceptional relative to the natural variability observed in the last millennium (Cook et al. 2016), increasing concerns that drought conditions will be further exacerbated by climate change.

A drought is a water-related hazard that has devastating impacts on social, economic, and environmental systems. Reduced crop output, increased fire hazard, increased livestock mortality, and decreased water levels are all examples of the direct impacts of droughts. An example of the direct effects of droughts is shown in figure 2.29, which compares wheat production data[21] with annual green water availability and precipitation[22] for Syria from 2001 to 2015. The peak drought year (2008) is also the year when wheat production was lowest, and lower than wheat production during the years at the beginning of the conflict. Although this analysis

FIGURE 2.29

Wheat Production, Green Water Anomaly, and Rainfall Anomaly during Drought and Conflict, Syria, 2001–15

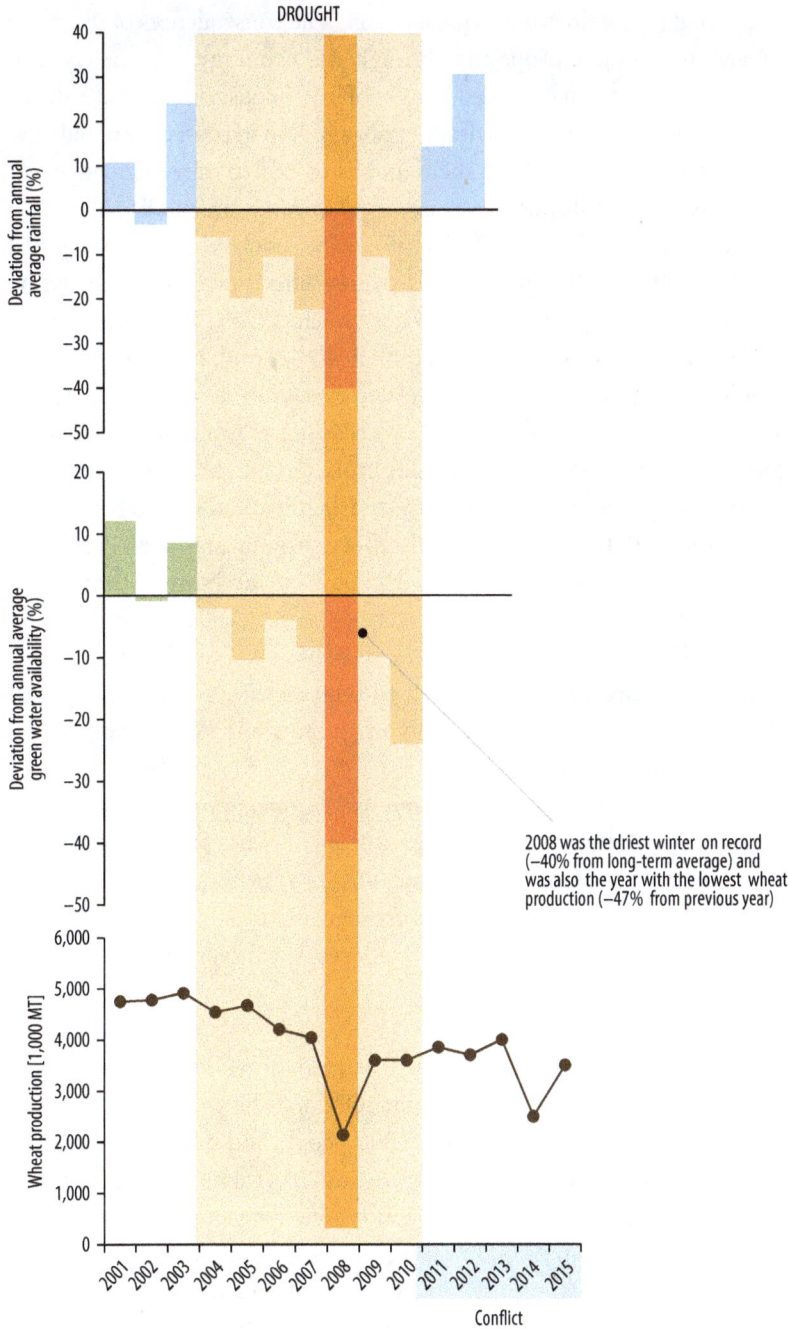

2008 was the driest winter on record (−40% from long-term average) and was also the year with the lowest wheat production (−47% from previous year)

Sources: Precipitation data from the World Bank's Climate Knowledge Portal. Wheat production data from the United States Department of Agriculture (USDA) Economics, Statistics and Market Information System. Green water data from Kummu et al. 2014.

Note: The annual precipitation anomaly was estimated using 1900–2012 annual rainfall totals. MT = metric tons.

ignores many factors, it shows the extent to which the recent drought in Syria was more damaging to wheat production than the armed conflict.

A drought can also act as a risk multiplier, destabilizing populations, amplifying inequalities in access to water services and water resources, and reinforcing perceptions of marginalization. The consequences of the direct impacts of drought propagate through the economy and society. For instance, failed crop harvests lead to loss of livelihoods, famine, and reduced incomes. In some instances, a drought can also lead to conflict or population displacement. Evidence from the Republic of Yemen suggests that people are often killed in disputes over access to groundwater wells (Almohsen 2015; Misiedjan and Van Rijswick 2015). Some scholars have also suggested that the 2007–10 drought in Syria, whose effects were exacerbated by decades of poor agricultural and water policies (De Châtel 2014), led to mass migration from rural to urban centers (Kelley et al. 2015). The government's failure to address this water-related disaster led to a progressive deterioration of Syria's social contract, contributing to grievances toward the government and unrest that eventually broke out into a full-scale civil war.

Poor people are more vulnerable to droughts than the average member of the population. Households affected by droughts or located in drought-prone regions such as the Middle East and North Africa have a higher risk of falling into poverty or face greater challenges in escaping poverty (Winsemius et al. 2015). These households can face more difficulty, for example, as they attempt to bounce back from challenges to livelihoods and health induced by crop failure, food shortages, and drought-related disasters.

A range of new technologies and institutional approaches are being implemented in the region to mitigate drought risks. These include integrated drought management systems (box 2.13) to monitor drought conditions and provide actionable information to decision makers and disaster risk reduction approaches to address the drivers of drought risk.

Floods

Floods are the most frequent natural disaster in the Middle East and North Africa. Between 1981 and 2011, about 300 floods hit the Middle East and North Africa (map 2.12), killing 19,000 people and negatively affecting more than 8.6 million people (Banerjee et al. 2014). The 2008 floods in the Republic of Yemen caused $1.6 billion in total damages—equivalent to 6 percent of the country's GDP (World Bank 2014). The 2009 floods in Jeddah, Saudi Arabia, resulted in $1.36 billion in losses (Banerjee et al. 2014). The 2004 floods in Djibouti led to 230 deaths and $11.1 million in losses, and adversely affected 100,000 people (World Bank 2014).

Population and economic growth have increased flood risks in the Middle East and North Africa. The percentage of the region's GDP

BOX 2.13

Integrated Drought Management Systems in the Middle East and North Africa

Droughts have devastating impacts, particularly on the vulnerable rural and urban poor. At present, there are no functioning drought management systems in the region. The lack of management systems combines with poor mitigation planning and integration across ministries/agencies to increase vulnerability to droughts.

Under a program funded by the United States Agency for International Development (USAID), the International Centre for Biosaline Agriculture and the University of Nebraska—Lincoln, in partnership with the Food and Agriculture Organization (FAO) of the United Nations, are supporting the development of integrated drought risk management systems. The program aims to empower decision makers from the national to regional levels in Jordan, Lebanon,

Morocco, and Tunisia, through comprehensive drought monitoring alongside practical mitigation activities and planning to improve resilience. In each of these countries, drought-related challenges are different, requiring definitions and approaches to these events tailored to the context. With droughts predicted to increase in intensity and frequency in light of climate change, these drought management systems are crucial across the entire region to protect the most vulnerable populations and environments.

The composite drought index system being developed by the International Centre for Biosaline Agriculture, together with subsequent technology and capacity transfer to the four partner countries teams, has already led to the production of monthly drought maps.

Source: Rachael McDonnell, International Centre for Biosaline Agriculture.

produced in areas exposed to floods tripled from 1979 to 2009 (Banerjee et al 2014). More economic growth and urban expansion close to surface water bodies exposes more people and assets to flooding. Sea-level rise will increase the risk of flooding in low-lying coastal areas such as the Nile Delta (Hallegatte et al. 2013). The combined dynamics of these socioeconomic changes along with climate change will increase flood risks for populations across the region.

Heavier downpours as a consequence of climate change may increase the risk of urban flooding in many cities in the Middle East and North Africa. In November 2015, approximately 40 minutes of torrential rains flooded large parts of Amman, causing significant direct and indirect economic losses (Lillywhite 2015). Rapid urbanization is increasing exposure to floods, and risks are particularly acute for households that are encroaching on natural drainage areas (*wadis*) (Verner 2012).

MAP 2.12

Number of Flood Events in the Middle East and North Africa, 1900–2011

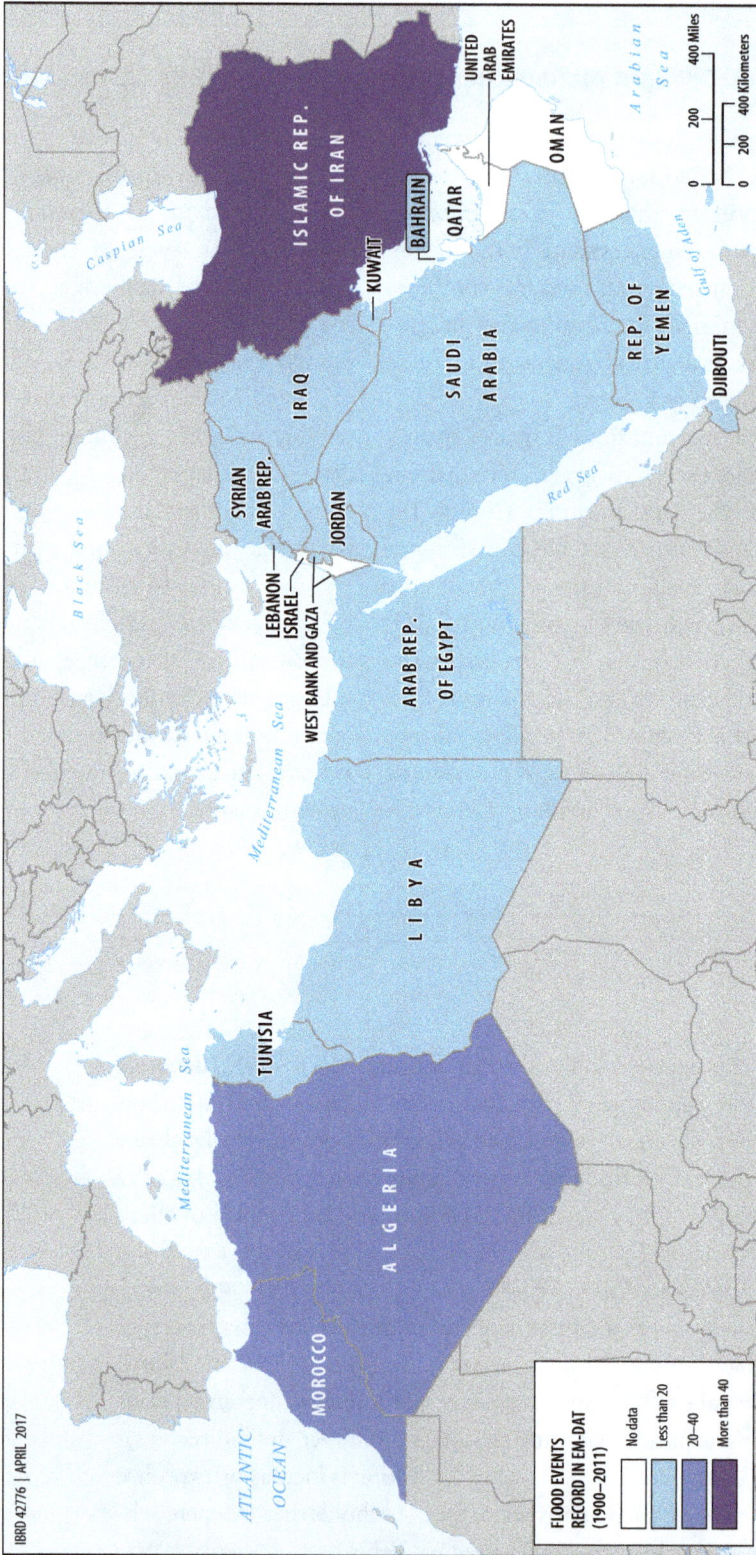

FLOOD EVENTS RECORD IN EM-DAT (1900–2011)

- No data
- Less than 20
- 20–40
- More than 40

Source: Banerjee et al. 2014.

Note: EM-DAT = Emergency Event Database; GFDRR = Global Facility for Disaster Reduction and Recovery.

BOX 2.14

Coping with Water-Related Disasters in Djibouti

Djibouti is very vulnerable to water-related disasters. The 2004 floods in Djibouti led to 230 deaths and $11.1 million in losses, and affected 100,000 people. Nine years later, in 2013, a similar flood event resulted in fewer victims, and there was a far briefer disruption of citizens' livelihoods.

During that nine-year period, multiple interventions were pursued to mitigate flood risk, which improved disaster preparedness and prevented damage during the 2013 event. The Djibouti Disaster Risk Management Programme started in 2006 with the construction of a dam to protect the country's capital from flash floods. Early warning systems and emergency preparedness plans were also put in place to assist the government in managing flood hazards.

Source: GFDRR 2016.

The urban poor are more exposed to floods (Hallegatte et al. 2016). As discussed for droughts, the poor are often more vulnerable to weather shocks. For example, they may lack the assets required to protect and maintain their property, they may reside on vulnerable land, and their livelihoods may be harmed by extreme rainfall. The failure of governments to guarantee protection from water-related hazards can challenge the social contract because the state is often perceived to be responsible for providing protection and relief following a flood.

Current and projected levels of flood risk suggest that Middle Eastern and North African countries may benefit greatly from investing in flood control measures (box 2.14). One effective measure will be controlling and preventing development on floodplains and in *wadis*, especially in urban areas. Other flood control measures might include rural land use management and construction of flood barriers. Flood relief and flood insurance programs will also need to be developed to respond to increasing flood risk in the region. Management of flood risks will require explicit discussions around targets for flood protection, and acceptable levels of risks and investments.

The Water-Energy-Food Nexus

Managing water-related risks also involves managing trade-offs and unintended consequences in the interrelated energy and food sectors. When water is allocated to one use such as agriculture, specific water services may be compromised for other uses. Understanding nexus trade-offs for multiple users can help mitigate water-related risks across society (boxes 2.15 and 2.16).

BOX 2.15

Subsidies and the Water-Energy-Food Nexus

The effects of energy subsidies on water withdrawals and depletion illustrate the consequences of unmanaged trade-offs in the water-energy-food nexus. A study of energy subsidies in the Middle East and North Africa suggests that countries with lower-than-average diesel prices are characterized by much higher (and statistically significant) water-withdrawal-to-availability ratios (and thus unsustainable water use). In the Gulf Cooperation Council (GCC) countries, low energy prices have allowed for the large-scale rollout of desalination facilities. In other Middle Eastern and North African countries where desalination is not a major supply source, subsidized fuel causes high water-withdrawal-to-availability ratios by driving uncontrolled groundwater pumping (see figure B2.15.1).

The Republic of Yemen is often cited as an example of the adverse impact of energy subsidies on groundwater depletion. Pumping for irrigation accounts for 28 percent of the country's total electricity and diesel consumption. Irrigation supports the agricultural sector, which remains a key component of the Yemeni economy and a major source of direct and indirect income. Yet unsustainable groundwater withdrawals driven by fuel subsidies can severely harm agriculture in the long run by depleting the groundwater resources on which it depends.

FIGURE B2.15.1

Difference in Water Withdrawals for Countries with Above- and Below-Average Fuel Prices

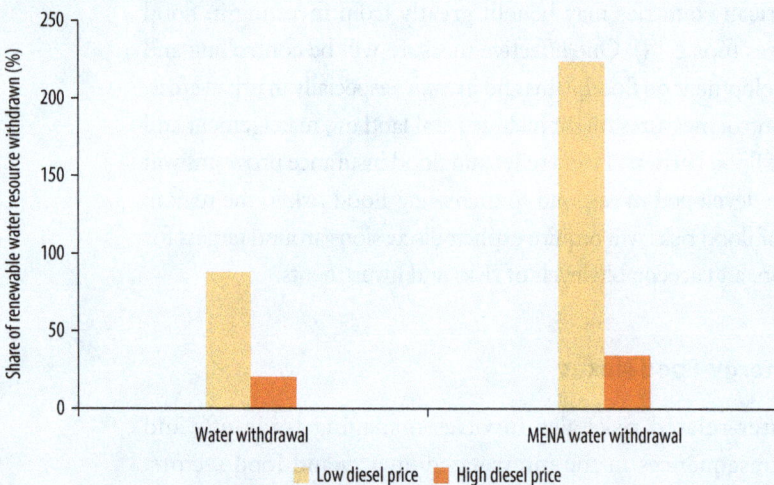

Source: World Bank elaboration based on Aquastat's database.
Note: The t-test between the average groups is significant at the 1 percent confidence level.

BOX 2.15 *Continued*

Intensive groundwater pumping supported by subsidized energy helps increase agricultural production and income for farmers. However, it also contributes to groundwater depletion.

Measures to strike a balance in this context may support the transition to less water-intensive crops, use of alternative water supply sources, or improvements in water productivity.

Source: Commander, Nikoloski, and Vagliasindi 2015.

BOX 2.16

Solar-Based Groundwater Pumping for Irrigation

Around the world, solar-powered water pumps have been proposed as a way to help farmers better irrigate crops in a more affordable way. These pumps allow farmers to irrigate their crops in areas where no electricity is distributed and where high fuel prices make running diesel-powered pumps expensive. Solar-based groundwater pumping for irrigation has increased agricultural productivity and has helped people move out of poverty in many rural areas. However, the financial and environmental sustainability of many solar-based pumping projects for groundwater irrigation is often overlooked.

Because solar energy is free, there is virtually no marginal cost of pumping water, so farmers have few economic incentives to stop pumping. This increases the risk of unsustainable groundwater abstraction and long-term groundwater depletion.

Meters and monitoring have been recommended as mechanisms to prevent groundwater overabstraction. In remote areas, however, regular and accurate meter readings may be difficult to ensure. Another way of managing this perverse incentive would be purchasing power generated by farmers and returning it to the grid to create an opportunity cost of excessive pumping; however, it is precisely the absence of a grid that pushes farmers to install solar pumps in the first instance. The development of solar-based groundwater pumping for irrigation needs to be carried out with careful considerations of the trade-offs at the water-energy-food nexus and of local issues around access to groundwater resources for marginalized farming communities.

Sources: Closas and Rap 2017; IRENA 2016; Weerasekera 2012.

Water scarcity results in particularly stark trade-offs among water, energy, and food in the Middle East and North Africa. The Jordan Valley Authority offers an example; the Authority manages the public irrigation infrastructure in the Jordan Valley, at present, it is unable to cover its operating and maintenance costs. Its irrigation water service fees have remained unchanged since 1994. The large operating and maintenance deficits, amounting to roughly 40 percent of total recurrent expenditures, have impaired the quality of service, as the Authority is forced to divert capital expenditures to cover operational losses (van den Berg et al. 2016). A World Bank study suggested a range of measures to improve the Authority's financial sustainability (van den Berg et al. 2016). These measures include traditional mechanisms to increasing the Authority's capacity to generate revenues, such as changing billing practices and increasing irrigation service fees, as well as more careful efficiency improvements and asset management planning. Improvements in service efficiency and asset planning will have to consider energy prices connected to requirements for pumping and municipal water requirements, including in underserved, marginal areas. The needs of multiple resource users, including the poor and vulnerable, must be balanced.

Reliance on cheap nonrenewable energy for desalination heightens the trade-offs in the water-energy-food nexus. In the GCC countries, in particular, municipal water services delivery depends heavily on energy-intensive desalination, groundwater pumping, and transportation. In Saudi Arabia, for instance, desalination and groundwater pumping account for about 10 percent of total annual energy consumption (Siddiqi and Anadon 2011). More generally, the region's dependence on energy to provide water services is higher than in other regions of the world (Siddiqi and Anadon 2011). For instance, in Tunisia, some water utilities spend over 20 percent of their operating budgets on electricity tariffs.[23] Quantifying the dependence of water security on cheap energy helps authorities and planners devise long-term water management strategies that are as robust as possible to volatile energy prices and that ensure sustainable water resource use over the long term (box 2.15).

Integrated thinking and approaches across the water-energy-food nexus are needed to mitigate water-related risks and achieve the SDG targets (El-Hajj et al. 2017). The importance of multisectoral, nexus approaches for solving complex resource management problems has been recognized by the League of Arab States' Strategic Framework for Sustainable Development (Gelil 2014). As part of the region's commitment to meeting the SDGs, nexus thinking will help improve resource efficiency and service delivery through market incentives and economic policy reform (Gelil 2014). Furthermore, by harnessing existing multistakeholder and multisector institutional platforms, nexus thinking will help harmonize policies targeted at adapting the SDGs and meeting targets to mitigate climate change.

Transboundary Waters

A large part of both the surface and groundwater resources in the Middle East and North Africa is transboundary. The combination of growing scarcity and growing climate-related risks is likely to drive competition and the increasing development of these waters. A large number of aquifers (map 2.13 and tables 2.3 and 2.4) and rivers (map 2.14 and table 2.4) are shared between countries in the Middle East and North Africa and with countries outside the region. This adds a layer of uncertainty and potential risks to many water resources management and planning decisions. Potential tensions might be heightened as river basins and aquifers "close"—meaning that water use equals or exceeds available resources—and as countries seek to develop water resources to foster economic growth.

Every Middle Eastern and North African country and economy shares at least one aquifer with a neighbor. Countries in the Maghreb have an even greater proportion of transboundary groundwater resources. Libya and Algeria top the list in terms of areal extent of shared aquifers. The current knowledge on the storage of these aquifers is uncertain, so it is difficult to estimate the volumetric percentage of a country's groundwater supplies that are transboundary. Transparent development and exchange of information on these important water supply sources are the first steps to ensure that these shared resources can be managed sustainably.

Climate change presents further challenges for transboundary waters. Climate change will alter patterns of water availability. Thus, there is a risk that existing transboundary water agreements may be challenged because these agreements are often based on multiyear averages, as opposed to percentages of flow (Falkenmark and Jägerskog 2010). Finally, even when dialogues and information sharing do occur, it is extremely difficult to disaggregate social and economic impacts of transboundary water management to ensure that policies and investments are inclusive and avoid unintended consequences for community stakeholders within the basin.

Transboundary waters also offer opportunities. More coordinated management and operation of water infrastructure on shared river systems can mitigate the impacts of droughts and floods on downstream countries and help improve the management of evaporative losses. Information sharing and the development of monitoring and early warning systems all promote the cooperative operation of water infrastructure, allowing for better decisions to be made to protect and benefit the environment, economies, and communities within the basin. With strategic planning, these data and information services can be holistically

MAP 2.13

Major Transboundary Aquifers in the Middle East and North Africa

IBRD 42540 | APRIL 2017

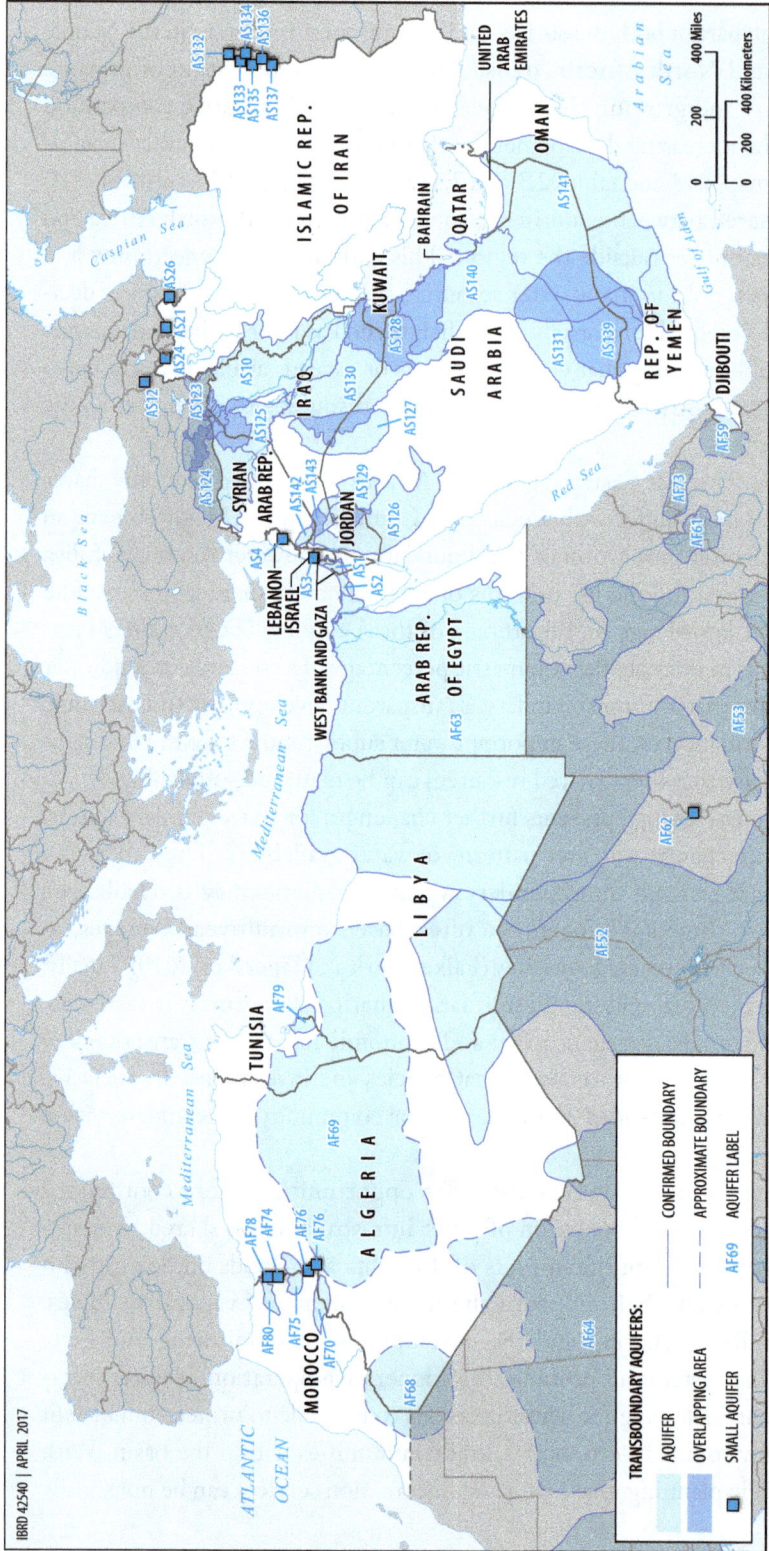

TRANSBOUNDARY AQUIFERS:

AQUIFER	—— CONFIRMED BOUNDARY
OVERLAPPING AREA	– – APPROXIMATE BOUNDARY
■ SMALL AQUIFER	AF69 AQUIFER LABEL

Source: International Groundwater Resource Assessment Centre (IGRAC and UNESCO-IHP 2015).

TABLE 2.3

Aquifer Names, Sharing Countries, and Areal Extent of the Aquifers Shown in Map 2.13

Code	Aquifer Name	Sharing Countries	Area [sqkm]
AF80	Triffa	Morocco, Algeria	11,530
AF75	Ain Beni Mathar	Morocco, Algeria	18,315
AF70	Système Aquifère d'Errachidia	Morocco, Algeria	20,721
AF68	Système Aquifère de Tindouf	Morocco, Western Sahara, Mauritania, Algeria	221,019
AF78	Jbel El Hamra	Morocco, Algeria	561
AF74	Angad	Morocco, Algeria	4,677
AF64	Taoudeni Basin	Algeria, Mali, Mauritania	1,260,940
AF56	Irhazer-Illuemeden Basin	Algeria, Benin, Mali, Niger, Nigeria	577,885
AF52	Lake Chad Basin	Chad, Niger, Nigeria, Cameroon, Central African Republic, Algeria	2,271,303
AF69	North-Western Sahara Aquifer System (NWSAS)	Algeria, Libya, Tunisia	1,279,963
AF79	Système Aquifère de la Djeffara	Tunisia, Libya	16,627
AF63	Nubian Sandstone Aquifer System (NSAS)	Chad, Arab Republic of Egypt, Libya, Sudan	2,892,867
AF59	Afar Rift valley / Afar Triangle Aquifer	Djibouti, Ethiopia	57,011
AS139	Wasia-Biyadh-Aruma Aquifer System (South): Tawila-Mahra/ Cretaceous Sands	Saudi Arabia, Republic of Yemen	180,087
AS131	Wajid Aquifer System	Saudi Arabia, Republic of Yemen	427,125
AS141	Umm er Radhuma-Dammam Aquifer System (South): Rub' al Khali	Oman, Saudi Arabia, United Arab Emirates, Republic of Yemen	791,877
AS140	Umm er Radhuma-Dammam Aquifer System (Centre): Gulf	Saudi Arabia, United Arab Emirates, Bahrain, Qatar	345,213
AS128	Neogene Aquifer System (South-East): DibdibbaKuwait Group	Iraq, Kuwait, Saudi Arabia	179,370
AS130	Umm er Radhuma-Dammam Aquifer System (North): Widyan-Salman	Iraq, Kuwait, Saudi Arabia	297,943
AS127	Wasia-Biyadh-Aruma Aquifer System (North): Sakaka-Rutba	Saudi Arabia, Iraq	103,778
AS126	Saq-Ram Aquifer System (West)	Jordan, Saudi Arabia	184,518
AS1	Wester Aquifer Basin	Arab Republic of Egypt, Israel, West Bank and Gaza	15,215
AS2	Coastal Aquifer Basin	Arab Republic of Egypt, Israel, West Bank and Gaza	23,338
AS3	Northeastern Aquifer	Israel, West Bank and Gaza	1,549
AS4	Anti-Lebanon	Lebanon, Syrian Arab Republic	3,850
AS129	Tawil Quaternary Aquifer System: Wadi Sirhan Basin	Jordan, Saudi Arabia	56,039
AS143	Basalt Aquifer System (South): Azraq-Dhuleil Basin	Jordan, Syrian Arab Republic	10,503
AS142	Basalt Aquifer System (West): Yarmouk Basin	Jordan, Syrian Arab Republic	8,574
AS124	Agh Darband	Syrian Arab Republic, Turkey	167,684
AS125	Neogene Aquifer System (North-West): Upper and Lower Fars	Syrian Arab Republic, Iraq	84,298
AS10	Upper Jezira & Taurus-Zagros	Iraq, Syrian Arab Republic, Turkey, Islamic Republic of Iran	13,236

Source: IGRAC and UNESCO-IHP 2015.

TABLE 2.4

Number of Shared Aquifers and River Basins, by Country and Economy

Country/economy	Number of shared aquifers	Number of shared river basins
Algeria	12	7
Iran, Islamic Rep.	11	8
Saudi Arabia	9	0
Morocco	6	0
Syrian Arab Republic	6	1
Iraq	6	7
Jordan	4	1
Libya	3	1
Kuwait	3	0
Yemen, Rep.	3	1
West Bank and Gaza	3	1
Israel	3	4
Egypt, Arab Rep.	3	1
United Arab Emirates	2	4
Tunisia	1	0
Qatar	1	0
Oman	1	4
Lebanon	1	1
Djibouti	1	1
Bahrain	1	0

Sources: World Bank, using data from International Groundwater Resources Assessment Centre (IGRAC); and Transboundary Freshwater Disputes Database, Oregon State University.

designed to be inclusive of all types of basin stakeholders, ensuring that vulnerable groups are incorporated.

A good example of cooperation in managing transboundary groundwater comes from the North-Western Sahara Aquifer System. This is a very large aquifer with considerable nonrenewable groundwater resources shared by Algeria, Libya, and Tunisia. In the 1980s, the three countries came together to cooperate on technical aspects related to evaluating the extent of the groundwater reserves and aquifer characteristics. Building on these findings and under the supervision of the Observatoire du Sahara et du Sahel, the three countries are developing institutional frameworks to share information and are establishing monitoring indicators and legal mechanisms for cooperation (Tropp and Jägerskog 2006).

Regional collaboration over transboundary surface water resources also is occurring. In 2013, senior Palestinian, Jordanian, and Israeli representatives signed a memorandum of understanding to support three major water sharing initiatives, including the development and use of a new desalination plant in Aqaba, Jordan, and increased releases of water by

MAP 2.14

Transboundary River Basins in the Middle East and North Africa

IBRD 42541 | APRIL 2017

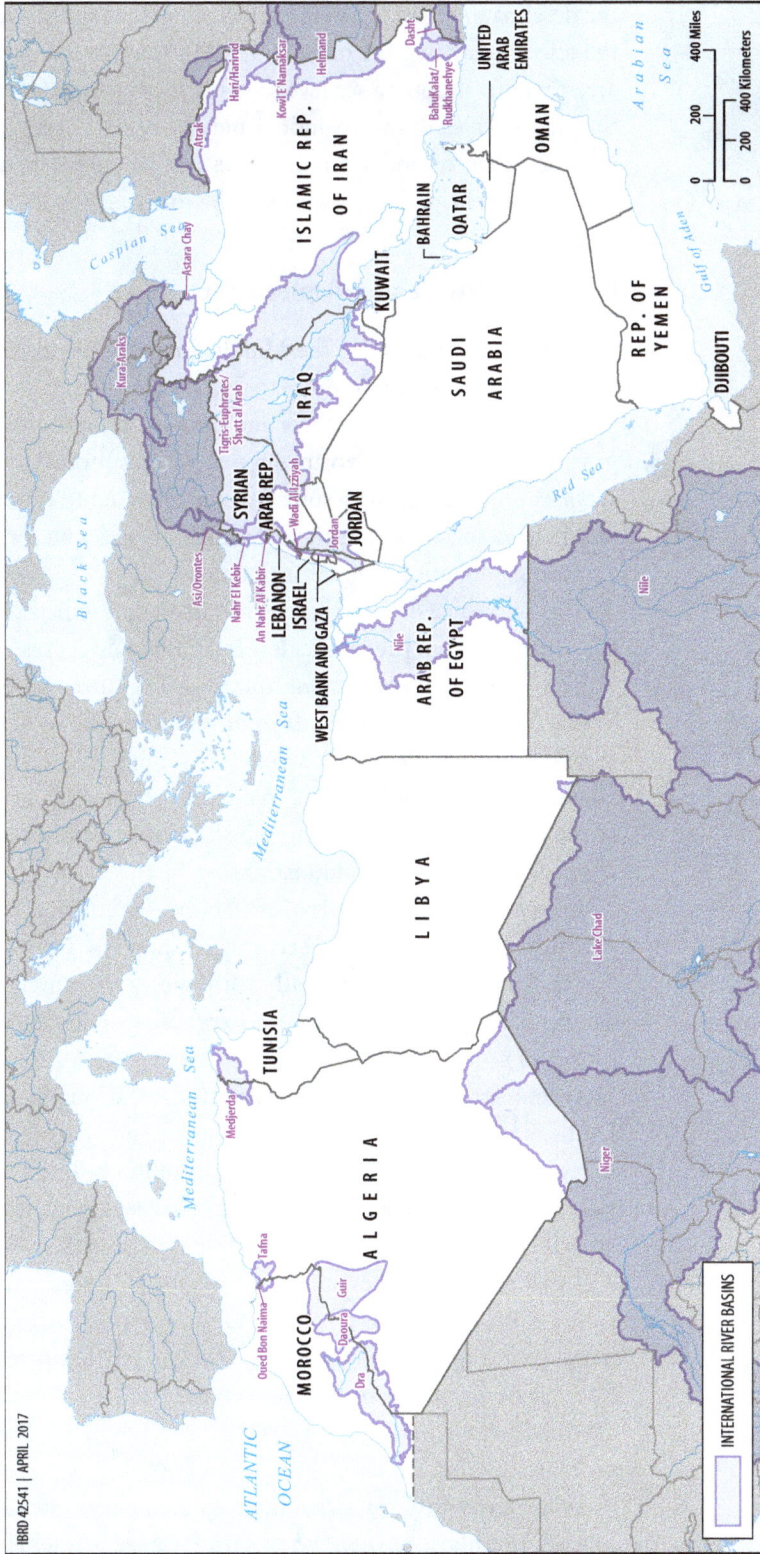

Source: Transboundary Freshwater Disputes Database, Oregon State University.

Israel from Lake Tiberias for use in Jordan. In addition, a pipeline from the desalination plant in Aqaba will convey brine to the Dead Sea to study the effects of mixing the brine with Dead Sea water as part of a scheme to arrest rapidly dropping sea levels.[24] Still, these new areas of cooperation in the Jordan River Basin are limited and not all-encompassing. Notably, the memorandum of understanding does not include Lebanon and Syria—two of the five riparian countries of the Jordan River Basin.

Fragility, Conflict and Displacement

Conflict and instability in the Middle East and North Africa are causing widespread damage to human lives, physical infrastructure, and governance systems. Conflicts and ensuing refugee crises compromise governments' abilities to manage water resources and deliver water services. In turn, this widespread damage has led to increased impacts of unsafe access to water supply and sanitation and widespread degradation and overexploitation of water resources.

The incidence of waterborne infections in conflict-affected countries has increased from preconflict levels. This is a direct result of the damage inflicted on water institutions and infrastructure, as well as the forced displacement of individuals. In Iraq, the Republic of Yemen, and Syria, access to safe drinking water supply and sanitation declined by as much as 70 percent (UN-Water 2015). In conflict-affected Gaza, only 10 percent of the population has access to piped, potable water because of groundwater depletion and contamination.

Water supply and sanitation facilities are often targeted during conflicts (ICRC 2015). Terrorist groups in the Middle East and North Africa have intentionally withheld or disrupted access to water, using water as a weapon or as a bargaining chip during negotiations (box 2.17).

Water security will be particularly precarious in fragile contexts. Unmanaged water scarcity leads to degradation of resources and a decline in regional agricultural prospects and livelihoods. Physical water scarcity, water shocks, unequal access to resources, and poor water services can contribute to displacement in already-fragile contexts. This is not to suggest that an environmental exodus related to water insecurity will take place—although it has been a factor in rural-urban migration in many places in the region. Rather it suggests that providing equitable water services, protecting from water-related disasters, and preserving adequate water resources can help prevent forced displacement and promote stability.

Water insecurity can drive the displacement of populations, and displaced populations can compound water insecurity. Temporary

BOX 2.17

The Weaponization of Water

The International Committee of the Red Cross (ICRC) has observed that water supply and sanitation infrastructure have been directly targeted during recent and ongoing armed conflicts in the Middle East and North Africa. Targeting water infrastructure during war has the immediate impact of leaving millions of people without safe access to water services. At the same time, it has the long-term impact of either causing significant or permanent damage to critical infrastructure or leading to long-term infrastructure deficits that cannot be easily addressed during and following an armed conflict, when financial resources are particularly limited. The ICRC has also observed how access to essential water supplies has been used as a "bargaining chip" during negotiations.

Recent conflicts in the Middle East and North Africa have also been characterized by water being used as a weapon to inflict direct or tactical damage on opponents. Swain and Jägerskog (2016) note that the use of water as weapon in the region "opens up new security challenges with repercussions on food security but also the risk that can be incurred by creating flooding events, potentially of catastrophic nature." A pronounced example of this was the brief takeover in August 2014 by Daesh of the Mosul Dam, which stores around 11 million cubic meters of water and produces a significant amount of energy. That takeover gave rise to fears that Mosul as well as Baghdad could be flooded by the intentional destruction of the dam.

Sources: ICRC 2015; and Swain and Jägerskog 2016.

displacement is a common response to short-term, adverse hydroclimatic conditions, such as floods or droughts. Chronic water scarcity can also lead to permanent displacement. For instance, a World Bank study of climate change, extreme weather events, and migration in five Middle Eastern and North African countries (Algeria, Egypt, Morocco, Syria, and the Republic of Yemen) found evidence of permanent displacement in response to climatic changes (Wodon et al. 2014).

These temporary or permanent population shifts can place abrupt and unanticipated burdens on water management in host communities. As displaced persons struggle to meet their needs, scarcity and conflict can lead to conflict within migrant groups and between migrants and their hosts. These trends can also weaken the social contract between affected communities and the government, as they attribute their vulnerabilities to inadequate action by authorities to mitigate these issues. These trends in turn can fuel fragility.

Water scarcity was a driver of significant internal displacement in Iraq. In 2012, the International Organization for Migration (IOM) reported that 11 percent of the internally displaced people in Iraq migrated from their place of origin because of water scarcity. In some Iraqi governorates, specifically those around the Mesopotamian marshes in the south, migration induced by water scarcity far exceeded migration related to security, conflicts, or a lack of employment opportunities (IOM 2012). In the Muthanna governorate, 94 percent of the assessed internally displaced persons were displaced for reasons related to water scarcity (UNESCO Iraq Office 2014, 92), as shown in panel a of map 2.15. Temporary migration is a common response to water scarcity, yet evidence from IOM's study suggests that water scarcity is also one of the main factors keeping displaced people from returning to their place of origin (map 2.15, panel b).

Population displacement also has significant impacts on water security in host communities. Forced displacement of Syrians to Jordan, Lebanon, and Turkey has increased water demand and generated more sewage and waste. In Lebanon, for instance, the annual per capita water availability has dropped some 225 m³ (a 25 percent drop) because of the arrival of forcefully displaced people from Syria (Jägerskog and Swain 2016).

Importing Water Security as Virtual Water

Middle Eastern and North African countries are net importers of virtual water. *Virtual water* is the water needed to produce a particular commodity. Using this concept of water embedded in products, scholars have analyzed the virtual water flows between countries—that is, the volume of virtual water "flowing" with traded products (Allan 2001).

Seven countries in the region are ranked among the top 30 importers of virtual water globally: Egypt, Saudi Arabia, Algeria, the Islamic Republic of Iran, Israel, Jordan, and Tunisia (Hoekstra and Hung 2002). The level of virtual water leaving the region is far lower. No Middle Eastern or North African country is among the top 30 exporters of virtual water.

Virtual water trading contributes to food security. Virtual water trading is a viable option, however, only where local incomes are high enough to afford imports to cover water and food scarcity (McLaughlin and Kinzelbach 2015). When regional and individual incomes are inadequate, as in Libya and the Republic of Yemen, virtual water trading (except in the form of food aid) is not an option, and local resources can become rapidly depleted.

MAP 2.15

Percentage of Internally Displaced People Citing Water Scarcity as the Main Reason for Preventing Their Return to Their Place of Origin, Iraq

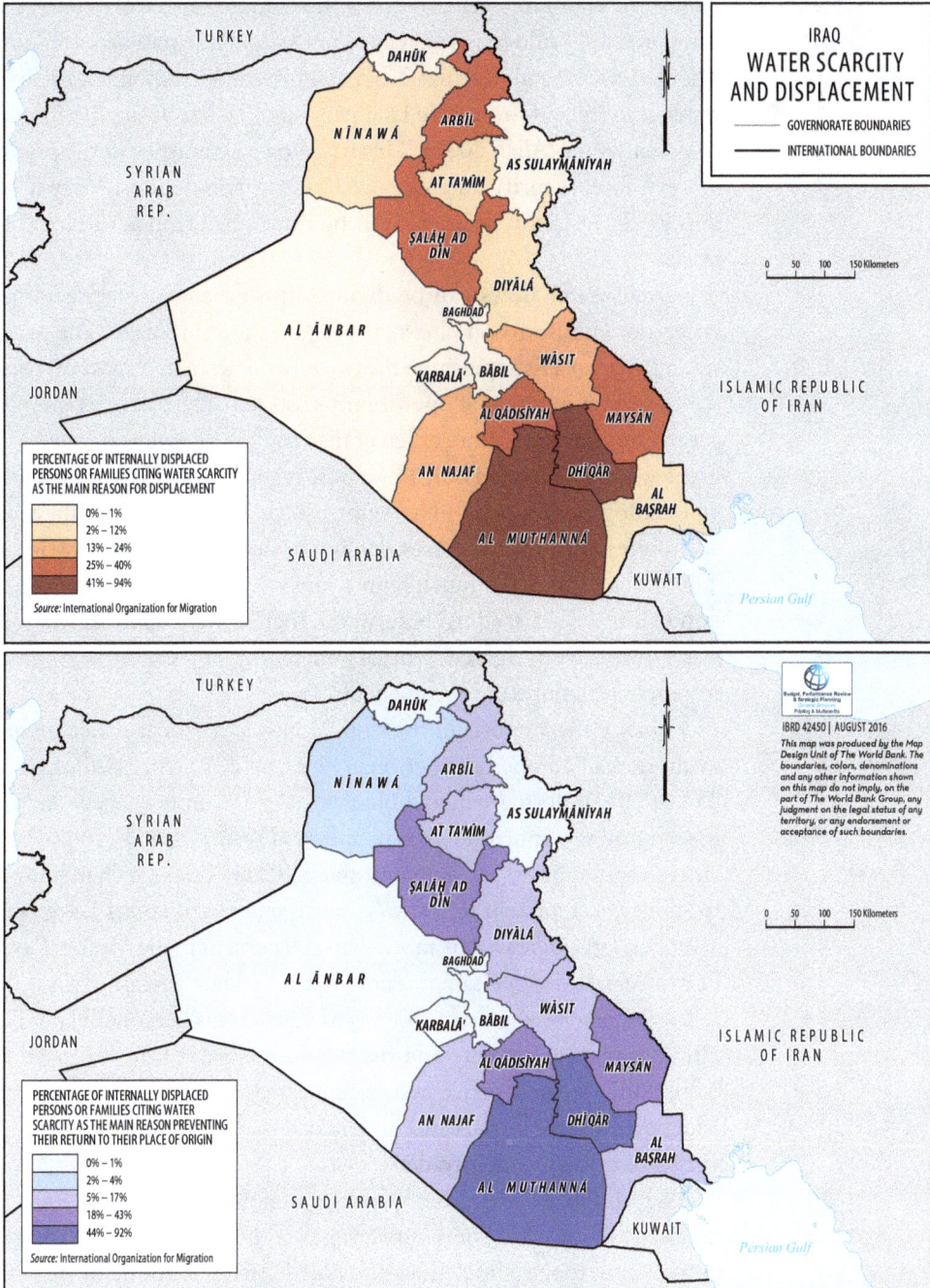

Source: Adopted from IOM 2012 and UNESCO Iraq Office 2014.

The Middle East and North Africa region is the world's largest importer of wheat. In 2010, the region imported 65.8 million tons of cereals, compared to 58.8 million tons in far more populous Asia (Solh 2014). On a per capita basis, the difference between these two regions is huge: 170 kilograms per capita for the Middle East and North Africa, compared to 25 kilograms per capita for Asia. These statistics suggest that Middle Eastern and North African countries have responded to physical water scarcity and low arable land per capita by becoming net importers of virtual water (Allan 2001). This has allowed countries in the region to achieve food security and support growing populations. Virtual water imports have partly been enabled by downward trends in global food prices.

Virtual water flows can be divided into green water (precipitation water stored in soil) and blue water (liquid water in surface and ground-water systems). Distinguishing the two types of water is important because the two differ in terms of opportunity costs and alternative uses. Trading green virtual water is more efficient than trading blue virtual water. While green water can be used only to support vegetation growth in agricultural and ecological systems, blue water can be used to meet other, more economically productive uses, including domestic and industrial uses. Thus, blue water has a much higher opportunity cost. Given this higher opportunity cost, trading blue water that is embedded in low-value, water-intensive irrigated crops is an inefficient use of scarce water resources (Gilmont and Antonelli 2013).

Virtual water imports in the Middle East and North Africa increased by more than 150 percent between 1986 and 2010 (Antonelli, Laio, and Tamea 2017). Both green and blue virtual water imports have increased in response to population growth and food security needs. In 2010, blue virtual water imports amounted to about 20 km^3/year, which is equivalent to about one-fourth of the Nile's discharge before it enters Lake Nasser. Water exports increased by more than 300 percent in the Middle East and North Africa over the same period, but have been declining since 2010, following new food polices and export restrictions (Antonelli and Tamea 2015). Increasing scarcity and reallocation of water from irrigated agriculture to more productive uses in some areas of the world, including the Middle East and North Africa, might lead to reductions in the amount of virtual blue water that is traded.

The Middle East and North Africa import virtual water from every region of the world. The United States is the single largest exporter of virtual water to the Middle East and North Africa, followed by Argentina, Australia, and Brazil (Antonelli and Tamea 2015), as shown in map 2.16. Egypt is the seventh-largest importer of blue virtual water traded in the world (Antonelli and Tamea 2015).

IBRD 43080 | AUGUST 2017

MAP 2.16

Net Virtual Water Trade with the Middle East and North Africa, by World Region, 2015

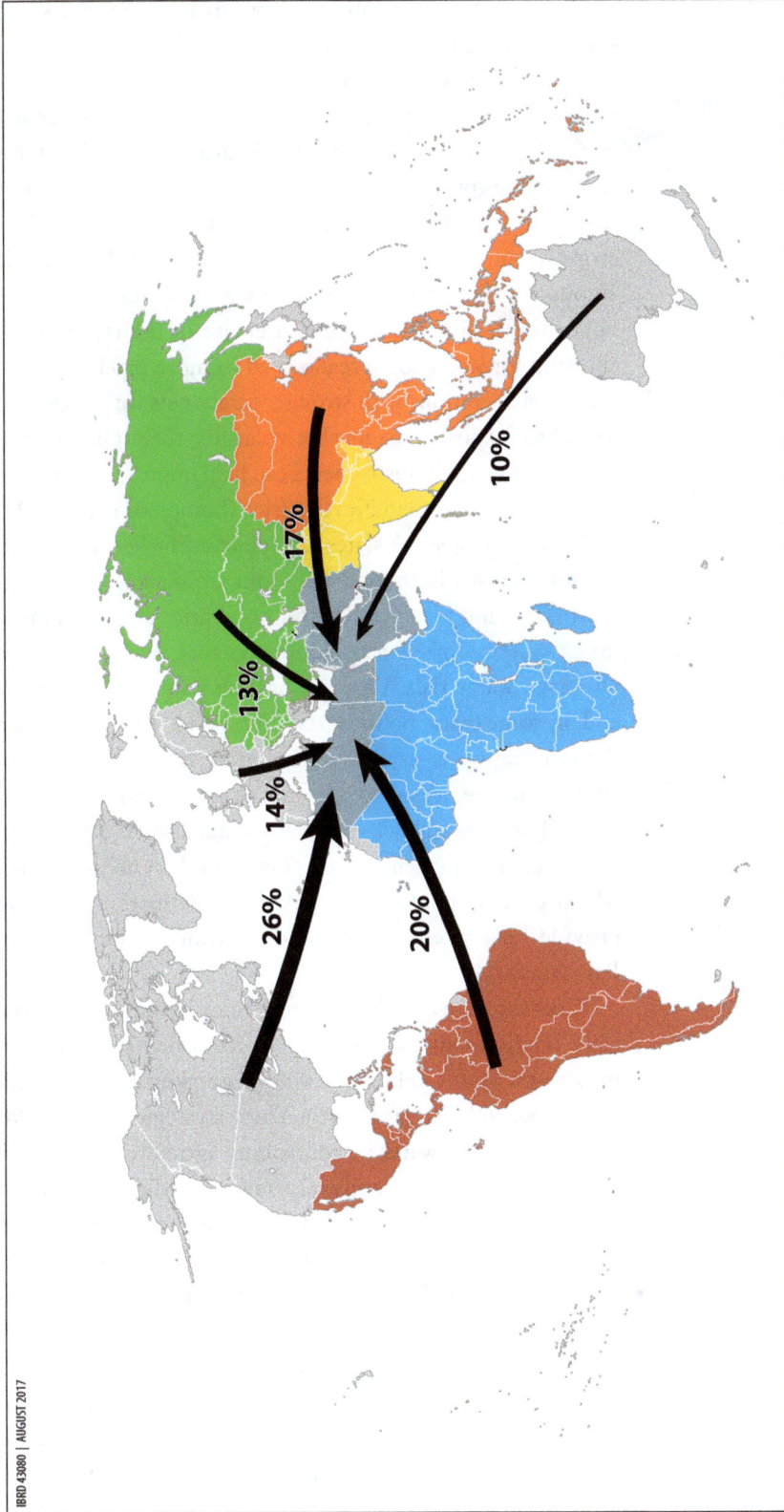

Source: World Bank, with data from Antonelli and Tamea 2015.

Note: Thickness of the arrow denotes relative amount of water imported to the Middle East and North Africa from that region.

Virtual water is an important tool to achieve water security in water-scarce countries and reduce blue water use in the Middle East and North Africa. In areas where freshwater resources are severely limited, virtual water trade has the potential to alleviate regional water scarcity (Konar et al. 2011) and strengthen food security. Trade of water embedded in commodities provides a conduit for water resources to be transferred to the water stressed Middle East and North Africa region. Given that many crops in the region are produced using more than the global average amount of blue water, expanding virtual water imports could provide opportunities to reduce blue water use in the region (Gilmont 2015), allowing for water to be reallocated to more productive uses. Balancing these considerations with stronger safety nets for the poor and strategies to reduce exposure to market volatility through better use of supply chains and financial instruments can help improve water and food security in the Middle East and North Africa (Lampietti et al. 2011).

Nonetheless, some states are reluctant to become too dependent on imports because both food and water are seen as issues of national security (Swain and Jägerskog 2016). Food price shocks, transportation, and other systemic risks can hamper virtual water trade, generating an imported water risk. This risk has the potential to affect food security and, in some cases, political stability. Water-rich countries could reduce their virtual water exports in the future because of population growth, climate change pressures, or other protectionist measures (Suweis et al. 2012). Food price shocks can lead to increases in demonstrations against the government (such as food riots) and discontent toward institutions, which may be perceived as taking inadequate action to protect and provide for citizens (Arezki and Bruckner 2011; Lagi, Bertrand, and Bar-Yam 2011).

Risks associated with imported water have led some countries, especially oil-rich countries, to invest in acquiring large blocks of arable land in foreign states (Hallam 2009; Jägerskog et al. 2012; Sandström, Jägerskog, and Ostigard 2016). These strategies seek to address the risks related to virtual water by controlling agricultural production in water-rich countries. They mainly rely on foreign direct investment in agricultural land in developing countries to secure long-term food supplies. Offsetting imported water risk by acquiring land has the potential to contribute to food security in water-scarce regions (Grindle, Siddiqi, and Anandan 2015). However, this practice has the potential to increase local conflict in areas where land is being acquired. Evidence from large-scale land acquisitions suggests the practice is a threat to lives and livelihoods of rural communities in these locations. It may also affect transboundary relations between countries that share a surface or groundwater resource.

Summary

Climate change will increase water stress in the Middle East and North Africa. Water is the primary medium through which the impacts of climate change will be felt. Climate projections point toward a drier and hotter Middle East and North Africa region, where increasing water stress could reduce GDP growth rates between 6 and 14 percent by 2050 (World Bank 2016). Not only will climate change lead to less water in many areas, it will also increase variability in terms of when rain occurs, thus presenting added challenges for the region's agriculture.

Climate change will also intensify flood and drought risks (Hoerling et al. 2012; Kelley et al. 2015). More severe and intense droughts are expected as a consequence of climate change. Climate change and development close to coastlines and surface water bodies are increasing flood risks in the Middle East and North Africa. Low-lying coastal areas, such as the Nile and Shatt-al-Arab Deltas, are particularly vulnerable to sea-level rise. Improved forecast and early warning systems can help reduce the impacts of droughts and floods. This will entail investing in monitoring and data archiving systems, but also developing transmission protocols to ensure that forecasts reach all users in actionable formats. Responding to droughts and floods will also require contingency plans.

Managing water-related risks will also entail managing trade-offs and unintended consequences in the interrelated energy and food sectors. The reliance of the water sector on energy for desalination is just one example of the risks arising from the water-energy-food nexus and the need to account for linkages among multiple sectors when addressing water security.

Many countries in the region rely heavily on freshwater resources originating outside their boundaries. In the face of increasing demand and scarcity, some of these shared resources are being exploited to their full potential. Constructive, transparent, and equitable relationships for transboundary water resources are essential to ensure that these shared resources are exploited fairly and to the benefit of all parties concerned. Cases of cooperation are emerging in the region, offering useful examples of frameworks for technical and institutional cooperation. Nonetheless, transboundary relations are coupled with political challenges and conflicts in the region, with significant power imbalances often leading to unequal outcomes. Moreover, governments can often overlook the needs of marginalized groups in these negotiations, potentially resulting in unintended negative consequences. For all these reasons, inclusive and equitable sharing of transboundary water should become a priority.

Fragility and political instability challenge recent progress in water security. At the same time, water security has a role to play in reducing risks related to fragility and political instability. The lack of appropriate responses to water-related disasters or failure to provide water services can generate widespread discontent, weakening the social contract. This, in turn, can make it more difficult for weak governments with little credibility to address water security challenges, thus reinforcing a vicious circle of water insecurity and instability. Strategic investments in water security can break this cycle, contributing to stability and resilience in the face of socioeconomic changes.

Virtual water can alleviate regional water scarcity; however, its related risks need to be managed. The Middle East and North Africa region is the world's largest importer of wheat, and seven Middle Eastern and North African countries are among the top 30 food importing countries in the world. Food price shocks, transportation disruptions, and other systemic risks can impede virtual water trade, generating new water and food security risks in Middle Eastern and North African countries and economies. Furthermore, as significant parts of the population are depending for their livelihoods on agriculture, it is important to increase economic diversification to allow for a continued reallocation of water from agriculture to sectors that use less water per unit of value produced (Allan 2001).

Notes

1. Data from WRI and Veolia Water and IFPRI (2011).
2. http://www.fao.org/docrep/005/y4502e/y4502e04.htm.
3. http://www.fao.org/nr/water/aquastat/countries_regions/Profile_segments /LBY-WU_eng.stm.
4. USGS (U.S. Geological Survey), Groundwater Depletion. https://water .usgs.gov/edu/gwdepletion.html.
5. AQUASTAT definition.
6. FAO 2015, Productivity. http://www.fao.org/nr/water/topics_productivity .html.
7. A range of methods exist to measure water productivity. This report uses an accounting-based measure of water productivity that takes the ratio between GDP and total freshwater withdrawal. For an initial discussion of other metrics to measure water productivity, see Scheierling and Treguer (2016).
8. http://www.fao.org/docrep/006/y4525e/y4525e06.htm.
9. This means a fee to cover the costs of service delivery and provision.
10. It should be noted that this survey's sample is not representative. It is heavily weighted toward men over women and to middle- and high-income respondents. This makeup probably occurred because the survey was voluntary, conducted without interviewers, done online, and promoted via newspapers.
11. Based on World Resources Institute Aqueduct data.

12. Spate irrigation is an irrigation practice whereby flash floods (or spates) from mountainous catchments are channeled through canals to retention basins and irrigable fields. Spate irrigation is characterized by the arid environment in which it takes place, the unpredictability of the flash floods, and the high sediment loads of the waters (Van Steenbergen 2010).

13. See advances in small-scale solar desalination technologies based on plasmonics (Zhou et al. 2016).

14. http://www.isdb.org/irj/go/km/docs/documents/IDBDevelopments /Attachments/Projects/s18_OmanWater.pdf.

15. http://unstats.un.org/sdgs/indicators/indicators-list/.

16. SciDevNet. 2015. "Iraq Cholera Outbreak Threatens Region." http://www .scidev.net/global/disease/news/iraq-cholera-outbreak-threatens-region .html.

17. Oxfam International (2016), "Two-Thirds of People in Conflict-Hit Yemen without Clean Water." May 26 press release. https://www.oxfam.org/en /pressroom/pressreleases/2015-05-26/two-thirds-people-conflict-hit -yemen-without-clean-water.

18. For a complete explanation of how these estimates were generated, see Sadoff et al. (2015).

19. Data from the International Food Policy Research Institute's IMPACT model.

20. On-site source separation entails passing toilet waste (referred to as black water) to a separate tank in the household for collection. All other wastewater generated in the household (from showering, washing, laundering), commonly referred to as greywater, is conveyed to either a decentralized or centralized unit for rapid treatment. Separating the two streams of wastewater allows for the greywater to be rapidly treated and reused, given the lower levels of contaminants and undesirable substances in it.

21. USDA database, World Agricultural Production, Foreign Agricultural Service. http://usda.mannlib.cornell.edu/MannUsda/viewDocumentInfo. do?documentID=1860,

22. World Bank, Climate Change Knowledge Portal. http://sdwebx.worldbank .org/climateportal/.

23. Work from the World Bank in Tunisia.

24. World Bank, December 9, 2013, Press Release: "Senior Israeli, Jordanian and Palestinian Representatives Sign Milestone Water Sharing Agreement."

Bibliography

ACWUA (Arab Countries Water Utilities Association). 2014. *Water Utilities Reform in the Arab Region: Lessons Learned and Guiding Principles.* Amman: ACWUA.

———. 2015. *Water Supply and Sanitation Services in the Arab Region (MDG+ Initiative) First Report.* Amman: ACWUA.

Al-Ansari, N. A. 2013. "Management of Water Resources in Iraq: Perspectives and Prognoses." *Engineering* 5 (8): 667–84.

Al-Maktoumi, A., S. Zekri, and M. El Rawy. 2016. "Managed Aquifer Recharge Using Treated Wastewater: An Option to Manage a Coastal Aquifer in Oman for Better Domestic Water Supply." EGU General Assembly 2016, Vienna.

Allan, J. A. 2001. *The Middle East Water Questions: Hydropolitics and the Global Economy*. London: I. B. Tauris.

Almasri, M. N. 2008. "Assessment of Intrinsic Vulnerability to Contamination for Gaza Coastal Aquifer, Palestine." *Journal of Environmental Management* 88: 577–93.

Almohsen, R. A. 2015. "Thousands Die in Yemen in Fights over Water." *SciDevNet*. http://www.scidev.net/global/water/news/water-death-yemen -conflict.html.

Al-Zyoud, S., W. Rühaak, E. Forootan, and I. Sass. 2015. "Over-Exploitation of Groundwater in the Centre of Amman Zarqa Basin–Jordan: Evaluation of Well Data and Grace Satellite Observations." *Resources* 4 (4): 819–30.

Antonelli, M., F. Laio, and S. Tamea. 2017. "Water Resources, Food Security and the Role of Virtual Water Trade in the MENA Region." In *Governance of Environmental Change within a Human Security Perspective*, edited by M. Behnassi. New York: Springer.

Antonelli, M., and S. Tamea. 2015. "Food-Water Security and Virtual Water Trade in the Middle East and North Africa." *International Journal of Water Resources Development* 31 (3): 326–42.

Ardakanian, R., and J. L. Martin-Bordes, eds. 2010. *Proceedings of the 3rd Regional Activity on Non-Revenue Water Management: Solutions for Drinking Water Loss Reduction*. Arab Countries 3rd ACWUA Best Practices Conference, January 20–21, Rabat. Proceedings No. 5-UNW-DPC Publication Series.

Arezki, R., and M. Bruckner. 2011. "Food Prices and Political Instability." IMF Working Paper 11/62, International Monetary Fund, Washington, DC.

AWC (Arab Water Council). 2011. "Water Reuse in the Arab World: From Principle to Practice." Summary of Proceedings of the Expert Consultation on Wastewater Management in the Arab World. Dubai.

———. 2012. *2nd Arab State of the Water 2012 Report*. Arab Water Council (AWC) and Centre for Environment and Development for the Arab Region and Europe (CEDARE).

———. 2014. *3rd Arab Water Forum, Together towards a Secure Arab Water*. Final Report. Cairo: AWC.

Aylward, B., H. Seely, R. Hartwell, and J. Dengel. 2010. "The Economic Value of Water for Agricultural, Domestic and Industrial Uses: A Global Compilation of Economic Studies and Market Prices." Prepared for UN FAO by Ecosystem Economics.

Baghvand, A. T. Nasrabadi, G. N. Bidhendi, A. Vosoogh, and N. Mehrdadi. 2010. "Groundwater Quality Degradation of an Aquifer in Iran Central Desert." *Desalination* 260 (1–3): 264–75.

Banerjee, A., R. Bhavnani, C. H. Burtonboy, O. Hamad, A. Linares-Rivas Barandiaran, S. Safaie, D. Tewari, and A. Zanon. 2014. "Natural Disasters in the Middle East and North Africa: A Regional Overview." Working Paper 81658, Global Facility for Disaster Reduction and Recovery (GFDRR), World Bank, Washington, DC.

Barnes, J. 2014. "Mixing Waters: The Reuse of Agricultural Drainage Water in Egypt." *Geoforum* 57: 181–91.

Bashitialshaeer, R.A.I., K. M. Persson, and M. Aljaradin. 2011. "Estimated Future Salinity in the Arabian Gulf, the Mediterranean Sea and the Red Sea: Consequences of Brine Discharge from Desalination." *International Journal of Academic Research* 3 (1): 133–40.

Bazza, M. 2003. "Wastewater Recycling and Reuse in the Near East Region: Experience and Issues." *Water Science and Technology: Water Supply* 3 (4): 33–50.

Berglöf, E., and S. Devarajan. 2015. "Water for Development: Fulfilling the Promise." In *Water for Development: Charting a Water Wise Path*, edited by A. Jägerskog, T. J. Clausen, T. Holmgren, and K. Lexén. Report 35. Stockholm: Stockholm International Water Institute (SIWI).

Brixi, H., E. Lust, and M. Woolcock. 2015. *Trust, Voice, and Incentives: Learning from Local Success Stories in Service Delivery in the Middle East and North Africa.* Washington, DC: World Bank.

Bushnak, A. 2010. "Desalination." In *Arab Water: Sustainable Management of a Scarce Resource*, edited by M. El-Ashry, N. Saab, and B. Zeitoon. Beirut: Arab Forum for Environment and Development.

Closas, A., and E. Rap. 2017. "Solar-Based Groundwater Pumping for Irrigation: Sustainability, Policies and Limitations." *Energy Policy* 104: 33–37.

Comair, G. F., P. Gupta, C. Ingenloff, G. Shin, and D. C. McKinney. 2013. "Water Resources Management in the Jordan River Basin." *Water and Environment* 27 (4): 495–504.

Commander, S. J., Z. S. Nikoloski, and M. Vagliasindi. 2015. "Estimating the Size of External Effects of Energy Subsidies in Transport and Agriculture." Policy Research Working Paper WPS 7227, World Bank, Washington, DC.

Cook, B. I., K. J. Anchukaitis, R. Touchan, D. M. Meko, and E. R. Cook. 2016. "Spatiotemporal Drought Variability in the Mediterranean over the Last 900 Years." *Journal of Geophysics Research Atmospheres* 121: 2060–74.

Dawoud, M. A., and M. M. Al Mulla. 2012. "Environmental Impacts of Seawater Desalination: Arabian Gulf Case Study." *International Journal of Environment and Sustainability* 1 (3): 22–37.

De Châtel, F. 2014. "The Role of Drought and Climate Change in the Syrian Uprising: Untangling the Triggers of the Revolution." *Middle Eastern Studies* 50 (4): 521–35. doi: 10.1080/00263206.2013.850076.

Dubrovský, M., M. Hayes, P. Duce, M. Trnka, M. Svoboda, and P. Zara. 2014. "Multi-GCM Projections of Future Drought and Climate Variability Indicators for the Mediterranean Region." *Regional Environmental Change* 14 (5): 1907–19.

El-Hajj, R., N. Farajalla, T. Terpstra, and A. Jägerskog. 2017. "Middle East and North Africa: A Case for Regional Cooperation Water-Energy-Food Security Nexus." Policy Brief, Planetary Security Initiative 2 (3).

EcoPeace. 2015. "Regional NGO Master Plan for Sustainable Development in the Jordan Valley." http://foeme.org/www/?module=projects&record_id=205.

Esfandiari-Baiat, M., and G. Rahbar. 2005. "Monitoring of Inflow and Outflow Rate from Kaftari Artificial Recharge of Groundwater System in Dorz-Sayban Region in South-eastern Iran." In *Strategies for Managed Aquifer Recharge (MAR) in Semi-Arid Areas*, edited by Ian Gale. Paris: UNESCO IHP (International Hydological Programme).

Falkenmark, M., and A. Jägerskog. 2010. "Sustainability of Transnational Water Agreements in the Face of Socio-Economic and Environmental Change." In *Transboundary Water Management: Principles and Practice*, edited by A. Earle, A. Jägerskog, and J. Öjendal. London: Earthscan.

Falkenmark, M., and J. Rockström. 2006. "The New Blue and Green Water Paradigm: Breaking New Ground for Water Resources Planning and Management." *Journal of Water Resources Planning and Management*, May–June, 129.

Famiglietti, J. 2015. "The Global Groundwater Crisis." *Nature Climate Change* 4: 945–48.

FAO (Food and Agricultural Organization of the United Nations). 2011. *Global Food Losses and Waste: Extent, Causes and Prevention*. Rome: FAO.

———. 2015. "Water News: Climate Change & Water: Main Findings and Short- and Medium-Term Recommendations." http://www.fao.org/nr/water /news/clim-change.html.

Fawzi, N. A.-M., K. P. Goodwin, B. A. Mahdi, and M. L. Stevens 2016. "Effects of Mesopotamian Marsh Desiccation on the Cultural Knowledge and Livelihood of Marsh Arab Women." *Ecosystem Health and Sustainability* 2 (3): e01207.

Foster, S., F. van Steenbergen, J. Zuleta, and H. Garduno. 2010. *Conjunctive Use of Groundwater and Surface Water from Spontaneous Coping Strategy to Adaptive Resource Management*. GW MATE Strategic Overview Series 2. Washington, DC: World Bank.

Fuente, D., J. Gakii Gatua, M. Ikiara, J. Kabubo-Mariara, M. Mwaura, and D. Whittington. 2016. "Water and Sanitation Service Delivery, Pricing, and the Poor: An Empirical Estimate of Subsidy Incidence in Nairobi, Kenya." *Water Resources Research* 52: 4845–62.

Gale, Ian, ed. 2005. *Strategies for Managed Aquifer Recharge (MAR) in Semi-Arid Areas*. Paris: UNESCO IHP (International Hydological Programme).

García, L. D. J. Rodriquez, M. Wijnen, and I. Pakulski, eds. 2016. *Earth Observation for Water Resources Management: Current Use and Future Opportunities for the Water Sector*. Washington, DC: World Bank Group.

García, N., I. Harrison, N. Cox, and M. F. Tognelli. 2015. *The Status and Distribution of Freshwater Biodiversity in the Arabian Peninsula*. Arlington, VA: IUCN.

Garnier, J., A. Beusen, V. Thieu, and G. Billen. 2010. "N:P:Si Nutrient Export Ratios and Ecological Consequences in Coastal Seas Evaluated by the ICEP Approach." *Global Biogeochemical Cycles* 24 (4). doi: 10.1029/2009GB003583.

Gassert, F., M. Luck, M. Landis, P. Reig, and T. Shiao. 2014. "Aqueduct Global Maps 2.1: Constructing Decision-Relevant Global Water Risk Indicators." Working Paper, World Resources Institute, Washington, DC.

Gelil, I. A. 2014. "Proposal for an Arab Strategic Framework for Sustainable Development, 2015–2025." Arab High-Level Forum on Sustainable Development, Amman, April 2–4. Economic and Social Commission for Western Asia (ESCWA), United Nations.

GFDRR (Global Facility for Disaster Reduction and Recovery). 2016. "Managing Drought and Sustaining Growth in Djibouti." Stories of Impact. https://www .gfdrr.org/sites/default/files/publication/Djibouti.pdf.

Ghaffour, N., T. M. Missimer, and G. L. Amy. 2013. "Technical Review and Evaluation of the Economics of Water Desalination: Current and Future Challenges for Better Supply Sustainability." *Desalination* 309 (15): 197–207.

Gilmont, M. 2015. "Water Resource Decoupling in MENA through Food Trade as a Mechanism for Circumventing National Water Scarcity." *Food Security* 7 (6): 1113–31.

Gilmont, M., and M. Antonelli. 2013. "Analyse to Optimise: Sustainable Intensification of Agricultural Production through Investment in Integrated

Land and Water Management in Africa." In *Handbook of Land and Water Grabs in Africa: Foreign Direct Investment and Food and Water Security*, edited by J. A. Allan, M. Keulertz, S. Sojamo, and J. Warner, 403–15. Abingdon, UK: I.B. Tauris.

GIZ (Deutsche Gesellschaft für Internationale Zusammenarbei). 2014. "Guidelines for Water Loss Reduction: A Focus on Pressure Management." https://www.giz.de/fachexpertise/downloads/giz2011-en-guideline-water -loss-reduction.pdf.

Gleeson, T., Y. Wada, M. F. P. Bierkens, L. P. H. van Beek. 2012. "Water Balance of Global Aquifers Revealed by Groundwater Footprint." *Nature* 488: 197–200.

Global Water Intelligence. 2016. "Global Water Market 2017: Meeting the World's Water and Wastewater Needs until 2020." Global Water Intelligence, Oxford.

Goode, D. J., L. A. Senior, A. Subah, and A. Jaber. 2013. *Groundwater-Level Trends and Forecasts, and Salinity Trends, in the Azraq, Dead Sea, Hammad, Jordan Side Valleys, Yarmouk, and Zarqa Groundwater Basins, Jordan.* Open-File Report 2013–1061 prepared in cooperation with the U.S. Agency for International Development and the U.S. Army Corps of Engineers.

Gorelick, S. M., and C. Zheng. 2015. "Global Change and the Groundwater Management Challenges." *Water Resources Research* 51 (5): 3031–51.

Grindle, A. K., A. Siddiqi, and L. D. Anandan. 2015. "Food Security amidst Water Scarcity: Insights on Sustainable Food Production from Saudi Arabia." *Sustainable Production and Consumption* 2 (April): 67–78.

Guillame, D., R. Zytek, and M.R. Farzin. 2011. "Iran: The Chronicles of the Subsidy Reform." IMF Working Paper WP/11/167, International Monetary Fund, Washington, DC.

Hall, J. W., D. Grey, D. Garrick, F. Fung, C. Brown, S. J. Dadson, and C. W. Sadoff. 2014. "Coping with the Curse of Freshwater Variability: Institutions, Infrastructure, and Information for Adaptation." *Science* 346 (6208): 429–30.

Hallam, D. 2009. "Foreign Investment in Developing Country Agriculture: Issues, Policy Implications and International Response." Paper prepared for the OECD Global Forum on International Investment, December 7–8.

Hallegatte, S., M. Bangalore, L. Bonzanigo, M. Fay, T. Kane, U. Narloch, J. Rozenberg, D. Treguer, and A. Vogt-Schilb. 2016. *Shock Waves: Managing the Impacts of Climate Change on Poverty.* Washington, DC: World Bank.

Hallegatte, S., C. Green, R. J. Nicholls, and J. Corfee-Moriot. 2013. "Future Flood Losses in Major Coastal Cities." *Nature Climate Change* 3: 802–06.

Hoekstra, A., and P. Q. Hung. 2002. "Virtual Water Trade: A Quantification of Virtual Water Flows between Nations in Relation to International Crop Trade." Value of Water Research Report Series 11, IHE Delft, Delft, Netherlands.

Hoerling, M., J. Eischeid, J. Perlwitz, X. Quan, T. Zhang, and P. Pegion. 2012. "On the Increased Frequency of Mediterranean Drought." *Journal of Climate* 25: 2146–61. doi: http://dx.doi.org/10.1175/JCLI-D-11-00296.1.

Hope, R., Foster, T., Money, A. and Rouse, M. 2012. "Harnessing Mobile Communications Innovations for Water Security." *Global Policy* 3: 433–42.

Hope, R., and M. Rouse. 2013. "Risks and Responses to Universal Drinking Water Security." *Philosophical Transactions of the Royal Society A* (September) 371: 20120417.

Hussain, I., L. Raschid, M. A. Hanjra, F. Marikar, and W. van der Hoek. 2002. "Wastewater Use in Agriculture: Review of Impacts and Methodological Issues in Valuing Impacts." Working Paper 37, International Water Management Institute, Colombo.

Hutton, G. 2013 "Global Costs and Benefits of Reaching Universal Coverage of Sanitation and Drinking-Water Supply." *Journal of Water and Health* 11 (1): 1–12.

ICBA (International Center for Biosaline Agriculture). 2015. *Innovative Agriculture in Saline and Marginal Environments.* Dubai: ICBA.

ICRC (International Committee of the Red Cross). 2015. *Bled Dry: How War in the Middle East Is Bringing the Region's Water Supplies to Breaking Point.* Geneva: ICRC.

IGRAC (International Groundwater Resources Assessment Centre) and UNESCO-IHP (UNESCO International Hydrological Programme). 2015. *Transboundary Aquifers of the World [map].* Edition 2015. Scale 1: 50 000 000. Delft, Netherlands: IGRAC.

IOM (International Organization for Migration). 2012. *IOM Iraq Special Report: Water Scarcity.* https://environmentalmigration.iom.int/iom-iraq-special -report-water-scarcity.

IPCC (Intergovernmental Panel on Climate Change). 2014. *Climate Change 2014: Impacts, Adaptation, and Vulnerability. Part B: Regional Aspects, Contribution of Working Group II to the Fifth Assessment Report of the Intergovernmental Panel on Climate Change,* 1327–70. Cambridge: Cambridge University Press.

IRENA (International Renewable Energy Agency). 2016. *Solar Pumping for Irrigation: Improving Livelihoods and Sustainability.* Abu Dhabi: IRENA.

Jägerskog, A., A. Cascao, M. Hårsmar, and K. Kim. 2012. "Land Acquisitions: How Will They Impact Transboundary Waters?" Report 30. Stockholm: SIWI. http://www.siwi.org/latest/report-land-acquisitions-how-will-they -impact-transboundary-waters/.

Jägerskog, A., and A. Swain. 2016. "Water, Migration and How They Are Interlinked." Working Paper 27, Stockholm Water Institute (SIWI), Stockholm.

Jarvis, L. S., and J. P. Pétraud. 2013. "Climate Change and Increasing Aridity: The Fate of Agriculture and Rural Communities in the Middle East and North Africa." Paper presented at the Rosenberg International Forum on Water Policy, Aqaba, Jordan, March 24–25.

Jasechko, S. D. Perrone, K. M. Befus, M. Bayani Cardenas, G. Ferguson, T. Gleeson, E. Luijendijk, J. J. McDonnell, et al. 2017. "Global Aquifers Dominated by Fossil Groundwaters but Wells Vulnerable to Modern Contamination." *Nature Geoscience* 10: 425–29. doi:10.1038/ngeo2943.

Jeuland, M. 2015. "Challenges to Wastewater Reuse in the Middle East and North Africa." *Middle East Development Journal* 7: 1–25.

Kaniewski, D., E. Van Campo, and H. Weiss. 2012. "Drought Is a Recurring Challenge in the Middle East." *PNAS (Proceedings of the National Academy of Sciences)* 109 (10): 3862–67.

Kelley, C. P., S. Mohtadi, M. A. Cane, R. Seager, and Y. Kushnir 2015. "Climate Change in the Fertile Crescent and Implications of the Recent Syrian Drought." *PNAS (Proceedings of the National Academy of Sciences)* 112 (11): 3241–46.

Kfouri, C., P. Mantovani, and M. Jeuland. 2009. "Water Reuse in the MENA Region: Constraints, Experiences and Policy Recommendations." In *Water in the Arab World: Management Perspectives and Innovations*, edited by N. V. Jagannathan, A. S. Mohamed, and A. Kremer. Washington, DC: World Bank.

Klein Goldewijk, K., A. Beusen, and P. Janssen. 2010. "Long-Term Dynamic Modeling of Global Population and Built-Up Area in a Spatially Explicit Way, HYDE 3.1." *The Holocene* 20 (4): 565–73. http://dx.doi .org/10.1177/0959683609356587.

Kochhar, K., C. Pattillo, Y. Sun, N. Suphaphiphat, A. Swiston, R. Tchaidze, B. Clements, S. Fabrizio, V. Flamini, L. Redifer, H. Finger, and an IMF Staff Team. 2015. "Is the Glass Half Empty or Half Full? Issues in Managing Water Challenges and Policy Instruments." Staff Discussion Note SDN/15/11, International Monetary Fund, Washington, DC.

Konar, M., C. Dalin, S. Suweis, N. Hanasaki, A. Rinaldo, and I. Rodriques-Iturbe. 2011. "Water for Food: The Global Virtual Water Trade Network." *Water Resources Research* 47 (5). doi: 10.1029/2010WR010307.

Kummu, M., H. de Moel, M. Porkka, S. Siebert, O. Varis, and P. J. Ward. 2012. "Lost Food, Wasted Resources: Global Food Supply Chain Losses and Their Impacts on Freshwater, Cropland and Fertilizer Use." *Science of the Total Environment* 438: 477–89.

Kummu, M., D., Gerten, J., Heinke, M., Konzmann, O., Varis 2014. "Climate-Driven Interannual Variability of Water Scarcity in Food Production Potential: A Global Analysis." *Hydrology and Earth Systems Sciences* 18: 447–61.

Lagi, M., K. Z. Bertrand, and Y. Bar-Yam. 2011. "The Food Crises and Political Instability in North Africa and the Middle East." New England Complex Systems Institute, arXiv:1108.2455 (August 10).

Lampietti, J. A., S. Michaels, N. Magnan, A. F. McCalla, M. Saade, and N. Khouri. 2011. "A Strategic Framework for Improving Food Security in Arab Countries." *Food Security* 3 (Supplement 1): 7–22.

Lange, J., S. Husary, A. Gunkel, D. Bastian, and T. Grodek. 2012. "Potentials and Limits of Urban Rainwater Harvesting in the Middle East." *Hydrology and Earth Systems Sciences* 16: 715–24.

Lelieveld, J., Y. Proestos, P. Hadjinicolaou, M. Tanarhte, E. Tyrlis, and G. Zittis. 2016. "Strongly Increasing Heat Extremes in the Middle East and North Africa (MENA) in the 21st Century." *Climatic Change* 137 (1): 245–60.

Lillywhite, J. 2015. "Jordan: Heavy Rain Causes Flooding Chaos in Amman." *International Business Times*, November 5. http://www.ibtimes.co.uk/jordan -heavy-rain-causes-flooding-chaos-amman-1527402.

Mabrouk, M. B., A. Jonoski, D. Solomatine, and S. Uhlenbrook. 2013. "A Review of Seawater Intrusion in the Nile Delta Groundwater System: The Basis for Assessing Impacts due to Climate Changes and Water Resources Development." *Hydrology and Earth Systems Sciences* 10: 10873–911.

Madani, K. 2014. "Water Management in Iran? What Is Causing the Looming Crisis?" *Journal of Environmental Studies and Sciences* 4 (4): 315–28.

Mateo-Sagasta, J., and P. Salian. 2012. "Global Database on Municipal Wastewater Production, Collection, Treatment, Discharge and Direct Use in Agriculture." FAO (Food and Agricultural Organization) and AQUASTAT.

McLaughlin, D., and W. Kinzelbach. 2015. "Food Security and Sustainable Resource Management." *Water Resources Research* 51: 4966–85.

MDPS (Ministry of Development Planning and Statistics). 2016. *Water Statistics in the State of Qatar 2013.* Doha: Ministry of Development Planning and Statistics.

MENA NWC (Middle East and North Africa Network of Water Centers of Excellence). 2015. *Excellence and Impact of Research.* Amman: MENA NWC.

Misiedjan, D., and H. F. M. W. Van Rijswick. 2015. "A Human Right to Water while the Well Runs Dry: Analyzing the Legal and Regulatory Framework of Yemen Water Law." *Journal of Water Law* 24 (5/6): 199–206.

MOE/EU/UNDP (Ministry of Environment of Lebanon, European Union, and United Nations Development Programme). 2014. "Lebanon Environmental Assessment of the Syrian Conflict and Priority Interventions." http://www .undp.org/content/dam/lebanon/docs/Energy%20and%20Environment /Publications/EASC-WEB.pdf.

Molden, D., T. Y. Oweis, S. Pasquale, J. W. Kijne, M. A. Hanjra, P. S. Bindraban, B. A. M. Bouman, S. Cook, O. Erenstein, H. Farahani, A. Hachum, J. Hoogeveen, H. Mahoo, V. Nangia, D. Peden, A. Sikka, P. Silva, H. Turral, A. Upadhyaya, and S. Zwart. 2007. "Pathways for Increasing Agricultural Productivity." In *Water for Food, Water for Life: A Comprehensive Assessment of Water Management in Agriculture*, edited by D. Molden, 279–310. London: Earthscan and Colombo: International Water Management Institute (IWMI).

Ndaw, M. F. 2015. *Unlocking the Potential of Information Communications Technology to Improve Water and Sanitation Services.* Washington, DC: Water and Sanitation Program, World Bank.

OECD (Organisation for Economic Co-operation and Development). 2015. *Drying Wells, Rising Stakes: Towards Sustainable Agricultural Groundwater Use.* OECD Studies on Water. Paris: OECD Publishing. http://dx.doi .org/10.1787/9789264238701-en.

O'Neill, B. C., E. Kriegler, K. K. Ebi, E. Kemp-Benedict, K. Riahi, D. S. Rothman, B. J. van Ruijven, D. P. van Vuuren, and J. Berkmann. 2015. "The Roads Ahead: Narratives for Shared Socioeconomic Pathways Describing World Futures in the 21st Century." *Global Environmental Change* 42 (January): 169–80.

Pal, J. S., and E. A. Eltahir. 2016. "Future Temperature in Southwest Asia Projected to Exceed Threshold for Human Adaptability." *Nature Climate Change* 6: 197–200.

Richey, A. S., B. F. Thomas, M.-H. Lo, J. S. Famiglietti, S. Swenson, and M. Rodell. 2015. "Uncertainty in Global Groundwater Storage Estimates in a Total Groundwater Stress Framework." *Water Resources Research* 51: 5198–216. doi:10.1002/2015WR017351.

Rosegrant, M. W., C. Ringler, S. Msangi, T. B. Sulser, T. Zhu, and S. A. Cline. 2008. "International Model for Policy Analysis of Agricultural Commodities and Trade (IMPACT): Model Description." International Food Policy Research Institute, Washington DC.

Rosenberg, D. E., R. E. Howitt, and J. R. Lund. 2008. "Water Management with Water Conservation, Infrastructure Expansions, and Source Variability in Jordan." *Water Resources Research* 44: W11402.

Saab, N. 2015. "Consumption Patterns in Arab Countries." AFED Public Opinion Survey. Arab Forum for Environment and Development.

Sadoff, C. W., E. Borgomeo, and D. de Waal. 2017. *Turbulent Waters: Pursuing Water Security in Fragile Contexts.* Washington, DC: World Bank.

Sadoff, C. W., J. W. Hall, D. Grey, J. C. J. H. Aerts, M. Ait-Kadi, C. Brown, A. Cox, S. Dadson, D. Garrick, J. Kelman, P. McCornick, C. Ringler, M. Rosegrant, D. Whittington, and D. Wiberg. 2015. *Securing Water, Sustaining Growth: Report of the GWP/OECD Task Force on Water Security and Sustainable Growth.* Oxford: University of Oxford.

Sandström, E., A. Jägerskog, and T. Ostigard, eds. 2016. *Water Politics in the Nile River Basin: Land Grabs, Energy Investments and Changing Hydropolitical Landscapes.* London: Routledge / Taylor & Francis.

Scheierling, S. M., and D. O. Treguer. 2016. "Enhancing Water Productivity in Irrigated Agriculture in the Face of Water Scarcity." *CHOICES* (3rd Quarter 2016) 31: (3).

Scheierling, S. M., R. A. Young, and G. E. Cardon. 2006. "Public Subsidies for Water-Conserving Irrigation Investments: Hydrologic, Agronomic, and Economic Assessment." *Water Resources Research* 42: W03428. doi:10.1029 /2004WR003809.

Sefelnasr, A., and M. Sherif. 2014. "Impacts of Seawater Rise on Seawater Intrusion in the Nile Delta Aquifer, Egypt." *Ground Water* 52 (2): 264–76. doi:10.1111/gwat.12058.

Seitzinger, S. P., E. Mayorga, A. F. Bouwman, C. Kroeze, A. H. W. Beusen, G. Billen, G. van Drecht, E. Durmont, B. M. Fekete, J. Garnier, and J. A. Harrison. 2010. "Global River Nutrient Export: A Scenario Analysis of Past and Future Trends." *Global Biogeochemical Cycles* 24 (4). doi. 10.1029/2009GB003587.

Shamout Nouar, M. 2015. "The Euphrates in Crisis: Channels of Cooperation for a Threatened River." Research Paper, Chatham House, the Royal Institute of International Affairs, London.

Sherif, M., A. Kacimov, A. Javadi, and A. M. Ebraheem. 2012. "Modeling Groundwater Flow and Seawater Intrusion in the Coastal Aquifer of Wadi Ham, UAE." *Water Resource Management* 26 (3): 751–74. doi:10.1007 /s11269-011-9943-6.

Siddiqi, A., and L. D. Anadon. 2011. "The Water-Energy Nexus in the Middle East and North Africa." *Energy Policy* 39 (6): 4529–40.

Smakhtin, V. U., C. Revenga, and P. Döll. 2004. "A Pilot Global Assessment of Environmental Water Requirements and Scarcity." *Water International* 29: 307–17.

Snoussi, M., T. Ouchani, and S. Niazi. 2008. "Vulnerability Assessment of the Impact of Sea-Level Rise and Flooding on the Moroccan Coast: The Case of the Mediterranean Eastern Zone." *Estuarine, Coastal and Shelf Science* 77 (2): 206–13.

Solh, M. 2014. "Finding a Road to Stability in the Arab Region." IFPRI (blog), October 15. http://www.ifpri.org/blog/finding-road-stability-arab-region.

Stadler, S., M. A. Geyh, D. Ploethner, and P. Koeniger. 2012. "The Deep Cretaceous Aquifer in the Aleppo and Steppe Basins of Syria: Assessment of the Meteoric Origin and Geographic Source of the Groundwater." *Hydrogeology Journal* 20 (6). doi: 10.1007/s10040-012-0862-2.

Suweis, S., A. Rinaldo, A. Maritan, and P. D'Odorico. 2012. "Water-Controlled Wealth of Nations." *PNAS (Proceedings of the National Academy of Sciences)* 110 (11): 4230–33.

Swain, A., and A. Jägerskog. 2016. *Emerging Security Threats in the Middle East: The Impact of Climate Change and Globalization*. Lanham, MD: Rowman and Littlefield Publishers.

SWIM-SM (Sustainable Water Integrated Management- Support Mechanism) 2013. "Documentation of Best Practices in Non-revenue Water in Selected Mediterranean Countries-Algeria, Israel, Jordan and Morocco." Project funded by the European Union. SWIM-SM.

Tessler, Z. D., C. Vorosmarty, M. Grossberg, I. Gladkova, H. Aizenman, J. P. M. Syvitski, and E. Foufoula-Georgiou. 2015. "Profiling Risk and Sustainability in Coastal Deltas of the World." *Science* 349 (6248): 638–43.

Tropp, H., and A. Jägerskog. 2006. "Water Scarcity Challenges in the Middle East and North Africa." Occasional Paper 2006/31 for the *Human Development Report 2006*. New York: United Nations Development Programme.

Van Lavieren, H., J. Burt, D. A. Feary, G. Cavalcante, E. Marquis, L. Benedetti, C. Trick, B. Kjerfve, and P. F. Sale. 2011. *Managing the Growing Impacts of Development on Fragile Coastal and Marine Ecosystems: Lessons from the Gulf*. A policy report. Hamilton, ON, Canada: UNU-INWEH.

Van Steenbergen, F. P. Lawrence, A. Mehari-Haile, M. Salman, and J-M Faurès. 2010. "Guidelines on Spate Irrigation." FAO Irrigation and Drainage Paper 65, Food and Agricultural Organization of the United Nations, Rome.

Verme, P. 2016. "Subsidy Reforms in the Middle East and North Africa Region." Policy Research Working Paper 7754, World Bank, Washington, DC.

UNDP (United Nations Development Programme). 2013. *Water Governance in the Arab Region: Managing Scarcity and Securing the Future*. New York: UNDP, Regional Bureau for Arab States.

UNESCO (United Nations Educational, Scientific, and Cultural Organization). 2014. "Opportunities for Managed Aquifer Recharge. Second Learning Workshop for MENARID Project Managers, 11–14 December, Amman, Jordan." Final Report. UNESCO Series on Groundwater for MENARID 2. Paris: UNESCO.

UNESCO Iraq Office. 2014. *Integrated Drought Risk Management DRM: National Framework for Iraq*. Analysis Report. UNESCO Iraq. http://unesdoc.unesco.org/images/0022/002283/228343E.pdf.

UNFPA and UNHCR (United Nations Population Fund and Office of United Nations High Commissioner for Refugees). 2015. "Sexual and Gender-Based Violence: Refugees in Jordan." http://www.syrialearning.org/resource/20593.

UNICEF (United Nations Children's Fund). 2015. "Ministry of Water & Irrigation and UNICEF Launches Cost Efficient Waste Water Treatment Units in Za'atari Refugee Camp." March 3 bulletin. http://childrenofsyria.info/2015/03/03/ministry-of-water-irrigation-and-unicef-launches-cost-efficient-waste-water-treatment-units-in-zaatari-refugee-camp/.

UNICEF and WHO (United Nations Children's Fund and World Health Organization). 2015a. "Keeping Up with Population Growth." In *Progress on Sanitation and Drinking Water 2015: Update and MDG Assessment*. Geneva: WHO Press.

———. 2015b. *Progress on Sanitation and Drinking Water 2015: Update and MDG Assessment*. Geneva: WHO Press.

UN Water. 2015. *Water for a Sustainable World*. United Nations World Water Development Report. Paris: UNESCO (United Nations Educational, Scientific, and Cultural Organization).

Vagliasindi, M. 2012. *Implementing Energy Subsidy Reforms: Evidence from Developing Countries*. Directions in Development. Washington, DC: World Bank.

van den Berg, C., S. Kh. H. Agha Al Nimera, T. Fileccia, L. M. Gonzalez, and S. Wahsehl. 2016. "The Cost of Irrigation Water in the Jordan Valley." Working Paper 104504, World Bank, Washington, DC.

Van Loon, A. F., and H. A. J. Van Lanen. 2013. "Making the Distinction between Water Scarcity and Drought Using an Observation-Modeling Framework." *Water Resources Research* 49: 1483–1502.

Veolia Water and IFPRI (International Food Policy Research Institute). 2011. *Sustaining Growth via Water Productivity: 2030/2050 Scenarios*. http://growing-blue.com/wp-content/uploads/2011/05/IFPRI_VEOLIA_STUDY_2011.pdf.

Verner, D. 2012. *Adaptation to a Changing Climate in the Arab Countries: A Case for Adaptation Governance and Leadership in Building Climate Resilience*. MENA Development Report. Washington, DC: World Bank.

Wada, Y., and M. F. P. Bierkens. 2014. "Sustainability of Global Water Use: Past Reconstruction and Future Projection." *Environmental Research Letters* 9: 104003.

Ward, C. 2015. *The Water Crisis in Yemen: Managing Extreme Water Scarcity in the Middle East*. London: I. B. Tauris.

Ward, F. A., and M. Pulido-Velazquez. 2008. "Water Conservation in Irrigation Can Increase Water Use." *PNAS (Proceedings of the National Academy of Sciences)* 105: 18215–20.

Werber, J. R., C. O. Osuji, and M. Elimelech. 2016. "Materials for Next-Generation Desalination and Water Purification Membranes." *Nature Reviews Materials* 1: 16018.

Weerasekera, Dharshani. 2012. "Solar Pumps Lift More Than Just Groundwater in Parts of India" (blog), November 28. CGIAR. https://wle.cgiar.org/thrive/2012/11/28/solar-pumps-lift-more-just-groundwater-parts-india.

Whittington, D., C. Nauges, D. Fuente, and X. Wu. 2015. "A Diagnostic Tool for Estimating the Incidence of Subsidies Delivered by Water Utilities in Low- and Medium-Income Countries, with Illustrative Simulations." *Utilities Policy* 34: 70–81.

WHO (World Health Organization). 2015. "Cholera-Iraq." *Disease Outbreak News*.

Winsemius, H. C., B. Jongman, T. I. E. Vedlkamp, S. Hallegatte, M. Bangalore, and P. J. Ward. 2015. "Disaster Risk, Climate Change, and Poverty: Assessing the Global Exposure of Poor People to Floods and Droughts." Policy Research Working Paper 7480, World Bank, Washington, DC.

Wodon, Q., A. Liverani, G. Joseph, and N. Bougnoux, eds. 2014. *Climate Change and Migration: Evidence from the Middle East and North Africa*. World Bank Studies. Washington, DC: World Bank Group.

World Bank. 2005. *A Water Sector Assessment Report on the Countries of the Cooperation Council of the Arab States of the Gulf*. Report 32539-MNA. Washington, DC: World Bank.

———. 2007. *Making the Most of Scarcity: Accountability for Better Water Management Results in the Middle East and North Africa*. MENA Development Report. Washington, DC: World Bank.

———. 2012. *Renewable Energy Desalination: An Emerging Solution to Close the Water Gap in the Middle East and North Africa*. MENA Development Report. Washington, DC: World Bank.

———. 2014. "Water in the Arab World: From Droughts to Flood, Building Resilience against Extremes." *News Feature*, March 21. http://www.worldbank .org/en/news/feature/2014/03/20/floods-and-droughts-in-mena.

———. 2016. *High and Dry: Climate Change, Water, and the Economy.* Washington, DC: World Bank.

———. 2017. *World Development Report 2017: Governance and the Law.* Washington, DC: World Bank.

World Bank and Arab Water Council. 2011. "Water Reuse in the Arab World: From Principle to Practice." A Summary of Proceedings of the Expert Consultation Wastewater Management in the Arab World, May 22–24, Dubai.

Zawahri, N., J. Sowers, and E. Weinthal. 2011. "The Politics of Assessment: Water and Sanitation MDGs in the Middle East." *Development and Change* 42 (2011): 1153–77.

Zekri, S., M. Ahmed, R. Chaieb, and N. Ghaffour. 2014. "Managed Aquifer Recharge Using Quaternary-Treated Wastewater: An Economic Perspective." *International Journal of Water Resources Development* 30 (2): 246–61.

Zhou, L., Y. Tan, J. Wang, W. Xu, Y. Yuan, W. Cai, S. Zhu, and J. Zhu. 2016. "3-D Self-Assembly of Aluminium Nanoparticles for Plasmon-Enhanced Solar Desalination." *Nature Photonics* 10: 393–98.

CHAPTER 3

The Water Security Dividend

Challenges and Emerging Priorities

Water security is a priority for long-term stability and prosperity in the Middle East and North Africa. As the region seeks to achieve the targets of the Sustainable Development Goals (SDGs), water issues could prove to be a major obstacle. This report shows how water poses both opportunities and constraints for sustained economic growth and stability in the region. This section describes the most salient challenges and priorities in the areas of water resources, water services, and water-related risk.

Physical water scarcity is not going away. To reverse current trends in the unsustainable consumption and depletion of freshwater resources, policies need to continue to improve the efficiency of water use, pursue nonconventional water supplies, and promote conjunctive management of freshwater resources. Dealing with scarcity also means signaling the value of scarcity to water users with incentives, service fees, and public awareness campaigns.

To address the challenges identified in this assessment, a diversified portfolio of investments in information, institutions, and infrastructure is required. Investments are required to protect lives and livelihoods from water-related risks and disasters, provide reliable water supply, and harness the productive potential of water. Information can contribute to water security, for instance by improving the monitoring of hydrological variables to inform agricultural decisions or by supporting early warning systems in the face of water-related disasters. Investments in institutions might include setting up regulations or organizations with specific mandates to improve water security. The construction of physical infrastructure, such as irrigation systems and wastewater treatment and recycling facilities, can also enhance water security. Investment in water security will be context specific and will increasingly need to simultaneously address a range of concerns and their interactions.

Improving governance of water resources and water services is fundamental to achieving water security. Depletion of water resources and unsustainable consumption are a direct result of poor governance and regulation arrangements. The case of the Republic of Yemen is emblematic, with experts calling its current groundwater abstraction regime "anarchic" (Alderwish and Wa'el 2015). Innovative experiences in the governance of water resources are also taking place in the region (De Gooijer et al. 2009). Countries are paying increasing attention to the importance of integrity, transparency, accountability, and a lack of corruption in promoting water security.[1]

Working toward inclusive and financially sustainable water services is a high priority for the region. Many water services in the region are not financially sustainable because of high operation and maintenance costs, low water service fees, and high subsidies. Inadequate financing can undermine service quality and limit utilities' abilities to expand service networks to include all potential users. In addition, the wealthy members of society often benefit more than the poor from high subsidies. Thus, water services are often not inclusive and do not adequately benefit poor people in the region.

Transparent and comprehensive data collection mechanisms and evaluation tools are needed to inform evidence-based policy debates and the selection of water policies. For instance, comprehensive systems for monitoring agricultural water usage are needed to inform policies seeking to improve water efficiency through market-based incentives or other mechanisms. The increased recognition of the role of improved governance in promoting water security also calls for closer analysis and development of tools able to track progress and evaluate performance with respect to water governance (De Stefano 2014), such as the Middle East and North Africa Regional Water Governance Benchmarking Project of the U.S. Agency for International Development (USAID) (Svendsen 2010).

Water security is a crucial component of adapting to climate change in the region. Climate change will increase the risk of coastal and riverine flooding, causing potentially very severe damage to Middle Eastern and North African economies. Climate change will also increase temperatures, leading to higher crop water requirements and potentially higher agricultural water demands. Diversifying water supplies, improving water use efficiency, and—more important—building flexible and transparent water governance arrangements are needed for water security under a changing climate.

Achieving water security in the Middle East and North Africa increasingly entails dealing with the region's highly complex political context. Political instability and population displacement exacerbate water challenges and can increase social tensions if unaddressed. Similarly, a lack of collaboration over transboundary waters prevents countries from being able to share the benefits of water for growth and prosperity. Continued dialogue and transparent policies will be essential to help the region make the transition toward water security and achieve the SDGs.

Pursuing Water Security during Protracted Crises

Conflict and protracted crises in the Middle East and North Africa have resulted in large-scale destruction and damage to water infrastructure, institutions, and information systems. Conflict has also reversed or delayed progress toward water security by preventing investments in water management and diminishing the ability of governments to deliver services. Given the scale of the disruption caused by conflicts and the protracted nature of the crisis, the traditional approach of waiting for the conflicts to end before carrying out reconstruction plans will not be enough (Devarajan 2015).

The World Bank's Regional Strategy calls for dynamic needs assessments and for interventions to be undertaken during conflict and situations of protracted crisis. At the level of the water sector, this entails developing a framework to differentiate interventions that need to be prioritized during times of protracted crisis as opposed to interventions and investments that can be carried out only during times of postconflict development opportunity. Table 3.1 presents a list of possible interventions that can be carried out during times of crisis and during times of development opportunity.

During a protracted crisis, recovery programs need to ensure that the water resource base is not unduly undermined and that basic water services are maintained or quickly restored. Accordingly, water sector interventions should prioritize the protection of critical water infrastructure and water sources, alongside highly visible improvements in the delivery of water services to conflict-affected and displaced communities (table 3.1). This will contribute to improving living conditions as well as helping restore confidence in government institutions.

As situations of development opportunity materialize following the conflict period, water policies need to capitalize on the opportunity provided by peace. These efforts will require financing water-related employment opportunities, such as labor-intensive water infrastructure rehabilitation and expansion, and strengthening the sustainable management of water resources so as to provide long-term livelihood opportunities. More importantly, water sector interventions during situations of development opportunity following the conflict period should emphasize institutions and the governance of water, such as promoting accountability and the financial sustainability of water utilities (table 3.1).

Pursuing water security during protracted crisis and postconflict recovery often means working with nontraditional partners. During conflict or postconflict periods, there may not be a functioning national government or water management agency. In many cases in the Middle East and North Africa, water supplies are delivered by nongovernmental organizations (NGOs) and water vendors that have the

TABLE 3.1

Action Framework for Water Security during Protracted Crises and Situations of Development Opportunity

	SITUATIONS OF **DEVELOPMENT OPPORTUNITY**	SITUATIONS OF **SHOCKS AND PROTRACTED CRISIS**
Provide water services Guaranteeing water services that meet standards of affordability, reliability, and quality helps to reverse the vicious cycle of water insecurity and fragility. Investments to reduce inadequate and unequal access to water services can promote stability in fragile contexts.	Promote cost recovery and efficiency in water utilities Develop a customer database Finance labor-intensive irrigation, rehabilitation, and expansion Strengthen dam safety Construct small-scale hydropower for isolated communities	Support cost recovery with one-off subsidies or in-kind donations for operating needs Retain skilled staff Extend water utility services to IDPs and host communities
Protect from water-related disasters Preparedness and response to disasters are central elements of the social compact. Disaster impacts and recovery options vary widely, so investments need to account for different gender, social, and economic circumstances.	Develop disaster preparedness plans Integrate remote sensing data into information systems Upgrade hydrometeorological forecast and early warning systems Enhance flood protection and drought management systems Adopt conflict-sensitive approaches to DRR Strengthen communication for disaster response	Protect key hydrometeorological early warning and ICT systems Ensure equity and transparency in disaster response and relief efforts
Preserve surface, ground- and transboundary water resources Governments need to guarantee the adequacy of water resources for their populations and to preserve healthy aquatic ecosystems. Working toward sustainable water resources management and cooperative water sharing agreements is key to reverse the water security and fragility cycle.	Sustain water resources planning, monitoring, and enforcement Regulate and monitor groundwater abstraction Rehabilitate/develop water storage infrastructure, using labor-intensive methods Share information in transboundary basins Pursue cooperative transboundary water agreements	Protect critical interconnected infrastructure Prevent encroachment by private and fractional interests Prevent investments in nonsustainable solutions Monitor compliance with transboundary agreements

Source: Sadoff, Borgomeo, and de Waal 2017.
Note: ICT = information and communication technology; IDPs = internally displaced persons; DRR = disaster risk reduction.

capacity and flexibility to operate in fragile contexts. In some cases, pursuing water security during protracted crises means engaging with these actors as a starting point to begin a water sector recovery and reconstruction program.

Different policy instruments will be appropriate for different contexts. The list of actions given in table 3.1 provides some possible policy interventions. These should be prioritized depending on the context and insight gained from country-specific assessments. For these measures to be most effective, a long-term vision promoting adaptive approaches and system resilience in the face of unexpected changes is required. Furthermore, strong governmental and nongovernmental cooperation, accountability, and access to financial resources are all important for building resilience to risks (Verner 2012).

Transforming Water: Opportunities and Solutions for Water Security

Technological and governance innovations—in the region and globally—are accelerating to meet an urgent need for action. Some of the most notable water management innovations in the world are being implemented in the Middle East and North Africa. Initiatives include highly successful efforts to increase water use efficiency, along with state-of-the-art water recycling technologies, and policies that have successfully reallocated water from low- to high-value uses.

A range of new technologies for water resources management and water service delivery are available to promote efficiency. Smart metering, in particular, can be used to improve accuracy in billing, evaluate consumption, and increase users' awareness of their own consumption. As experiences in the region and globally show, smart metering also helps water service providers identify leaks, reduce operating costs, and communicate the value of water to users.

Technology also helps improve water service delivery, especially for the underserved and the poor. Mobile-based systems ensure improved customer service by allowing for real-time monitoring of water infrastructure. This is particularly important for identifying and fixing operational issues in remote areas, where many of the poor live and where the status of water infrastructure may be difficult to monitor. Furthermore, mobile technologies promote rapid access to information and data sharing, creating a system of accountability. In turn, this strengthens public participation and promotes a more equitable and transparent allocation of the resource. Finally, evidence from different parts of the world shows that the introduction of mobile water payment options improves collection efficiency and increases utilities' revenues, providing financial strength to extend services to the underserved.

Technologies and practices to recycle water and curb waste are increasingly being used in the region. Several countries have recognized the benefits of recycling water; some aim to recycle all their wastewater by 2030. Positive experiences in Jordan (As-Samra) and Tunisia (Souhil Wadi) show that wastewater can be safely recycled for use in irrigation and managed aquifer recharge. With recent decreases in the cost of desalination and advances in membrane technology, desalination is increasingly becoming a viable alternative to traditional freshwater resources.

Innovations in integrated urban water management can help improve the quality, reliability, and sustainability of urban and agricultural water services. Integrated urban water management considers the city's urban water services in close relation to its urban development dynamics on the one hand, and to the broader basin context on the other (World Bank 2012). These approaches have been tried, tested, and scaled up in many water-scarce regions in the world (box 3.1). Such approaches will encourage cities to create strong synergies within or outside the water basin, for example, through the development of reuse for agriculture or shared desalination with industries.

BOX 3.1

Water-Scarce Cities: A World Bank Initiative to Help Cities Move toward Integrated and Diversified Water Management Practices

The World Bank has launched the Water-Scarce Cities initiative to promote and scale up improved water management practices in water-scarce cities and to shift to more sustainable pathways toward long-term water security. Faced with chronic water scarcity, these cities are also confronting the pressures of a growing population, rapid urbanization, economic growth, and climate change. Despite these risks, even the most water-scarce cities continue to rely on traditional solutions based on abundant resources and engineering approaches to increasing water supplies. Unsustainable resource management practices compound the pressures, putting several cities on a dangerous path toward major water crises. The current mind-set needs to be shifted away from linear solutions to embrace more integrated and diversified approaches.

Through the promotion of experiences and good practices from around the world, the initiative supports developing countries in extremely water-scarce areas to engage on more sustainable pathways toward urban water security. A growing global network of

(continued on next page)

BOX 3.1 *Continued*

practitioners and experts on the subject of urban water management in water-scarce regions is already facilitating multistakeholder dialogue, knowledge flow, and collaboration by showcasing successful experiences like those of Malta, Namibia, Singapore, and the arid southwestern United States.

The initiative does not aim to simply scale up best practices, but rather to unleash the potential of developing countries to develop similarly integrated and resilient approaches specific to their own contexts. The initiative helps countries to demystify the array of available technologies, to provide the appropriate decision-making tools, and to develop context-specific institutional support, with more inclusion and public outreach, to overcome classic barriers to more sustainable pathways. These barriers include political or cultural issues (limited sensitivity to water risks, entrenched engineering approaches, complexity of cooperation and demand management, cultural resistance to recycling), as well as institutional issues (lack of accountability/autonomy of service providers, lack of mechanisms for integrated planning, rigid regulatory frameworks limiting innovations such as recycling and trading water, or using public-private partnerships).

Source: Richard Abdulnour, World Bank.

Water security also requires moving toward a diversified water management portfolio. Diversified solutions lead to greater resilience to systemic shocks—be they related to conflict, climatic changes, or economic shifts. Diversifying means first of all "closing the water resources loop" rather than thinking of water usage as "once through the system." Examples of diversification include conjunctive use of surface and groundwater resources; developing nonconventional water resources such as desalination; recycling; reducing leakage; and promoting conservation.

Increased institutional coordination among the water, energy, and agricultural sectors is strengthening water management efforts. Successfully reducing water use and reallocating water to higher-value uses requires coordination between different ministries, increased regulatory clarity, and data sharing (box 3.2). Around the world, successful water management is happening in concert with policies considering energy and agriculture.

Experiences from the region show that it is possible to implement the right incentives to encourage water savings and reallocation. These incentives can be developed in a way that avoids disproportionate impacts on the poor and social unrest. Well-designed incentives include accurate

---

BOX 3.2

Developing a Performance Management System for Middle Eastern and North African Water Agencies

For decades, water agencies throughout the region have been conducting research to identify and promote sustainable and innovative solutions to tackle water-related challenges. While knowledge has indeed been created, it needs to be applied concretely to efforts to determine and meet the national priorities of the countries and economies of the Middle East and North Africa. After reviewing annual reports of several agencies, the Middle East and North Africa Network of Water Centers of Excellence (MENA NWC) concluded that there is no real consensus among the water agencies on building strategies and defining priorities to serve their institutions, countries, and the region.

The Network of Water Centers of Excellence identified three priority areas to support water agencies to better manage their performance; build more concise and well-constructed plans; and align research priorities with national and regional strategies, such as the Arab Ministerial Water Council strategy.

The Network of Water Centers of Excellence also proposed a model to promote better performance based on three sets of indicators: strategic, operational, and financial. The performance measurement system will help water agencies evaluate their performance from short-, medium-, and long-term perspectives. It will also include the main pillars of sustainable development: environmental sustainability, social responsibility, and economic development.

Source: Ghazi Abu Rumman, World Bank.

---

targeting of water service fee changes—for instance, by targeting higher-consumption users—and public awareness campaigns explaining the reason for pricing changes and the availability of compensatory mechanisms.

Public-private partnerships have also been implemented in the region to tackle the operational constraints of water utilities. The Middle East and North Africa region has been the most active place in the world, along with China, in terms of public-private partnerships in water management. This has led to improved utility performance over the last six years. Across the region, almost 28 million people now have improved water services via public-private utility partnerships.

There is an increasing role for private sector financing of water infrastructure. Most of the public-private partnerships in the region have focused on service efficiency. Now there is growing interest in mobilizing private capital to meet the tremendous financing needs for water infrastructure. Wastewater treatment plants in Bahrain, the Arab Republic of Egypt, Jordan, and the Islamic Republic of Iran, along with irrigation projects in Morocco, demonstrate that the private sector is motivated to bring financing to public-private partnerships and work toward achieving creditworthy water utilities—which, in turn, could attract more private sector financing when issues of service fees, partial subsidies, and assurance of payments are addressed.

Achieving water security means acting together, from the household level to the regional level. From a household water perspective, this means engaging women, who often have the main responsibility for using and conserving water. Women's rights, representation, and resources need to be acknowledged and addressed, both for social inclusion and sustainable development. Youth should also be engaged in developing the next generation's water expectations and practices.

At the regional level, cooperation on water can foster greater trust and collaboration. As part of its regional strategy (box 3.3), the World Bank is promoting regional cooperation around water and other regional public goods and sectors such as energy and education. The purpose of this action area is not to promote cooperation for its own benefits, but to serve as a means to bring about greater peace and stability in the region (Devarajan 2015). The efforts of the League of Arab States to strengthen water management in the region need to continue. The work by the Arab Countries Water Utilities Association (ACWUA) on benchmarking water utilities and tracking the performance of water services across the region will become more valuable as part of the SDGs.

BOX 3.3

The World Bank Group's Strategy for the Middle East and North Africa

The World Bank Group's strategy, "Economic and Social Inclusion for Peace and Stability in the Middle East and North Africa," is centered on the goal of promoting peace and social stability in the Middle East and North Africa region. The strategy is built around four pillars ("the 4 Rs") that respond to both the underlying causes of conflict and violence as well as the urgent consequences through development interventions that foster inclusion and shared prosperity. The four pillars of the strategy are as follows:

1. *Renewing the social contract* to generate a new development model that is built on greater citizen trust; more effective protection of the poor and vulnerable; inclusive and accountable service delivery; and a stronger private sector that

(continued on next page)

BOX 3.3   *Continued*

can create jobs and opportunities for Middle East and North Africa's youth.

2. *Regional cooperation*—particularly around regional public goods and sectors such as education, water, and energy—so as to foster greater trust and collaboration across Middle Eastern and North African countries.

3. *Resilience* to refugee and migration shocks by promoting the welfare of

refugees, internally displaced persons (IDPs), and host communities by focusing on building trust and building their assets.

4. *Reconstruction and recovery* through a dynamic approach that brings in external partners, leverages large-scale financing, and moves beyond humanitarian response to longer-term development wherever and whenever conflict subsides.

Source: Devarajan 2015.

Similarly, collaboration between researchers and universities through established and emerging networks such as the Middle East and North Africa Network of Water Centers of Excellence (MENA NWC) is essential. Finally, NGOs—such as the regional Israeli, Palestinian, and Jordanian NGO EcoPeace Middle East—and international organizations can contribute with knowledge and financial resources to help Middle Eastern and North African countries and economies address some of their water challenges.

Engaging and educating civil society on water issues and water conservation is also crucial to guarantee success. Changing water management practices to ensure better service delivery and sustainability of water use requires changing the attitudes of individuals and government officials as much as putting in place institutional incentives and arrangements. Promoting water conservation in schools has been identified as a potential mechanism to change people's awareness and attitudes about water, with examples from Jordan showing the success of such initiatives (MENA NWC 2015).

While the opportunities and experiences presented here can serve as points of entry for action, solutions will depend on the context. There is a rich menu of technological, financial, and institutional options, but the right mix of actions will be different for any particular country, river basin, or city. This is because of the diversity of environmental, economic, and sociopolitical characteristics in the Middle East and North Africa. Some interventions will need to be prioritized during times of protracted crisis, as opposed to interventions and investments that can be carried out during times of development following conflict. Given the scale of the disruption caused by conflicts and the protracted nature of some of the region's crises, the traditional approach of waiting for conflicts to end before carrying out reconstruction plans will not work (Devarajan 2015). As discussed in the World Bank's Regional Strategy, the Middle East and North Africa region requires a dynamic approach that brings in external partners, leverages large-scale financing, and moves beyond humanitarian responses to longer-term development wherever and whenever conflict subsides.

A host of potential solutions to various water management challenges have been demonstrated in the region, but clear, strong incentives are needed to spur action. Incentives for water conservation and innovation are needed to change the way water is managed. These can come through policies, pricing, allocation, or regulation. If water becomes unavailable, or too expensive, water users will respond. They will innovate. They will find better ways of doing more with less. They will adopt proven solutions and adapt or create new solutions.

The most important lesson from global and regional experience is that technology, policy, and institutional management must evolve together to achieve water security. Strategies that seek to "desalinate their way out of water insecurity" have made limited progress toward attaining water security. Global experience shows that countries and cities that have arguably overcome the limits of water scarcity have done so through the integrated management of both water resources (conventional and non-conventional) and water services and the mitigation of water-related risks (figure 3.1). This has allowed them to effectively surpass the constraints of their scant natural water endowments. These cutting-edge water managers are effectively aligning water resource planning, management, institutions, information systems, infrastructure, risk management, and incentives to access and store more water, allocate it more efficiently, and deliver it more effectively to customers. And they have done so while guarding the quality and sustainability of their water resources.

Failure to seize these opportunities will have significant implications for political, economic, and environmental stability in the region and beyond. As the current conflict and migration crisis unfolding in the Middle East and North Africa shows, political failure to address water challenges can have a severe impact on people's well-being and political stability.

The strategic question for the region is whether its countries will act with foresight and resolve to strengthen water security, or whether they will wait to react to the inevitable disruptions of water crises.

FIGURE 3.1

Governance and Incentives to Seize Emerging Opportunities in Water Resources Management and Water Services Delivery and to Mitigate Water-Related Risks

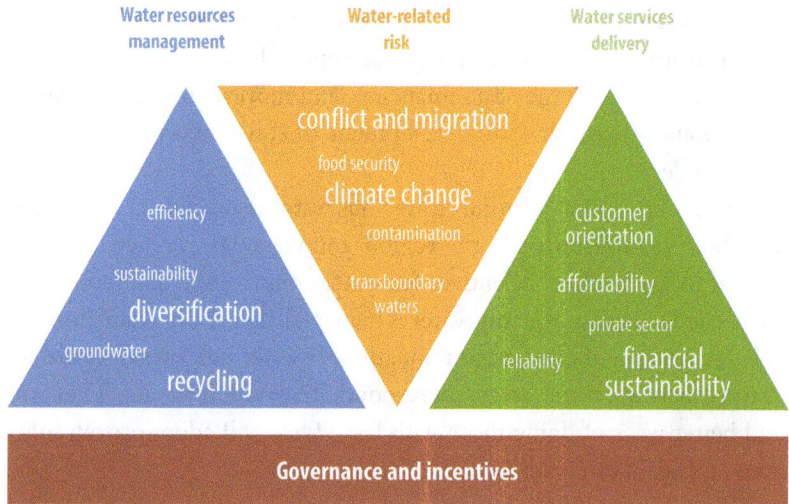

Source: World Bank.

Note

1. See, for example, SIWI's capacity building programme: http://www.siwi.org /what-we-do/capacity-building/.

References

Alderwish, A. M., and I. M. Wa'el. 2015. "Review of Yemen's Control of Groundwater Extraction Regime: Situation and Options." Yemenwater.org.

De Gooijer, G., R. Löfgren, J. Granit, A. Jägerskog, and A. Renck. 2009. "Innovations in Groundwater Governance in the MENA Region." Middle East North Africa Seminar report from World Water Week 2010. Paper 14, Stockholm International Water Institute, Stockholm.

De Stefano, L. 2014. "Water Governance Benchmarking: Concepts and Approach Framework as Applied to Middle East and North Africa Countries." *Water Policy* 16: 1121–39.

Devarajan, Shantayanan. 2015. "An Exposition of the New Strategy, 'Promoting Peace and Stability in the Middle East and North Africa.'" Working Paper 102936, World Bank, Washington, DC.

MENA NWC (Middle East and North Africa Network of Water Centers of Excellence). 2015. "Excellence and Impact of Research." Working Paper. MENA NWC.

Sadoff, Claudia W., Edoardo Borgomeo, and Dominick de Waal. 2017. *Turbulent Waters: Pursuing Water Security in Fragile Contexts*. Washington, DC: World Bank.

Svendsen, M. 2010. "MENA Regional Water Governance Benchmarking Project. Final Report." International Resources Group, Washington, DC.

Verner, D. 2012. *Adaptation to Climate Change in Arab Countries: A Case for Adaptation Governance and Leadership in Building Climate Resilience*. MENA Development Report. Washington, DC: World Bank.

World Bank. 2012. *Integrated Urban Water Management: A Summary Note*. Washington, DC: World Bank.

Appendix

A set of indicators was identified to summarize the regionally comparable aspects of water security for each country and economy in the Middle East and North Africa. The indicators were grouped following the three dimensions of water security described in the report: water resources, water services, and water-related risks. The selection of the indicators was dictated by data quality and availability. For many important aspects of water security, such as continuity of water supply or affordability of water services, reliable and up-to-date country-level data were not available.

As with any set of indicators, this set is incomplete and captures only a portion of the numerous aspects of water security. However, it allows initial country comparisons to be carried out and provides a framework into which data and information can be added as they become available. The country profile pages in this appendix present these indicators for each country in the Middle East and North Africa.

The indicators and data sources are summarized in table A.1, and table A.2 lists references for each country profile.

TABLE A.1

Definition of Indicators and Data Sources

Dimension	Indicator	Description	Source	Year
Water resources	**Sustainability of freshwater use**	Percentage of human water consumption that does not result in either environmental flow degradation or abstraction of nonrenewable groundwater resources.	World Bank	2016
	Agricultural water productivity	Agricultural GDP in U.S. dollars per cubic meter of total freshwater withdrawal (normalized by best performer in the Middle East and North Africa). This indicator has important limitations, in that it measures the economic activity of both rainfed and irrigated agriculture, while only irrigation contributes to freshwater withdrawals. Hence, for countries with large rainfed agricultural systems, this indicator provides an overestimate of productivity.	Arab Water Council *2nd Arab State of the Water Report*	2012
Delivery of water services	**Access**[a]	Access to "improved" sanitation facilities: For MDG monitoring, an improved sanitation facility is defined as one that hygienically separates human excreta from human contact.	Joint Monitoring Programme for Water Supply and Sanitation (JMP) (WHO/UNICEF)	2015
		Access to "improved" drinking water source: An improved drinking-water source is defined as one that, by nature of its construction or through active intervention, is protected from outside contamination, in particular from contamination with fecal matter.		
		Both indicators of coverage can be misleading. First, a piped water connection on the premises is counted as an improved source in both Joint Monitoring Programme (JMP) definitions, but there is no assurance that the quality of water delivered to the household is potable. Similarly, for the second definition, water from the other types of improved sources may be contaminated, and the household will still be counted as having an improved source.		
		Second, water sources considered by the JMP to be "unimproved" may, in fact, provide a household with potable water. For example, water vendors (both tanker trucks and distributing vendors) and bottled water are counted as "unimproved sources," even though they may reliably supply a household with sufficient quantities of safe (high-quality) water.		
		Third, both indicators of coverage implicitly assume that a household uses only one source for its drinking water. Households may collect drinking water from both improved and unimproved sources, even if their "improved" water source is a piped water connection on the premises.		
		Despite these limitations, the JMP data on improved water coverage are the best available, and they are used here to examine water supply and sanitation access statistics in the Middle East and North Africa.		

(continued on next page)

TABLE A.1 *Continued*

Dimension	Indicator	Description	Source	Year
	Efficiency of water service delivery	Share of produced water that is not lost before it reaches the customer. It is the complement of nonrevenue water.	International Benchmarking Network for Water and Sanitation Utilities (IBNET) and country-specific sources, as indicated in the references	—
Risk management	**Climate robustness**	This indicator captures the robustness of a country's freshwater supplies to climate change. It includes indicators of projected changes in annual runoff, projected changes in annual groundwater recharge, and dam capacity. It is independent of the socioeconomic context. It is the complement of the water vulnerability index in the ND-GAIN database.	ND-GAIN (University of Notre Dame Global Adaptation Index) Country Index	2015
	Transboundary water security	Transboundary water security expresses the share of the total renewable water resources originating inside the country as a percentage. This indicator may theoretically vary between 100 percent (the country receives no water from neighboring countries) and 0 percent (the country receives all its water from outside). This ratio does not consider the possible allocation of water to downstream or upstream countries. Actual dependence on external sources is lower in some countries than these numbers suggest, notably in Bahrain and Kuwait, because these figures do not consider the use of internal nonrenewable groundwater and nonconventional water sources. The transboundary water security indicator is the complement of the water dependency ratio in FAO's AQUASTAT database. The FAO indicator is limited in that it does not fully account for transboundary aquifers nor for the existence of water treaties which might increase transboundary water security.	FAO (Food and Agriculture Organization of the United Nations) AQUASTAT and expert elicitation[b]	—
People	**Percentage of deaths of children under age five due to diarrhea**	This indicator reflects the impact on people of inadequate water services. It is measured as the percent of deaths of children under five attributable to diarrhea. Deaths due to other waterborne diseases (such as cholera) are not accounted for, suggesting that this indicator gives a lower bound on the effects of inadequate water supply and sanitation on people.	WHO and Maternal and Child Epidemiology Estimation Group (MCEE) estimates, 2015	2015

(continued on next page)

TABLE A.1 *Continued*

Dimension	Indicator	Description	Source	Year
	Population exposure to high or very high water stress	Population exposure to surface water stress is calculated by combining water stress data with population data. Water stress is estimated using administrative units for each country from the Global Database of Administrative Areas. In high or very high water stress areas, water withdrawals are 40 percent or more of surface water availability. Population data is from PBL Netherlands Environmental Assessment Agency. This calculation does not account for seasonal variability in water availability or for upstream developments that may cause shortages in downstream countries.	World Bank	2017
	Total number of people affected by floods, 1980–2016	This indicator corresponds to the total number of people affected by floods contained in the EM-DAT database for each country. A "flood" is here intended as a general term for the overflow of water from a stream channel onto normally dry land in the floodplain (riverine flooding), higher-than-normal levels along the coast and in lakes or reservoirs (coastal flooding), as well as ponding of water at or near the point where the rain fell (flash floods). People "affected" are people requiring immediate assistance during a period of emergency: for instance, requiring basic survival needs, such as food, water, shelter, sanitation, and immediate medical assistance.	EM-DAT database	1980–2016
The economy	**Economic losses from inadequate water supply and sanitation**	The estimated economic losses associated with inadequate water supply and sanitation have been estimated by the World Health Organization (WHO). The estimated economic losses include the value of time savings that result from using a water source or latrine closer to home than existing facilities, health care costs, lost productive time because of illness, and premature mortality.	Hutton (2013)	2010
	GDP exposure to high or very high water stress	Percent of country's GDP exposed to water stress (where water withdrawals are 40 percent or more of surface water availability). GDP exposure to surface water stress. Water stress is estimated using administrative units for each country from the Global Database of Administrative Areas. GDP data is from PBL Netherlands Environmental Assessment Agency.	World Bank	2017
	Expected annual property damage due to fluvial and coastal flooding	The expected annual property damage due to fluvial and coastal flooding is expressed as a percentage of 2015 GDP. It has been estimated by quantifying the damage to assets located in fluvial or coastal floodplains.	Sadoff et al. (2015)	2015

(continued on next page)

TABLE A.1 *Continued*

Dimension	Indicator	Description	Source	Year
The environment	**Water quality threat**	Pollution threat includes the effects of nitrogen loading, phosphorus loading, organic loading, salinization, acidification, and sediment loading on water quality. The index is measured on a scale from 0 (low threat) to 100 (high threat).	Sadoff et al. (2015); Vörösmarty et al. (2010)	2010

a. Access statistics can be misleading. For instance, households may collect drinking water from both improved and unimproved sources, even if their "improved" water source is a piped water connection on the premises. Despite these limitations, the JMP data on improved water coverage are the best available, and they are used here to examine water supply and sanitation access statistics in the Middle East and North Africa.
b. Expert elicitation is a tool used to develop estimates of unknown or uncertain quantities based on careful assessment of the knowledge of experts about those quantities. It is often considered the best way to develop credible estimates when data are sparse or lacking.

TABLE A.2

Data Sources for the Country Profiles

Country/economy	Data sources
Algeria	ACWUA 2014; AWC 2012; Hamiche, Stambouli, and Flazi 2015
Bahrain	FAO 2016a
Djibouti	GFDRR 2016
Egypt, Arab Rep.	AWC 2012; World Bank 2014a, 2015a
Iran, Islamic Rep.	Madani 2014; Madani, AghaKouchak, and Mirchi 2016
Iraq	World Bank 2016a
Israel	FAO 2016b; Yinon 2013
Jordan	World Bank 2016b
Kuwait	Ismail 2015; PwC 2014
Lebanon	World Bank 2012
Libya	FAO 2016c; WHO 2016
Morocco	World Bank 2015b, 2015c
Oman	Kalbus, Zekri and Karimi 2016; Lehane 2015
Qatar	Darwish and Mohtar 2012
Saudi Arabia	PwC 2014
Syrian Arab Republic	De Châtel 2014; ICRC 2015
Tunisia	CEDARE 2014; World Bank 2014b, 2016c
United Arab Emirates	PwC 2014
West Bank and Gaza	Ghosheh 2016; Rammal 2016
Yemen, Rep.	Ward 2015

ALGERIA

Impacts of water insecurity

	Economy	People	Environment
Regional maximum			71%
Regional minimum		38%	

	1.08%	0.06%	5%	38%	298,476	71%
	Economic losses from inadequate water supply and sanitation (% of GDP)	GDP exposure to water stress (% of GDP)	Expected annual property damage due to fluvial and coastal flooding (% of GDP)	Percent deaths of children under five due to diarrhea	Population exposure to water stress	Total number of people affected by floods (1980–2016)	Water quality threat

RISK MANAGEMENT

Algeria shares a large portion of its water resources, in particular, its aquifers, with neighboring countries. This adds significant uncertainty to assessments of Algeria's water availability, especially because data on storage in these large transboundary aquifers is lacking. Scenario simulations suggest that large increases in water stress and flood exposure are to be expected from changing socioeconomic conditions and climate change.

WATER RESOURCES MANAGEMENT

Algeria's surface water resources are concentrated along the coastline, with the Saharan regions having the largest portion of groundwater reserves. Abstraction of Algeria's groundwater resources exceeds recharge rates by about 10 percent, and groundwater levels have been dropping significantly. Growing nonconventional water resources are an essential component of the present and future water supply portfolio to address the limited availability of freshwater resources and the growing demands.

Transboundary water security

Sustainability of freshwater use

Agricultural water productivity

Access (drinking water)

Access (sanitation)

Climate change robustness

Efficiency of water services

HIGH

LOW

No data

DELIVERY OF WATER SERVICES

Coverage rates in urban and rural environments have been steadily improving in the last decades, with more than 85 percent of the users served by a connection. Reliability of water supplies is varied, with about 20 percent of the users receiving water every other day. Non-revenue water in Algeria is estimated between 40 and 50 percent. This has led the government to launch a large operation for the rehabilitation of drinking water supply systems in all major cities in the country based on network upgrade studies and support to Algerienne des Eaux.

BAHRAIN

Impacts of water insecurity

	Economy	People	Environment
Regional maximum	100%	100%	
Regional minimum	0%		No data

	1.65%		0.4%		No data		No data

Economic losses from inadequate water supply and sanitation (% of GDP)	GDP exposure to water stress (% of GDP)	Expected annual property damage due to fluvial and coastal flooding (% of GDP)	Percent deaths of children under five due to diarrhea	Population exposure to water stress	Total number of people affected by floods (1980–2016)	Water quality threat

Sustainability of freshwater use

Agricultural water productivity

Transboundary water security

HIGH

Access (drinking water)

Access (sanitation)

LOW

Climate change robustness

Efficiency of water services

RISK MANAGEMENT

Bahrain's groundwater reserves are part of the large transboundary Dammam aquifer, which is increasingly threatened by salinization as a result of seawater intrusion and overpumping from the sharing countries.

WATER RESOURCES MANAGEMENT

Bahrain is characterized by high temperature, erratic rainfall and extremely high evapotranspiration rates. Lack of perennial surface water bodies and limited groundwater supplies have led to investments in desalination plants to meet domestic water demands and increased interest in the reuse of treated wastewater.

DELIVERY OF WATER SERVICES

Bahrain has achieved universal access to water and sanitation services. The water sector is not financially sustainable. Water tariffs in Manama are at the bottom of regional and global charts. Lack of financial sustainability prevents the water sector from achieving cost recovery and incentivizes consumptive behavior.

DJIBOUTI

Impacts of water insecurity

	Economy		People	Environment

Regional maximum

Regional minimum

1.44%	No data	0.52%	No data	8.1%	No data	13%	492,300

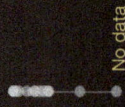

Economic losses from inadequate water supply and sanitation (% of GDP)	GDP exposure to water stress (% of GDP)	Expected annual property damage due to fluvial and coastal flooding (% of GDP)	Percent deaths of children under five due to diarrhea	Population exposure to water stress	Water quality threat	Total number of people affected by floods (1980–2016)

RISK MANAGEMENT

Djibouti's exposure to imported water risk is significant, with most food needs being met with imports. Water-related disasters also have a large impact on Djibouti's society and economy. Droughts in the 2000s affected about 50 percent of the rural population and about 15 percent of total population, resulting in economic losses equivalent to an average of 3.9 percent of GDP per year between 2008 and 2011.

WATER RESOURCES MANAGEMENT

Djibouti has no permanent rivers, streams, or fresh-water lakes, and as a result of extreme evaporation, less than 5 percent of total rainfall replenishes groundwater reserves. Limited water planning and excessive exploitation of groundwater resources have also led to the salinization of aquifers. These challenges are compounded by high climate variability and rapid increases in water demand due to population growth. To respond to the water deficit, different projects are taking place at the level of the water utility ONEAD, such as a new desalination plant to increase water supplies and rehabilitation and expansion of distribution networks to manage leakage.

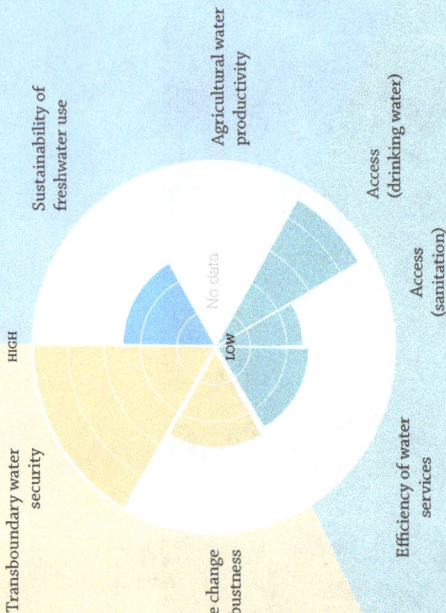

DELIVERY OF WATER SERVICES

Access statistics hide strong disparities on the ground. More than 20 percent of the rural population has no access to potable water, and access in rural areas is often limited during the dry season. In the slums of Balbala, most of the water supplies are provided by expensive tankers.

HIGH

LOW

No data

Sustainability of freshwater use

Agricultural water productivity

Access (drinking water)

Access (sanitation)

Transboundary water security

Climate change robustness

Efficiency of water services

ARAB REPUBLIC OF EGYPT

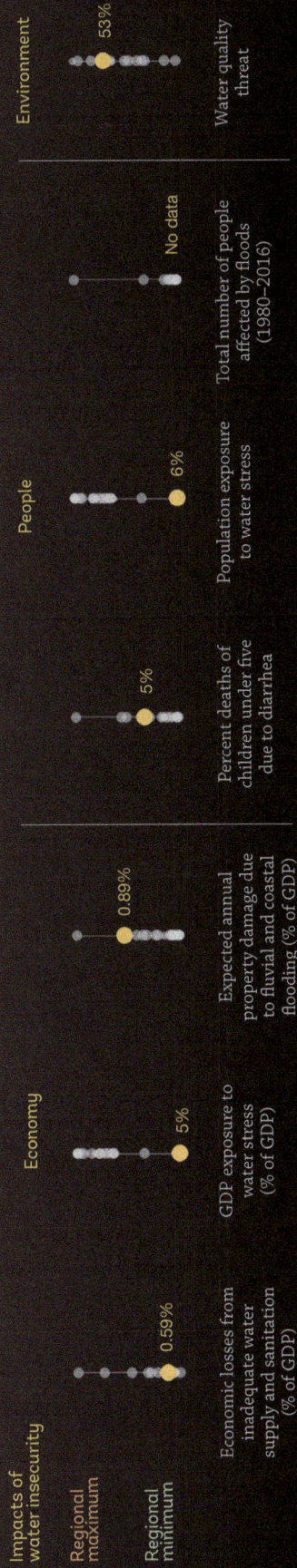

Impacts of water insecurity

Economy

Regional maximum — 0.89%

Regional minimum — 0.59% — 5%

Economic losses from inadequate water supply and sanitation (% of GDP)

GDP exposure to water stress (% of GDP)

Expected annual property damage due to fluvial and coastal flooding (% of GDP)

People

5%

6%

Percent deaths of children under five due to diarrhea

Population exposure to water stress

Environment

53%

No data

Total number of people affected by floods (1980–2016)

Water quality threat

RISK MANAGEMENT

Climate change is set to increase the risk of riverine and coastal floods, calling for immediate adaptation actions. Coastal areas will also suffer from salinity intrusion, which is already compromising groundwater quality in the Nile Delta. Addressing Egypt's water security challenges will require high-level regional support and fostering policy and technological innovations for sustainable urban water management and agricultural water productivity. It will also require enhanced cooperation on transboundary water resources via international water management agreements and diversification of water supplies.

WATER RESOURCES MANAGEMENT

Although Egypt shows a low exposure to water stress, it is highly dependent on a single source for its water supplies, with most water being supplied by Nile waters. Agricultural drainage water plays an important role in meeting irrigation water demands. Fragmented governance and lack of coordination among different agencies exacerbate some of the challenges of managing water resources. Deteriorating water quality, due to untreated sewage, industrial effluents, and agricultural runoff laden with fertilizers, is contributing to declining freshwater availability.

Sustainability of freshwater use

Agricultural water productivity

Transboundary water security

Access (drinking water)

Climate change robustness

Access (sanitation)

Efficiency of water services

HIGH

LOW

No data

DELIVERY OF WATER SERVICES

Most investment over the last 20 years has been on water supply, and this has raised access to safe drinking water from 39 percent to 93 percent, whereas sanitation services have lagged behind, with only about 50 percent of the population being connected to piped sewerage systems with adequate wastewater treatment (only 12 percent in rural areas). Country-wide estimates suggest that non-revenue water amounts to up to 30 percent of produced water but estimates vary by city. Egypt's irrigation and drainage infrastructure operate at only 50 percent efficiency and 40 percent cost recovery.

ISLAMIC REPUBLIC OF IRAN

Impacts of water insecurity

Economy

Regional maximum	94%	94%
Regional minimum	0.39%	0.11%

Economic losses from inadequate water supply and sanitation (% of GDP)	GDP exposure to water stress (% of GDP)	Expected annual property damage due to fluvial and coastal flooding (% of GDP)

People

94%

4.2%

Population exposure to water stress	Percent deaths of children under five due to diarrhea

4,119,894

Total number of people affected by floods (1980–2016)

Environment

No data

Water quality threat

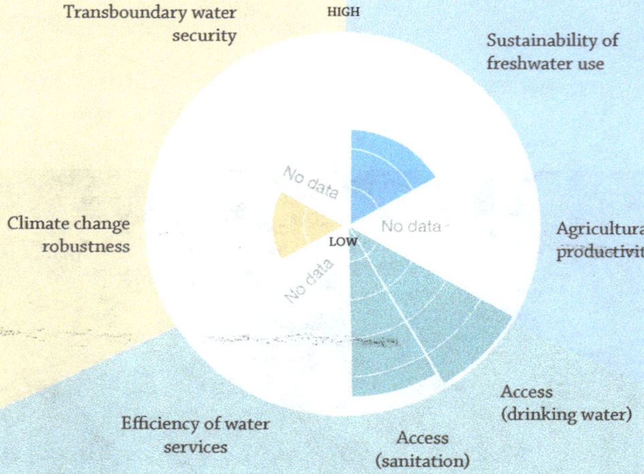

WATER RESOURCES MANAGEMENT

Iran faces significant water resources challenges, with high rates of unsustainable use. These challenges are compounded by a highly inefficient agricultural sector with low levels of water productivity. Deteriorating water quality, damage to aquatic ecosystems, desertification, and water shortages are all symptoms of Iran's potential water resources crisis. Unsustainable groundwater abstraction has also led to widespread sinkholes and land subsidence affecting about 50 percent of Iran's plains.

Radial chart labels:
- Sustainability of freshwater use
- Agricultural water productivity
- Access (drinking water)
- Access (sanitation)
- Efficiency of water services
- Climate change robustness
- Transboundary water security

HIGH — LOW

No data

RISK MANAGEMENT

Rapid urbanization and rural–urban migration will put pressure on Iran's water system. Iran has the highest number of transboundary groundwater resources in the region, calling for careful coordinated planning to prevent depletion of this strategic resource. Hydrological extremes also pose significant risks to the economy and society of Iran, and they are both set to increase under climate change.

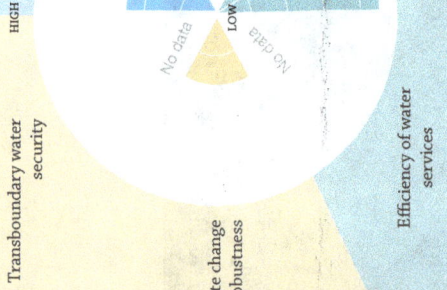

DELIVERY OF WATER SERVICES

Access to water services is generally good; however, water quality issues and the lack of wastewater treatment, especially in rural areas, are raising concerns about the quality of supplies in Iranian cities. Network losses are still quite significant, ranging from 15 to 50 percent. Water tariffs for domestic and agricultural users are far below the cost of water supply and treatment and also far below regional charges.

IRAQ

Impacts of water insecurity

Economy

People

Environment

Regional maximum

2.33%

75%

0.59%

75%

5%

138,511

37%

Regional minimum

| Economic losses from inadequate water supply and sanitation (% of GDP) | GDP exposure to water stress (% of GDP) | Expected annual property damage due to fluvial and coastal flooding (% of GDP) | Percent deaths of children under five due to diarrhea | Population exposure to water stress | Total number of people affected by floods (1980–2016) | Water quality threat |

RISK MANAGEMENT

Armed conflict and political instability challenge any action toward improving water security in Iraq. These challenges compound water-related risks by making it more difficult for governments to provide services and preserve water resources. Uncertainty over the shared waters of the Tigris-Euphrates River system means that Iraq's water supplies are at significant risk. Furthermore, lack of cooperation and environmental planning on this important river system is causing irreversible damage to Iraq's fragile aquatic ecosystems, including the Shatt-al-Arab marshes, whose size is now less than 90 percent of their original (pre-1970s) size.

WATER RESOURCES MANAGEMENT

Iraq's water is supplied by surface water from the Tigris-Euphrates River system and groundwater abstraction. Surface water use is largely unsustainable, with negative impacts on aquatic ecosystems. Water supplies are threatened by low availability and rapidly deteriorating water quality, affected by return flows from irrigation projects and industrial discharges upstream and within Iraq.

DELIVERY OF WATER SERVICES

Before the Gulf War, Iraq ranked among the best water service providers in the region. Following the war, sanctions and the deteriorating security situation, the level of access, and the quality of water services has dropped markedly. Only 52 percent of people whose houses are connected to the public water network report that their water supply is stable. Large investments are needed to restore basic water supply and sanitation services in major Iraqi cities to prevent human suffering and the spreading of waterborne diseases.

a. Access statistics can be misleading; for example, households may collect drinking water from both improved and unimproved sources, even if their 'improved' water source is a piped water connection on the premises. Despite these limitations, the JMP data on improved water coverage are the best available, and they are used here to examine water supply and sanitation access statistics in the region.

Sustainability of freshwater use

Agricultural water productivity

Access (drinking water)*

Access (sanitation)ᵃ

Efficiency of water services

Climate change robustness

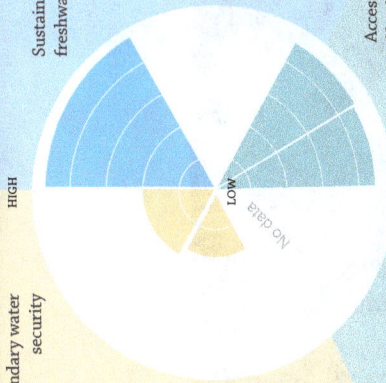

Transboundary water security

HIGH

LOW

No data

ISRAEL

Impacts of water insecurity

	Economy	People	Environment
Regional maximum	97%	95%	6%
Regional minimum	0.02%	0.5%	No data

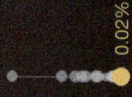

Economic losses from inadequate water supply and sanitation (% of GDP)	GDP exposure to water stress (% of GDP)	Expected annual property damage due to fluvial and coastal flooding (% of GDP)	Percent deaths of children under five due to diarrhea	Population exposure to water stress	Total number of people affected by floods (1980–2016)	Water quality threat
0.27%		0.02%	0.5%	95%	No data	6%

RISK MANAGEMENT

A large portion of Israel's water resources are shared, adding a layer of complexity to a fragile situation but also providing the opportunity for transboundary waters to be an instrument for peace and stability.

WATER RESOURCES MANAGEMENT

Israel's freshwater resources are being unsustainably exploited. To respond to this ongoing overexploitation, Israel has invested heavily in technology and infrastructure to develop nonconventional water supplies and to integrate the water resources systems.

DELIVERY OF WATER SERVICES

Israel has achieved universal access to water services and cost recovery in urban water service provision.

- Sustainability of freshwater use
- Agricultural water productivity
- Access (drinking water)
- Access (sanitation)
- Efficiency of water services
- Climate change robustness
- Transboundary water security

HIGH
LOW
No data

JORDAN

Impacts of water insecurity

	Economy	People	Environment

Regional maximum

Regional minimum

| 0.34% | 87% | 0.01% | 2.6% | 83% | 0.01% | 18,029 | No data |

Economic losses from inadequate water supply and sanitation (% of GDP)

GDP exposure to water stress (% of GDP)

Expected annual property damage due to fluvial and coastal flooding (% of GDP)

Percent deaths of children under five due to diarrhea

Population exposure to water stress

Total number of people affected by floods (1980–2016)

Water quality threat

WATER RESOURCES MANAGEMENT

Jordan is the fourth most water-scarce country in the world. The government constructed the last small dams and the Disi-Amman system to mobilize additional water. Jordan is also exploring additional sources of supply, such as large-scale seawater desalination. Efforts should be made to optimize the use of existing resources by reducing physical and commercial losses.

RISK MANAGEMENT

Economic development and demographic growth linked to the recent influx of refugees have added further strain on the very limited water supply of the country. Given Jordan's high vulnerability to transboundary water risks and climate change, investments in adaptation and water-sharing agreements are critical.

DELIVERY OF WATER SERVICES

Access statistics are high, however, reliability of services is low, with most households in urban centers receiving water one day a week. Water sector reform is underway to improve service delivery and financial sustainability. Improved governance of water services will also contribute to support ongoing government efforts.

Sustainability of freshwater use

Agricultural water productivity

Access (drinking water)

Access (sanitation)

Transboundary water security

Climate change robustness

Efficiency of water services

HIGH

LOW

KUWAIT

Impacts of water insecurity

Economy

Regional maximum — 100%

Regional minimum — 0.7%

0.49%

Economic losses from inadequate water supply and sanitation (% of GDP)

GDP exposure to water stress (% of GDP)

People

100%

0.4%

Percent deaths of children under five due to diarrhea

Expected annual property damage due to fluvial and coastal flooding (% of GDP)

Population exposure to water stress

Total number of people affected by floods (1980–2016) — 200

Environment

49%

Water quality threat

RISK MANAGEMENT

Kuwait has almost no internal source of freshwater, with most of its groundwater flowing from Saudi Arabia. Kuwait's imported water risk poses challenges for food security as it exposes the country to supply chain disruptions.

WATER RESOURCES MANAGEMENT

Kuwait's water consumption is among the highest in the world, mostly supplied via expensive desalinated water. Rates of groundwater abstraction far exceed recharge, which has led to significant unsustainble use and increased salinity. Kuwait's plans to reuse 100 percent of its wastewater are urgently needed to preserve dwindling freshwater resources.

Transboundary water security

Climate change robustness

Sustainability of freshwater use

Agricultural water productivity

Access (drinking water)

Access (sanitation)

Efficiency of water services

HIGH

LOW

DELIVERY OF WATER SERVICES

Most groundwater abstraction is not charged and not controlled, which leads to wasteful practices and over-abstraction. The high levels of subsidies mean that water prices are among the lowest in the world. Subsidies also eliminate the financial incentives for efficiency and reduced consumption, forcing investments in supply expansion.

LEBANON

Impacts of water insecurity

	Economy	People	Environment
Regional maximum	100%	100%	47%
Regional minimum	0.03%	2.1%	
	0.18%	18,500	

Economic losses from inadequate water supply and sanitation (% of GDP)

GDP exposure to water stress (% of GDP)

Expected annual property damage due to fluvial and coastal flooding (% of GDP)

Percent deaths of children under five due to diarrhea

Population exposure to water stress

Total number of people affected by floods (1980–2016)

Water quality threat

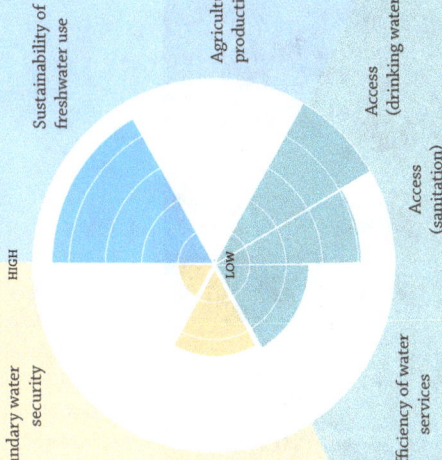

Transboundary water security

Climate change robustness

Sustainability of freshwater use

Agricultural water productivity

Access (drinking water)

Access (sanitation)

Efficiency of water services

HIGH — LOW

RISK MANAGEMENT

Refugees increased water demands by an estimated 61 million cubic meters and wastewater generation by an estimated 49 million cubic meters. Loss of winter precipitation storage in the snowpack may reduce runoff and streamflow in the warmer cropping period, creating climate change–related risks.

WATER RESOURCES MANAGEMENT

Although its per capita water endowment is relatively high, Lebanon is on the threshold of water scarcity, with surface water largely exploited and groundwater already in overdraft. Sustainability of water use is higher than regional averages but lower than global averages. There is a seasonal mismatch between supply (at its peak in the rainy winter) and demand (peaking in the hot, dry summer months). Factors exacerbating this seasonal water imbalance are the very low water storage capacity (6 percent of total resources, compared to the MENA average of 85 percent), the deficiency of water supply networks, and on the demand side, fast rising demand from the municipal and industrial sectors. An expensive but poorly sequenced investment program and absence of a viable business model for wastewater have left 92 percent of Lebanon's sewage running untreated into watercourses and the sea.

DELIVERY OF WATER SERVICES

Network coverage is relatively high (79 percent); however, there are big in-country differences. Unaccounted-for water averages 48 percent and supply continuity is low. Collection rates in 2010 averaged only 47 percent. As a result, maintenance is neglected: at 14 percent of total operations and maintenance expenditures, maintenance expenditures are well below the global benchmark of 20–80 percent. The Lebanese water sector is also characterized by lack of inclusiveness, with notable impact on the poor who spend up to 15 percent of total household income on alternative sources of water supply, often at high environmental and public health costs.

LIBYA

Impacts of water insecurity

Economy

Regional maximum

Regional minimum

4.96%

66%

66%

0.13%

1.9%

Economic losses from inadequate water supply and sanitation (% of GDP)

GDP exposure to water stress (% of GDP)

Expected annual property damage due to fluvial and coastal flooding (% of GDP)

Percent deaths of children under five due to diarrhea

People

66%

2000

Population exposure to water stress

Total number of people affected by floods (1980–2016)

Environment

39%

Water quality threat

WATER RESOURCES MANAGEMENT

Libya relies almost entirely on groundwater resources for its water supplies. Groundwater is being unsustainably exploited, with FAO estimates suggesting that water withdrawals exceed, by more than 800 percent, the renewable groundwater availability. This includes fossil groundwater, which constitutes an unrenewable yet crucial water supply source for Libya. More than half of the domestic water supplies in 2012 were provided by the Great Manmade River Project.

Sustainability of freshwater use

Agricultural water productivity

Transboundary water security

HIGH

LOW

No data

Access (drinking water)

Access (sanitation)

Climate change robustness

Efficiency of water services

DELIVERY OF WATER SERVICES

Five years of armed conflict and instability have reversed gains in access to water services. WHO estimates suggest that more than 10 percent of Libya's population, including refugees, internally displaced persons, and people affected by the conflict, are in need of assistance to ensure access to safe drinking water and sanitation.

RISK MANAGEMENT

Political stalemates and civil conflicts have resulted in damage to water infrastructure and institutions, preventing any progress toward water security. Climate change is expected to bring about increases in water stress and flood risk, compounding existing fragility challenges.

MOROCCO

Impacts of water insecurity

	Economy	People	Environment

Regional maximum

Regional minimum

0.54% — Economic losses from inadequate water supply and sanitation (% of GDP)

71% — GDP exposure to water stress (% of GDP)

0.17% — Expected annual property damage due to fluvial and coastal flooding (% of GDP)

4.6% — Percent deaths of children under five due to diarrhea

71% — Population exposure to water stress

232,896 — Total number of people affected by floods (1980–2016)

26% — Water quality threat

Radial chart axes (clockwise): Sustainability of freshwater use · Agricultural water productivity · Access (drinking water) · Access (sanitation) · Efficiency of water services · Climate change robustness · Transboundary water security

HIGH — LOW

RISK MANAGEMENT

The imbalance between demand and supply will be further accentuated by climate change, which is expected to result in a 10–35 percent decline in average annual precipitation by 2030. Climate change can also potentially alter the timing and amount of rainfall events and snowpack melting in the Atlas mountains.

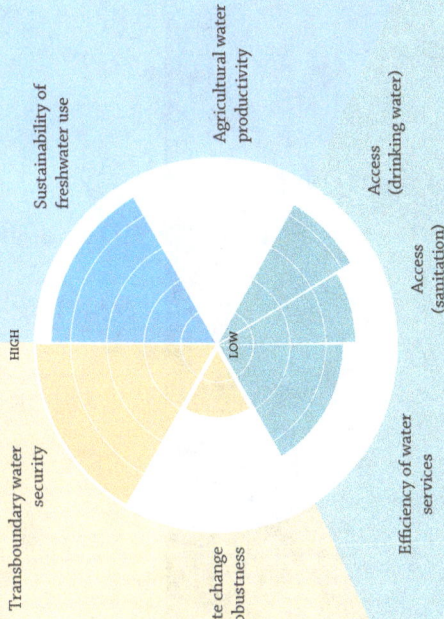

WATER RESOURCES MANAGEMENT

Morocco is a semi-arid country facing water resources challenges related to deteriorating water quality and unsustainable use. Most unsustainable use taps into groundwater resources, with key groundwater basins, such as the Tensift Basin, now close to depletion. To curb unsustainable water use, the government is developing policies targeted at conserving groundwater. Morocco also has one of the lowest values for water productivity in the region, suggesting that improvements and investments in irrigation networks and efficiency, such as in the National Irrigation Water Savings Program, can contribute to water security.

DELIVERY OF WATER SERVICES

Access has been improving in Morocco; however, rural access is still low compared to regional averages. Water tariffs are low compared to other MENA countries, which means that many utilities still need to achieve operating cost recovery.

OMAN

Impacts of water insecurity

Economy	People	Environment

Regional maximum
Regional minimum

0.66%
Economic losses from inadequate water supply and sanitation (% of GDP)

0.11%
GDP exposure to water stress (% of GDP)

67%
Expected annual property damage due to fluvial and coastal flooding (% of GDP)

1.3%
Percent deaths of children under five due to diarrhea

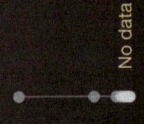

67%
Population exposure to water stress

No data
Total number of people affected by floods (1980–2016)

54%
Water quality threat

WATER RESOURCES MANAGEMENT

Oman has been working to secure its limited freshwater supplies and investing in nonconventional sources. Moves toward stricter regulation of groundwater use and source protection are needed to achieve long-term sustainable water management. Work to maintain and develop aflaj and water structures will need to be scaled up to enhance their performance.

Sustainability of freshwater use

Agricultural water productivity

Access (drinking water)

Access (sanitation)

HIGH

LOW

Transboundary water security

Climate change robustness

Efficiency of water services

DELIVERY OF WATER SERVICES

Oman has achieved almost universal access to water services; however, interruptions to the water supply are still common. Restructuring the water sector to combine supply and wastewater services is currently under way to achieve economic efficiency, improve nationwide service delivery, and encourage private sector involvement.

RISK MANAGEMENT

Coastal plains in Oman have experienced water quality deterioration due to seawater intrusion as a result of groundwater pumping for irrigation, which will be exacerbated by sea-level rise. As in the other Gulf countries, increased temperatures resulting from climate change will also increase water demands from agriculture.

QATAR

	Economy	People	Environment
	100%	100%	74%
Regional maximum			
	0.04%	0.5%	
	0.25%		14,500
Regional minimum			

Impacts of water insecurity			
Economic losses from inadequate water supply and sanitation (% of GDP)	GDP exposure to water stress (% of GDP)	Percent deaths of children under five due to diarrhea	Population exposure to water stress
	Expected annual property damage due to fluvial and coastal flooding (% of GDP)		Total number of people affected by floods (1980–2016)
			Water quality threat

RISK MANAGEMENT

Lack of strategic water reserves and diversity of supply sources means that Qatar's water security is fragile. This has led to ongoing investments to augment surface and groundwater storage. Qatar will face increases in heat extremes and an average rise in temperature, which requires adaptation to ensure livability in Qatar's highly urbanized settings.

WATER RESOURCES MANAGEMENT

Desalinated water supplies meet 99 percent of domestic water demand in Qatar. As this dependence on desalinated water increases, more attention needs to be paid to managing demands and developing clean energy desalination technologies to minimize environmental and economic costs. The potential for wastewater reuse still needs to be fully exploited, especially given that the cost of reuse is lower than the cost of desalinated water.

Sustainability of freshwater use

Agricultural water productivity

Access (drinking water)

Access (sanitation)

Transboundary water security

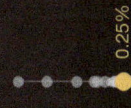

Climate change robustness

Efficiency of water services

HIGH

LOW

DELIVERY OF WATER SERVICES

Kahramaa has recently reduced subsidies, introducing stricter rules to promote the financial sustainability of water services. Water conservation measures, including pricing and awareness raising, are being employed to manage water demands and halt groundwater depletion.

SAUDI ARABIA

Impacts of water insecurity

Economy

Regional maximum 0.53%

Regional minimum 0.04%

Economic losses from inadequate water supply and sanitation (% of GDP)

GDP exposure to water stress (% of GDP)

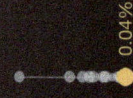

65%

People

1.1%

64%

Percent deaths of children under five due to diarrhea

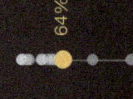

Population exposure to water stress

30,568

Total number of people affected by floods (1980–2016)

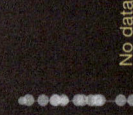

Environment

No data

Water quality threat

RISK MANAGEMENT

Risks associated with rapid population growth, volatile energy prices, and a high reliance on desalination challenge progress toward water security. Climate change will bring higher temperatures to Saudi Arabia, increasing evapotranspiration and crop water requirements. Increasing dependence on imported food also increases the exposure to "imported water risk," which has been partly offset by land purchases in foreign countries to directly control production and mitigate this risk.

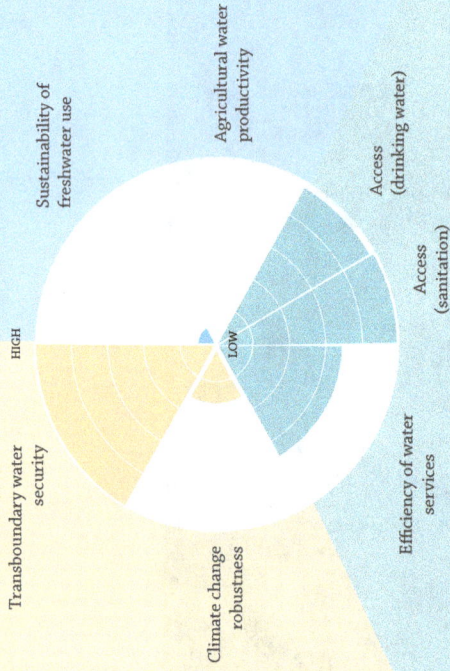

WATER RESOURCES MANAGEMENT

Saudi Arabia is the world's topmost producer of desalinated water. Desalination has secured the water supply; however, it comes with high energy costs and emissions, as well as negative impacts on marine environments due to brine discharge. Even though the rate of unsustainable groundwater abstraction has been decreasing in recent years, groundwater depletion still represents a challenge to Saudi water security. The National Water Company's efforts toward increased reuse of wastewater strengthens Saudi Arabia's water security prospects.

DELIVERY OF WATER SERVICES

Wasteful use of water in all sectors abounds, and tariffs are also extremely low, with cities in Saudi Arabia having the lowest tariffs in the region (and globally). Unless the costs of water supply and treatment are fully recovered, delivery of water services will not be financially sustainable in the long term.

Sustainability of freshwater use

Agricultural water productivity

Access (drinking water)

Access (sanitation)

Efficiency of water services

Climate change robustness

Transboundary water security

HIGH

LOW

SYRIAN ARAB REPUBLIC

Impacts of water insecurity

Economy

Regional maximum — 78%

Regional minimum — No data

Economic losses from inadequate water supply and sanitation (% of GDP)

23%

GDP exposure to water stress (% of GDP)

Expected annual property damage due to fluvial and coastal flooding (% of GDP)

People

14.4%

76.6%

Percent deaths of children under five due to diarrhea

Population exposure to water stress

Environment

32.5%

No data

Water quality threat

Total number of people affected by floods (1980–2016)

RISK MANAGEMENT

Armed conflict and instability challenge progress toward water security. The effects of climate change are already being felt in Syria, with recent studies suggesting that climate change is bringing about more extreme weather events and droughts.

Transboundary water security

Climate change robustness

Sustainability of freshwater use

HIGH

LOW

No data

Agricultural water productivity

Access (drinking water)

Access (sanitation)

Efficiency of water services

WATER RESOURCES MANAGEMENT

Decades of poor water resources management and planning have led Syria to a water crisis characterized by surface water overabstraction and groundwater depletion. High hydrological variability compounds this management challenge, making it more difficult to address Syria's water challenges.

DELIVERY OF WATER SERVICES

Armed conflict has severely damaged water supply and sanitation infrastructure. Forced displacement has caused immense human suffering and challenges in accessing water services. Lack of water services has resulted in up to 15 percent of the deaths of children under age 5. In 2014, local officials estimated they lost 60 percent of pumped water through gaps in the network, as a result of damage caused by the conflict as well as the aging infrastructure.

TUNISIA

Impacts of water insecurity

Economy	People	Environment

Regional maximum

Regional minimum

0.84%

0.22%

2.4%

83%

83%

218,008

No data

Economic losses from inadequate water supply and sanitation (% of GDP)

GDP exposure to water stress (% of GDP)

Expected annual property damage due to fluvial and coastal flooding (% of GDP)

Percent deaths of children under five due to diarrhea

Population exposure to water stress

Total number of people affected by floods (1980–2016)

Water quality threat

RISK MANAGEMENT

Rapid urbanization is putting immense pressure on water resources and services. Salinization of coastal aquifers due to sea level rise and uncontrolled groundwater pumping are also placing water supplies at risk. More than 70 percent of both shallow and deep aquifers have very high salinity content. In terms of transboundary waters, there is a need to strengthen agreements and management of the North-Western Saharan Aquifer System.

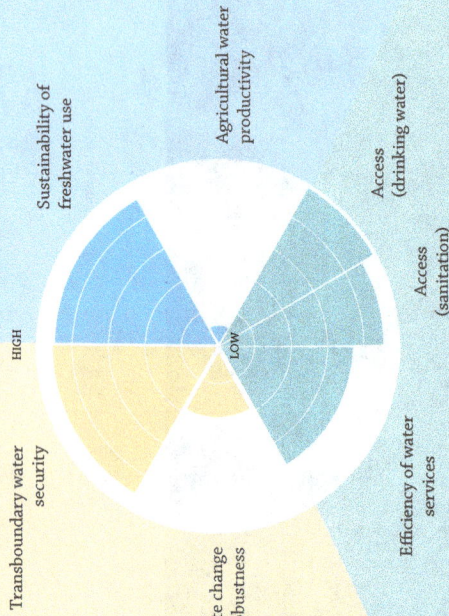

WATER RESOURCES MANAGEMENT

Water resources availability is spatially uneven, with the north receiving more than about 20 times the amount of rainfall than the south. Although Tunisia has invested significantly in the mobilization and conservation of water resources, defective irrigation systems and lack of enforcement and regulation are some of the factors requiring further interventions to improve water resources management.

Transboundary water security

Sustainability of freshwater use

Agricultural water productivity

Access (drinking water)

Access (sanitation)

Efficiency of water services

Climate change robustness

HIGH

LOW

DELIVERY OF WATER SERVICES

Tunisia has made progress toward universal access; however, sizable differences in access for water and sanitation persists between poor and non-poor. Inadequate coverage and institutional gaps mean that rural water services are significantly worse than services in urban settings. The cost of production of drinking water was 0.716 TD per cubic meter in 2011. The average sale price was 0.562 TD per cubic meter. This makes cost recovery standing at 78.5 percent. Moving forward, the government and SONEDE have launched a program and vision to ensure undisrupted water service delivery over the next decade.

UNITED ARAB EMIRATES

Impacts of water insecurity

	Economy	People	Environment
Regional maximum	100%	100%	49%
Regional minimum	0.08%	0.8%	No data
	0.47%		

Economic losses from inadequate water supply and sanitation (% of GDP)

GDP exposure to water stress (% of GDP)

Percent deaths of children under five due to diarrhea

Population exposure to water stress

Expected annual property damage due to fluvial and coastal flooding (% of GDP)

Total number of people affected by floods (1980–2016)

Water quality threat

RISK MANAGEMENT

The biggest water-related risk in the United Arab Emirates is the lack of a diversified water supply portfolio. This makes the United Arab Emirates vulnerable to threats to desalination production, such as algal blooms or oil spills at the intake. As with other Gulf countries, the United Arab Emirates face climate-related risks; for example, severe heat waves and extremely high temperatures by the middle of the century, as well as exposure to disruptions to food supply chains and to imported water.

WATER RESOURCES MANAGEMENT

The United Arab Emirates' abundant energy supplies have led to significant reliance on desalination, with more than 25 desalination plants meeting all domestic water demands. To respond to the depletion of renewable freshwater resources, the United Arab Emirates has invested in rain enhancement research and technology.

DELIVERY OF WATER SERVICES

Water services are generally reliable in the United Arab Emirates. Compared to other Gulf countries, water tariffs in the United Arab Emirates reflect the actual cost of supplying water, in line with the United Arab Emirates' natural resources conservation policy. The biggest challenges for sustained water service delivery in the United Arab Emirates is managing water demands and minimizing network losses.

Sustainability of freshwater use

Agricultural water productivity

Access (drinking water)

Access (sanitation)

Efficiency of water services

Climate change robustness

Transboundary water security

HIGH

LOW

WEST BANK AND GAZA

Impacts of water insecurity

Economy

Regional maximum — 100%

Regional minimum — 1.57%

Economic losses from inadequate water supply and sanitation (% of GDP)

0.02%

GDP exposure to water stress (% of GDP)

No data

Expected annual property damage due to fluvial and coastal flooding (% of GDP)

People

100%

Percent deaths of children under five due to diarrhea — No data

Population exposure to water stress

Total number of people affected by floods (1980–2016) — No data

Environment

62%

Water quality threat

RISK MANAGEMENT

The West Bank's reliance on the shared Mountain Aquifer means that transboundary water risks are high. This calls for water-sharing agreements to promote water security and promote peace and stability. Water infrastructure damage following conflict is another major risk hindering progress toward water security. Hostilities in 2014 caused extensive damage to the water and sanitation infrastructure, including damage to 12 sewage pumping stations, several thousand meters of water network pipes, and extensive damage to household-level water and sanitation infrastructure (tanks and sanitary installations).

WATER RESOURCES MANAGEMENT

Freshwater resources in the West Bank and Gaza are being overexploited. Water overabstraction and pollution mean that the coastal aquifer is undergoing irreversible damage, which may make its waters unsafe by 2020. More than half (52 percent) of Gaza's seashore is severely polluted and unsuitable for swimming, including nearly 90 percent of the shore in Gaza City. Recent institutional reforms, including a new water law and a new water regulator, are contributing to improved governance of water resources. Furthermore, the creation of performance monitoring and national water information systems aims to promote sustainable and efficient water resources management in the long-term.

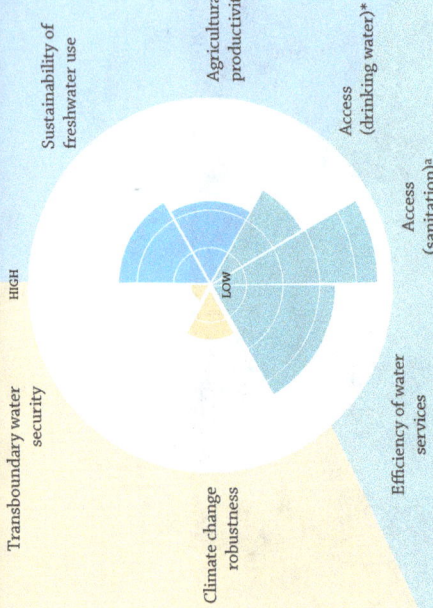

DELIVERY OF WATER SERVICES

Access statistics hide the reality on the ground. Only 10 percent of Gaza's population has access to improved drinking water, compared to 90 percent in the West Bank and 85 percent in MENA in general. Palestinians also experience very low levels of service: half of all households receive water less than once a day, and 10 percent get water only once a month. In Gaza, more than 65 percent of the population uses expensive water from tankers.

a. Access statistics can be misleading; for example, households may collect drinking water from both improved and unimproved sources, even if their "improved" water source is a piped water connection on the premises. Despite these limitations, the JMP data on improved water coverage are the best available, and they are used here to examine water supply and sanitation access statistics in the region.

Transboundary water security

Climate change robustness

Sustainability of freshwater use

Agricultural water productivity

Access (drinking water)*

Access (sanitation)a

Efficiency of water services

HIGH

LOW

REPUBLIC OF YEMEN

Impacts of water insecurity

	Economy	People	Environment

Economy

Regional maximum — 79%

Regional minimum — 0.33%

GDP exposure to water stress (% of GDP)

Economic losses from inadequate water supply and sanitation (% of GDP) — 3.7%

Expected annual property damage due to fluvial and coastal flooding (% of GDP)

People

82%

7.5%

Population exposure to water stress

Percent deaths of children under five due to diarrhea

Environment

32%

1,278,217

Water quality threat

Total number of people affected by floods (1980–2016)

RISK MANAGEMENT

The Republic of Yemen's water crisis is being exacerbated by protracted conflict, which has significantly damaged water infrastructure and institutions. The Republic of Yemen is also exposed to extreme weather events, such as tropical cyclones that compound the ongoing humanitarian crisis. Climate change is projected to bring about more intense rainfall events and increased risks of flash floods. High imported water risk, due to dependence on food imports, makes Yemeni households, especially nonfarming households in rural and urban areas, highly vulnerable to climate change and food price volatility.

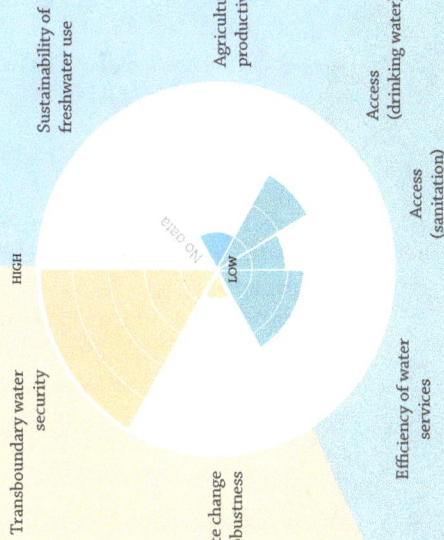

WATER RESOURCES MANAGEMENT

The Republic of Yemen is in a water crisis. Annual per capita renewable water resource availability is 1 percent of world averages and 14 percent of regional averages. Groundwater is being depleted at an alarming rate, with abstraction exceeding recharge rates by about 200–300 percent and water tables dropping by 1–7 meters per year. Efforts to preserve the Republic of Yemen's water resources have been piecemeal and hindered by armed conflict, strong economic and political interests, and weak state authority. Irrigation efficiency is low at 35–40 percent, calling for improvements in irrigation systems. Since the agricultural sector consumes about 90 percent of the available water resources, any effective intervention to conserve water and stabilize water levels requires a consideration of the irrigated agriculture sector.

Sustainability of freshwater use

Agricultural water productivity

Access (drinking water)

Access (sanitation)

Efficiency of water services

Climate change robustness

Transboundary water security

HIGH

LOW

NO DATA

DELIVERY OF WATER SERVICES

In the Republic of Yemen, access to water is a daily struggle. Armed conflict means that about 14.5 million Yemenis are now in need of water and sanitation assistance. This has had severe human impacts, with about 50 percent of children under age 5 suffering from stunting, and 7 percent of them dying from water-borne diseases. Water tankers supply about 80 percent of urban water demands with low quality and expensive water, greatly affecting the poor.

References

ACWUA (Arab Countries Water Utilities Association). 2014. *Management of Water Utilities: Case Studies from the Arab Region.* Amman: ACWUA.

AWC (Arab Water Council). 2012. *2nd Arab State of the Water 2012 Report.* Cairo: AWC and CEDARE.

CEDARE (Centre for Environment and Development for the Arab Region and Europe). 2014. "Tunisia Water Sector M&E Rapid Assessment Report, Monitoring & Evaluation for Water." In *North Africa (MEWINA) Project.* Cairo: Water Resources Management Program, CEDARE.

Darwish, M.A., and R. Mohtar. 2012. "Qatar Water Challenges." *Desalination and Water Treatment* 51 (3): 75–86.

De Châtel, Francesca. 2014. "The Role of Drought and Climate Change in the Syrian Uprising: Untangling the Triggers of the Revolution." *Middle Eastern Studies* 50 (4): 521–35.

FAO (Food and Agriculture Organization of the United Nations). 2016a. *Bahrain.* AQUASTAT.

———. 2016b. *Israel.* AQUASTAT.

———. 2016c. *Libya.* AQUASTAT.

GFDRR (Global Facility for Disaster Risk Reduction). 2016. *Djibouti Country Profile.* Washington, DC: GFDRR. https://www.gfdrr.org/sites/gfdrr/files/region/DJ.pdf.

Ghosheh, A. 2016. "Water Situation Alarming in Gaza" (blog), November 22. http://www.worldbank.org/en/news/feature/2016/11/22/water-situation-alarming-in-gaza.

Hamiche, A. M., A. B. Stambouli, and S. Flazi. 2015. "A Review of the Water and Energy Sectors in Algeria: Current Forecasts, Scenario and Sustainability Issues." *Renewable and Sustainable Energy Reviews* 41: 261–76.

Hutton, G. 2013. "Global Costs and Benefits of Reaching Universal Coverage of Sanitation and Drinking-Water Supply." *Journal of Water and Health* 11 (1): 1–12.

ICRC (International Committee of the Red Cross). 2015. *Bled Dry—How War in the Middle East Is Bringing the Region to the Brink of a Water Catastrophe.* Geneva: ICRC.

Ismail, H. 2015. *Kuwait: Food and Water Security.* Strategic Analysis Paper, Future Directions International.

JMP (WHO/UNICEF Joint Monitoring Programme for Water Supply and Sanitation). 2015. *Progress on Sanitation and Drinking Water–2015 Update and MDG Assessment.* Geneva: WHO.

Kalbus, E., S. Zekri, and A. Karimi. 2016. "Intervention Scenarios to Manage Seawater Intrusion in a Coastal Agricultural area in Oman." *Arabian Journal of Geosciences* 9: 472. doi:10.1007/s12517-016-2442-6.

Lehane, S. 2015. *The Sultanate of Oman: Food and Water Security to 2025.* Strategic Analysis Paper. Dalkeith, Australia: Future Directions International.

Madani, K. 2014. "Water Management in Iran: What Is Causing the Looming Crisis?" *Journal of Environmental Studies and Sciences* 4 (4): 315–28.

Madani, K., Amir Agha Kouchak, and Ali Mirchi. 2016. "Iran's Socio-Economic Drought: Challenges of a Water-Bankrupt Nation." *Iranian Studies* 49 (6): 997–1016.

PwC. 2014. *Achieving a Sustainable Water Sector in the GCC: Managing Supply and Demand, Building Institutions.* Beirut and Dubai: Strategy &.

Rammal, I. 2016. *West Bank and Gaza—Water Security Development Program for Results Project.* Washington, DC: World Bank Group.

Sadoff, C. W., J. W. Hall, D. Grey, D., J. C. J. H. Aerts, M. Ait-Kadi, C. Brown, A. Cox, S. Dadson, D. Garrick, J. Kelman, P. McCornick, C. Ringler, M. Rosegrant, D. Whittington, and D. Wiberg. 2015. *Securing Water, Sustaining Growth.* Report of the GWP/OECD Task Force on Water Security and Sustainable Growth. Oxford: University of Oxford.

Vörösmarty, C. J., P. B. McIntyre, M. O. Gessner, D. Dudgeon, A. Prusevich, P. Green, S. Glidden, S. E. Bunn, C. A. Sullivan, C. R. Liermann, and P. M. Davies. 2010. "Global Threats to Human Water Security and River Biodiversity." *Nature* 467 (7315): 555–61.

Ward, C. 2015. *The Water Crisis in Yemen: Managing Extreme Water Scarcity in the Middle East.* London: I. B. Tauris.

WHO (World Health Organization). 2016. *Libya Humanitarian Response Plan.* Geneva: WHO.

WHO and Maternal and Child Epidemiology Estimation Group. http://data.unicef.org/topic/child-health/diarrhoeal-disease/.

World Bank. 2012. *Lebanon Country Water Sector Assistance Strategy (2012–2016).* Washington, DC: World Bank.

———. 2014a. *FY2015–2019 Country Partnership Framework for Arab Republic of Egypt.* Washington, DC: World Bank Group.

———. 2014b. *Water: Tunisia's Other Development Challenge.* (blog), September 4. Washington, DC: World Bank. http://www.worldbank.org/en/news/feature/2014/09/04/water-tunisia-s-other-development-challenge.

———. 2015a. *Egypt—Promoting Poverty Reduction and Shared Prosperity: A Systematic Country Diagnostic.* Washington, DC: World Bank Group.

———. 2015b. *Project Information Document (Concept Stage)—Morocco Integrated Urban Water Management—P151128.* Washington, DC: World Bank Group.

———. 2015c. *Morocco—Large-Scale Irrigation Modernization Project.* Washington, DC: World Bank Group.

———. 2016a. *Iraq—Emergency Water Supply Project.* Washington, DC: World Bank Group.

———. 2016b. *Jordan—Promoting Poverty Reduction and Shared Prosperity: Systematic Country Diagnostic.* Washington, DC: World Bank Group.

———. 2016c. *Tunisia—Country Partnership Framework for the Period FY 2016-2020.* Washington, DC: World Bank Group.

Yinon, Y. 2013. *Documentation of Best Practices in Non-Revenue Water Management in Selected Mediterranean Countries.* Brussels: SWIM (Sustainable Water Integrated Management Support Mechanism) Programme, European Union.

www.ingramcontent.com/pod-product-compliance
Lightning Source LLC
Chambersburg PA
CBHW080420270326
41929CB00018B/3098